Find A Federal Job Fast

Books and CD-ROMs by Drs. Ron and Caryl Krannich

R

FIND A FEDERAL JOB FAST
How to Cut the Red Tape and Get Hired

Fourth Edition

Ronald L. Krannich, Ph.D.
Caryl Rae Krannich, Ph.D.

IMPACT PUBLICATIONS
Manassas Park, VA

he Red Tape and Get Hired

Library of Congress Cataloguing-in-Publication Data

Krannich, Ronald L.
 Find a federal job fast: how to cut the red tape and get hired /
Ronald L. Krannich, Caryl Rae Krannich.—4th ed.
  p. cm.
 Includes bibliographical references and index.
 ISBN 1-57023-068-4 (alk. Paper)
  1. Civil service positions—United States. I. Krannich, Caryl Rae.
II. Title.
 JK716.K684 1999
 352.6'4'0973—dc21   97-25276
                                                         CIP

Publisher: For information on Impact Publications, including current and forthcoming publications, authors, press kits, online bookstore, and submission requirements, visit Impact's Web site: *www.impactpublications.com*

Publicity/Rights: For information on publicity, author interviews, and subsidiary rights, contact the Public Relations Department: Tel. 703/361-7300.

Sales/Distribution: All bookstore sales are handled through Impact's trade distributor: National Book Network, 15200 NBN Way, Blue Ridge Summit, PA 17214, Tel. 1-800-462-6420. All other sales and distribution inquiries should be directed to the publisher: Sales Department, IMPACT PUBLICATIONS, 9104-N Manassas Drive, Manassas Park, VA 20111-5211, Tel. 703/361-7300, Fax 703/335-9486, or Email *fed@impactpublications.com*

Contents

Preface

Find a federal job fast? Isn't that an oxymoron in today's substantially "downsized" and "reinvented" government? Doesn't it really take longer than ever to get a federal job?

Yes and no. If you lack qualifications and don't know how the hiring process operates—from locating vacancies to developing an outstanding application package—finding a federal job can take forever! However, if you have the right skills, know where the jobs are, and can put together a dynamite application, finding a federal job can be fast.

Despite all the talk about "reinventing" and "downsizing" government, somewhere between 300,000 and 400,000 people find a federal job each year. What is it they do that others don't to find a job? Are they more qualified than others? Or do they know something about the hiring process that others have yet to learn?

Within the past few years the federal government has taken important initiatives to streamline the application and hiring processes. Unknown to many outsiders, finding a job with the federal government can be fast. It is particularly fast for those who know the details of where and how to find jobs in today's federal job market.

Effective job seekers do some things differently from the ordinary job seeker. First of all, they know how the hiring process operates in both theory and practice. Avoiding myths and being job search smart, they understand the realities of government. They know where they can quickly find job vacancies on the Internet, in print, over the telephone, or by visiting personnel offices. They produce effective applications to clearly communicate required qualifications to potential employers. They know what they want to do and identify specific positions involving their interests and skills. They understand which agencies they want to work for and target them accordingly. Most important of all, they go beyond the formal system of rules and regulations with good "street smarts."

We wrote this book because there is a need for a current perspective on how to get a federal job. Many significant changes continue to take place in the federal hiring process that have not been adequately communicated to job seekers who still believe that finding a federal job is complicated, time-consuming, and frustrating. We also see a need to put federal employment in the larger context of effective job search strategies. Most examinations of how to get a federal job primarily focus on the formal rules and regulations. While important to know and follow, the formal system only tells you part of the larger story on how thousands of job seekers really get hired each year.

Find a Federal Job Fast is designed as your passport for both under-standing and action relevant to finding federal employment. This new edition has been substantially updated to reflect the new digital era of federal hiring. In today's new federal government, the Internet plays a central role in linking candidates to agencies and positions.

This new edition builds on the foundation we developed since 1989. We've updated statistical data and telephone numbers and included a great deal of new information on how to use the Internet to research agencies, identify vacancies, and complete application packages. Today's new "reinvented" government is one that is increasingly wired via the Internet. If you are Internet savvy, you may be surprised to discover how easy it is to get information on agencies, vacancies, and applications.

Regardless of what others may tell you, the public sector does offer interesting and rewarding jobs for those who know where and how to find them. The pages that follow are designed to give you that "extra edge" in finding a federal job by focusing on important "where" and "how" questions of the federal employment process. If you put the following pages into practice, you may well join the many thousands of other job applicants who are learning that finding a federal job is much faster than they had ever thought possible. Better still, you may quickly join thousands of others who enjoy working for the federal government and pursuing public service goals and careers.

Ron and Caryl Krannich

FIND A FEDERAL JOB FAST

GOVERNMENT OF THE UNITED STATES

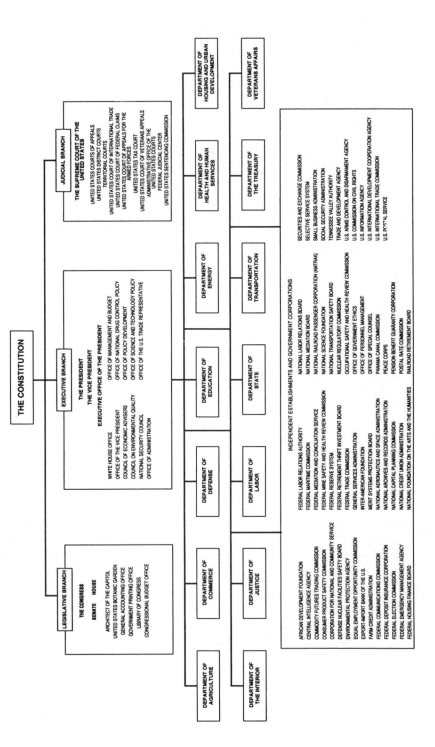

THE CONSTITUTION

LEGISLATIVE BRANCH

THE CONGRESS

SENATE   HOUSE

ARCHITECT OF THE CAPITOL
UNITED STATES BOTANIC GARDEN
GENERAL ACCOUNTING OFFICE
GOVERNMENT PRINTING OFFICE
LIBRARY OF CONGRESS
CONGRESSIONAL BUDGET OFFICE

EXECUTIVE BRANCH

THE PRESIDENT
THE VICE PRESIDENT

EXECUTIVE OFFICE OF THE PRESIDENT

WHITE HOUSE OFFICE
OFFICE OF THE VICE PRESIDENT
COUNCIL OF ECONOMIC ADVISERS
COUNCIL ON ENVIRONMENTAL QUALITY
NATIONAL SECURITY COUNCIL
OFFICE OF ADMINISTRATION

OFFICE OF MANAGEMENT AND BUDGET
OFFICE OF NATIONAL DRUG CONTROL POLICY
OFFICE OF POLICY DEVELOPMENT
OFFICE OF SCIENCE AND TECHNOLOGY POLICY
OFFICE OF THE U.S. TRADE REPRESENTATIVE

JUDICIAL BRANCH

THE SUPREME COURT OF THE UNITED STATES

UNITED STATES COURTS OF APPEALS
UNITED STATES DISTRICT COURTS
TERRITORIAL COURTS
UNITED STATES COURT OF INTERNATIONAL TRADE
UNITED STATES COURT OF FEDERAL CLAIMS
UNITED STATES COURT OF APPEALS FOR THE ARMED FORCES
UNITED STATES TAX COURT
UNITED STATES COURT OF VETERANS APPEALS
ADMINISTRATIVE OFFICE OF THE UNITED STATES COURTS
FEDERAL JUDICIAL CENTER
UNITED STATES SENTENCING COMMISSION

DEPARTMENT OF AGRICULTURE

DEPARTMENT OF COMMERCE

DEPARTMENT OF DEFENSE

DEPARTMENT OF EDUCATION

DEPARTMENT OF ENERGY

DEPARTMENT OF HEALTH AND HUMAN SERVICES

DEPARTMENT OF HOUSING AND URBAN DEVELOPMENT

DEPARTMENT OF THE INTERIOR

DEPARTMENT OF JUSTICE

DEPARTMENT OF LABOR

DEPARTMENT OF STATE

DEPARTMENT OF TRANSPORTATION

DEPARTMENT OF THE TREASURY

DEPARTMENT OF VETERANS AFFAIRS

INDEPENDENT ESTABLISHMENTS AND GOVERNMENT CORPORATIONS

AFRICAN DEVELOPMENT FOUNDATION
CENTRAL INTELLIGENCE AGENCY
COMMODITY FUTURES TRADING COMMISSION
CONSUMER PRODUCT SAFETY COMMISSION
CORPORATION FOR NATIONAL AND COMMUNITY SERVICE
DEFENSE NUCLEAR FACILITIES SAFETY BOARD
ENVIRONMENTAL PROTECTION AGENCY
EQUAL EMPLOYMENT OPPORTUNITY COMMISSION
EXPORT-IMPORT BANK OF THE U.S.
FARM CREDIT ADMINISTRATION
FEDERAL COMMUNICATIONS COMMISSION
FEDERAL DEPOSIT INSURANCE CORPORATION
FEDERAL ELECTION COMMISSION
FEDERAL EMERGENCY MANAGEMENT AGENCY
FEDERAL HOUSING FINANCE BOARD

FEDERAL LABOR RELATIONS AUTHORITY
FEDERAL MARITIME COMMISSION
FEDERAL MEDIATION AND CONCILIATION SERVICE
FEDERAL MINE SAFETY AND HEALTH REVIEW COMMISSION
FEDERAL RESERVE SYSTEM
FEDERAL RETIREMENT THRIFT INVESTMENT BOARD
FEDERAL TRADE COMMISSION
GENERAL SERVICES ADMINISTRATION
INTER-AMERICAN FOUNDATION
MERIT SYSTEMS PROTECTION BOARD
NATIONAL AERONAUTICS AND SPACE ADMINISTRATION
NATIONAL ARCHIVES AND RECORDS ADMINISTRATION
NATIONAL CAPITAL PLANNING COMMISSION
NATIONAL CREDIT UNION ADMINISTRATION
NATIONAL FOUNDATION ON THE ARTS AND THE HUMANITIES

NATIONAL LABOR RELATIONS BOARD
NATIONAL MEDIATION BOARD
NATIONAL RAILROAD PASSENGER CORPORATION (AMTRAK)
NATIONAL SCIENCE FOUNDATION
NATIONAL TRANSPORTATION SAFETY BOARD
NUCLEAR REGULATORY COMMISSION
OCCUPATIONAL SAFETY AND HEALTH REVIEW COMMISSION
OFFICE OF GOVERNMENT ETHICS
OFFICE OF PERSONNEL MANAGEMENT
OFFICE OF SPECIAL COUNSEL
PANAMA CANAL COMMISSION
PEACE CORPS
PENSION BENEFIT GUARANTY CORPORATION
POSTAL RATE COMMISSION
RAILROAD RETIREMENT BOARD

SECURITIES AND EXCHANGE COMMISSION
SELECTIVE SERVICE SYSTEM
SMALL BUSINESS ADMINISTRATION
SOCIAL SECURITY ADMINISTRATION
TENNESSEE VALLEY AUTHORITY
TRADE AND DEVELOPMENT AGENCY
U.S. ARMS CONTROL AND DISARMAMENT AGENCY
U.S. COMMISSION ON CIVIL RIGHTS
U.S. INFORMATION AGENCY
U.S. INTERNATIONAL DEVELOPMENT COOPERATION AGENCY
U.S. INTERNATIONAL TRADE COMMISSION
U.S. POSTAL SERVICE

The Great Federal Job Factory

S o you want to work for the Feds, America's single largest employer. You've probably heard numerous stories—both good and bad—about the federal government and federal employment. That it's engulfed in crises and scandals. No one seems to get respect these days. There's lots of deadwood, unskilled people, and spoiled employees with serious attitude problems hanging around in too many poorly managed agencies. Morale is awful. You won't like where and with whom you have to work. It's difficult to find a federal job given today's budget-cutting, downsizing, and "reinventing" government environment. On a more positive note, federal employees receive generous benefits and have great job security. Many federal jobs lead to exciting career opportunities.

There's lots of truth to all these statements as well as many myths and misunderstandings. This is a big and diverse government complex that defies simple stereotypes and generalizations. The "truth" often depends on where you stand—or sit—in this colossal called the federal government!

Questions, Questions, Questions

Perhaps you are less concerned with macro trends and micro cultures. You want to be "shown the way" to land a federal job, maybe any job.

1

Indeed, your needs are very simple: you want to know where are the jobs, how can I get one, and where do I start? You have other questions. What do they pay, and what benefits can I expect to receive? What type of examinations must I take? Is there a Civil Service examination? What is the SF-171, OF-612, and a federal-style resume? Which ones should I complete, how do they differ from one another, and how do I get started? Do I need personal "connections" to land a job? How do I get a rating as well as placed on a registry? What are the roles of the Office of Personnel Management (OPM), the Federal Employment Information System, and agency personnel offices in the hiring process? How can I access the federal "Employment Information Highway" electronically? Where can I find federal vacancies listed on the Internet? What are my chances of landing a federal job? How long will it take—one month, three months, or six months? How secure is a federal job given today's economic uncertainties, political changes, and cutbacks in government? Will I really enjoy working for the federal government? The questions seem to go on and on and on.

These and many other questions are often raised by those interested in federal employment. Some of the questions are inappropriate, reflecting a general lack of knowledge about changes in the federal government. Others can be easily answered. And still others require a thorough knowledge of the government hiring process.

> **The federal government hires nearly 1,000 people a day.**

We'll answer these and many other questions you may have about this large and fascinating employment arena that literally hires nearly 1,000 people a day. You'll learn some basic facts about federal employment as well as acquire some very useful knowledge for landing a federal job. Much of this knowledge relates to the formal rules and regulations, whereas other knowledge might be best termed "street smarts." How fast you find a job will largely depend on your federal job finding knowledge and skills.

Faster and Easier Than Ever

Finding a federal job today is fast compared to the situation five or ten years ago. Indeed, hiring for some jobs is much faster than for comparable jobs in the private sector—so fast that you may be forced to make up your mind immediately upon application!

But finding a federal job is especially fast for those who know how the system works; who use the Internet for acquiring agency, vacancy, and application information and even for applying online; who target a well organized job search toward specific positions and agencies; and who clearly communicate their qualifications to hiring officials through tests, applications, and interviews.

That's what this book is all about—understanding how the system works and how to quickly move into a federal job you really want. While it is not a "magic pill" for getting a federal job, the book is designed to make the application process much easier for you.

Misinformation

While many people are interested in working for the federal government, few know how to find a job in the most efficient and effective manner possible. Many people believe federal jobs offer good pay and security, and many jobs are extremely interesting and rewarding. But few of these same people ever apply for a federal job, or they give up prematurely because they believe the hiring process is complicated, time consuming, and too competitive for them. In many cases, they use a weak approach to finding a federal job—respond to a vacancy announcement with a brief Standard Form 171 (SF-171), OF-612, or an inappropriate resume and then wait to be called for an interview. Others believe they still need to take a civil service examination, get an OPM "rating," and be placed on a registry. And still others don't know even the basics of where to go or what to do. They've never heard of the SF-171, OF-612, or a federal-style resume; they don't know how to "customize" these application forms for maximum impact; they're not sure what to do with their applications; they are uncertain about where to find job vacancy announcements as well as offices of agencies; they struggle with understanding the retirement system and such related concepts as CSRS, FERS, and COLAS. All in all, they see the federal government as one big swamp filled with hundreds of confusing agencies and hiring procedures that are best left alone.

Despite numerous attempts by the federal government to publicize its hiring procedures, streamline the hiring process, and decentralize hiring authority to individual agencies, the federal government still has a reputation for operating a slow, cumbersome, and confusing hiring system. In the minds of many people, federal hiring is anything but fast!

However, changes in federal personnel practices during the past five years have created a more favorable climate for those interested in finding a federal job.

Internet "Haves" and "Have Nots"

Information on federal hiring, from applications to vacancy announcements and details on agency operations, is easily accessed via the Internet (for starters, try *www.usajobs.opm.gov* and *www.whitehouse.gov*). As the federal government has become increasingly "wired" via the Internet, information is now readily available on agencies and the application process. For those who are Internet and computer savvy, applying for a federal government job has never been as easy. Using your computer mouse, your government, your favorite agency, and perhaps your next job may be just a few clicks away. You may be very surprised just how easy it is to access information relevant to finding a federal job.

> Information on federal hiring is easily accessed via the Internet. If you're Internet savvy, your next job could be just a few clicks away!

Unfortunately, for those who lack computer skills and access to the Internet, the federal application process will be much more difficult and cumbersome. Increasingly, federal applicants fall into two major categories—the "haves" (Internet access) and "have nots" (traditional mail, telephone, and walk-in access). The "haves" move through the information and application processes much faster than the "have nots." To be a "have not" in today's federal job market is to be at a distinct disadvantage. If you are really serious about getting a federal job, make sure you are wired to the federal government's information superhighway, or at least get access. Many public libraries now provide such access to patrons.

It Can Really Be Fast

One of the best kept secrets in the federal government today is that hiring can be very fast. In some cases, especially for hard-to-fill clerical and technical positions, the time between submitting an application for a federal job and being hired may be only 24 to 48 hours! Other cases may only take two to four weeks. Many positions still take two to four months to fill. Except for special positions requiring lengthy security clearances—which can add 4-6 months to the screening process—today's federal government hiring process is surprisingly fast.

Changing the System

In recent years the federal government has taken major steps to streamline its hiring procedures. These changes are in part due to complaints from job applicants about the old centralized hiring system managed by the government's central personnel agency—the Office of Personnel Management (OPM). In part it was due to complaints from agency personnel who needed greater hiring flexibility to meet the particular personnel needs of their agencies. In part it is related to continuing shortages of key clerical and technical personnel who are extremely difficult to recruit given present salary levels. And in part it is due to what many experts see as a crisis in the public service—the continuing inability to recruit the best and the brightest people for the federal government, especially those with high demand skills in the private sector where they can earn two to four times more than in the federal government. For positions requiring technical skills, the private sector usually offers more attractive job opportunities than federal agencies.

> The federal government has adapted many decentralized hiring practices of the private sector by moving key recruitment and hiring decisions to the agency level.

Whatever the causes for such changes, one thing appears certain: during the past eight years the federal hiring process has been on what is proving to be an irreversible trend toward greater decentralization. More and more agencies now have authority to make their own hiring decisions. Others are sharing a greater percentage of hiring responsibilities with OPM than ever before—from announcing vacancies and collecting applications to assessing and selecting candidates. The federal government, in effect, has adapted many decentralized hiring practices of the private sector by moving key recruitment and hiring decisions to the agency level. It has literally "re-invented" its hiring process.

While the Office of Personnel Management stands at the apex of the federal personnel system, its role today is primarily to assist agencies in meeting their personnel needs. It accomplishes this by providing information to the public on how to apply for federal jobs; compiling and publishing job vacancies; maintaining online services; helping agencies disseminate information on vacancies; reviewing applications; certifying; auditing; and assisting in managing important personnel functions such as training and retirement which must be carried out on a much larger scale than at the agency level.

But these changes have also left in their aftermath more complexity and confusion concerning federal hiring practices. The very act of decentralizing hiring authority to agencies and increasing application options makes the application process more difficult for individuals who must now contact many different agencies about job vacancies as well as complete more application forms—from SF-171s and OF-612s to federal-style resumes—in applying for different types of positions. Understanding federal personnel procedures of ten years ago, many applicants still believe they need to take lengthy examinations and get an OPM rating before applying for agency job vacancies. In fact, OPM still spends time trying to explain that it no longer gives general "ratings," administers PACE or ACWA exams, or forwards SF-171s to agency personnel. Above all, the system is decentralized. In most cases you simply complete a SF-171, OF-612, or federal-style resume and submit one of these applications directly to an agency in response to the qualifications and requirements outlined in the agency's vacancy announcement. OPM still plays important roles in the hiring process, but not the highly centralized role it played ten or twenty years ago.

Best of all, this application and hiring process may only take a few days or weeks. Similar to applying for jobs in the private sector, most federal hiring these days is both decentralized and fast.

Implications For You

What are the implications of these changes for today's federal job seekers? Decentralization and streamlined hiring practices mean you should:

1. **Plan to go online to quickly find agency, job vacancy, and application information.** The federal government has been undergoing a massive electronic transformation within the past five years. Not only is this government highly computerized,

with the application of the latest technology to agency functions, its agencies are increasingly wired to the Internet. A great deal of federal agency and employment information that used to be available through printed materials in bookstores and libraries or acquired through agencies by mail is now quickly accessed via the Internet 24-hours a day. If you're not connected to the Internet and the federal government's information superhighway, you simply will be at a disadvantage in today's federal job market. Indeed, you are competing with many savvy applicants who use the Internet to quickly find vacancies and research agencies.

> **If you're not connected to the Internet and the federal government's information superhighway, you simply will be at a disadvantage in today's federal job market.**

2. **Be prepared to spend more time applying for positions**. Gone are the days when you could just submit one SF-171 for a rating, get ranked and placed on a registry, and wait to be called for an interview with an agency that selected you from the registry. You must now spend more time locating vacancies and responding to each with a SF-171, OF-612, or a federal-style resume and any other required documents. In most cases you will not be considered for a job unless you take action by locating the vacancy and meeting all application and deadline requirements.

3. **Know what you want to do, especially which positions you're interested in applying for.** Under the old system you could approach federal employment by submitting a general SF-171 for a "rating" which, in turn, qualified you for many different positions. While this occurs on a limited scale today, especially in the case of hard-to-fill "Open Continuous Positions," in most cases you get "rated" for a specific position. Using a "case examining" rather than a "central inventory" approach, this personnel system requires you to focus on specific positions. Rather than ask *"Where are the jobs?"* you must inquire *"Where are the jobs for position X?"* Begin by

deciding what you want to do (specific positions) and then locate those positions in specific agencies. You then apply for those positions with your SF-171, OF-612, or federal-style resume as well as take any required examinations.

4. **Monitor job vacancies at the agency level rather than go through OPM.** Most agencies issue their own vacancy announcements, although OPM still announces many Open Continuous Positions and screens some candidates. The key to making this process work is to keep in contact with particular agencies that interest you so you will know when vacancies are announced. If you do this, you will be in a better position to meet specific application deadlines, which sometimes can be as short as a 10-day period between when the position is announced and the application period ends.

5. **Apply directly to agencies or through OPM.** Always read vacancy announcements carefully. Vacancy announcements specify the procedures for submitting an application. In most cases the procedure is the same—send a SF-171, OF-612, or federal-style resume and other supporting documents directly to the agency personnel office; in some cases OPM requests and screens applications for agencies. Any required examinations will be specified in the vacancy announcement.

6. **Customize or "target" your SF-171, OF-612, or federal-style resume so it best responds to the knowledge, skills, and abilities specified for particular positions.** Please remember that the old "rating" system no longer exists. And do OPM personnel a favor by not asking them *"How do I get a rating?"* This question will demonstrate your ignorance of current hiring procedures. Since you no longer receive a general OPM rating to be used in applying for all positions, you no longer need to produce a general SF-171 that would meet the rating criteria of OPM examiners that used to specify whether or not you were "qualified" for a particular class of positions. Under this new case examining system, you normally get rated each time you apply for a position. Therefore, your SF-171, OF-612, or federal-style resume must clearly

communicate your qualifications for specific positions rather than for classes of positions. Given this procedure, it's best to carefully examine each vacancy announcement and customize the knowledge, skills, and abilities (KSA) sections of your application so they best respond to the detailed requirements of the particular position. Your choice of language becomes extremely important in this new application system.

7. **Use informal job finding strategies, such as networking and informational interviewing, that are most commonly associated with the "hidden job market" in the private sector.** Regardless of attempts to coordinate information on job vacancies through OPM's Federal Employment Information System, which is updated daily and can be accessed by phone, fax, touch screen computers, and the Internet, information on agency job vacancies is at best both formalized and incomplete. Decentralization means that information on job vacancies will be highly fragmented and chaotic. In addition to monitoring job vacancies with individual agencies, you should network and engage in informational interviewing so that you will learn when and where vacancies are likely to be announced. In the process of doing so, you may become the subject of "wiring" a position around your qualifications.

8. **Keep an eye open for special recruiting events amongst agencies that have critical personnel needs for certain types of positions.** Many federal agencies have difficulty recruiting for positions at two different ends of the hiring spectrum— clerical and high-tech. These are high-demand occupations for which most federal agencies have extreme difficulty recruiting qualified personnel. The problem is due to a combination of the overall nationwide shortage of such skilled workers and the sometimes more attractive salaries offered in the private sector. In response to this crisis, OPM and agencies have stepped up their public information and advertising campaigns to interest more clerical and high-tech personnel in federal work. Most agencies have job hotline phone numbers that announce current vacancies and application procedures. Many agency personnel offices will send you via email, fax, or mail a copy

of a particular vacancy announcement upon request. In addition, some agencies occasionally sponsor job fairs for the purpose of quickly hiring much needed personnel. While job fairs were very popular in the early 1990s, they are rarely used today given major cutbacks and staffing uncertainties of many agencies. However, job fairs may become popular sometime in the future as agencies need to once again recruit hard-to-find personnel. Participating in such job fairs is the quickest way to survey numerous employment options and get hired in the federal government. Ads announcing upcoming federal job fairs will periodically appear in local newspapers or such events will be announced on radio and television.

9. **Expect to encounter greater career mobility due to recent changes in the federal retirement system that is eroding the old "golden handcuff" system that discouraged individuals from seeking career mobility outside their agencies or the federal government.** Adapting the concept of a portable retirement system from the private sector, the federal government is opening up its personnel system to greater fluidity of personnel. No longer should federal employees feel locked into positions after ten years of service because of being vested in a retirement system that discourages them from moving to other jobs or careers. With the portable retirement system (FERS), federal workers will participate in career development systems more closely approximating those found in corporations in the private sector.

The major implication of all these changes for you and many thousands of other federal job seekers is that finding a federal job today is much easier than ever before. It's especially fast for those individuals who possess the most important ingredients for success in today's federal job market:

- Computer and Internet savvy skills for researching agencies, finding vacancies, and submitting first-class applications.

- Highly marketable work-content skills and an aptitude for learning new skills required by federal agencies.

- A powerful SF-171, OF-612, or federal-style resume that clearly communicates one's specific qualifications in the specialized language of agencies and hiring officials.

- Knowledge of how to best penetrate both the formal (advertised) and informal (hidden) federal job markets.

While we are not in a position to provide you with nor enhance your repertoire of marketable work-content skills, we can provide you with important information and knowledge on how the federal job market works as well as suggest key job search strategies that will give you that "extra edge" in finding the federal job that is right for you. That precisely is our mission in the chapters that follow—show you how to find a federal job as fast as possible assuming you already have the necessary skills agencies seek in today's federal job market.

The Public Service Crisis

We would be the last to suggest you take advantage of crises. However, in the case of the federal government, you can do both yourself and your country a favor by finding a federal job fast!

Today's public service has been battered by political pundits, a poor image, public relations failures, and real budgetary, program, and personnel cutbacks. During the past decade we have witnessed what many seasoned observers call a quiet "public service crisis." This is essentially a **crisis of competence** as federal agencies increasingly face difficulties in recruiting and retaining highly qualified personnel who prefer private sector jobs. Why, for example, should you work for the federal government when you may be able to make more money and probably have just as much security and perhaps receive better benefits working in the private sector? This is a tough question for many would-be, as well as current, federal employees to answer, especially if they are oriented toward public service work but appreciate the value of cash!

Unless major steps are taken to reverse recent trends, the federal government faces two major problems in the decade ahead:

- **Salaries will become increasingly noncompetitive, especially for high-skill jobs in the most expensive areas of the country.** Federal government salaries face stiff competition from the private sector in such areas as New York City, the Northeast, and the West Coast. Despite federal pay differentials for major metropolitan areas, many agencies in these areas will experience even greater difficulty in recruiting and retaining individuals with high-tech skills as well as senior managers.

- **Public attitudes toward, student interest in, and prestige of the public service will continue to decline and thus accentuate the growing government performance crisis.** Fewer talented individuals will decide to enter government given a public environment of disdain and hostility toward the public service. Skill levels and capabilities of new recruits may not be adequate for the increased performance requirements of government in the decade ahead. The result will be to further contract-out government services to capable private consultants and contractors who have the skills to provide necessary services.

Overall, the federal government in the decade ahead faces a frustrating double-whammy: demands for increased government performance but fewer qualified individuals to perform at even present levels. The picture is one of continuing drift in the public service unless certain changes take place in the very near future.

> The federal government faces a frustrating double-whammy: demands for increased government performance but fewer qualified employees.

Nonetheless, hope for a better public service is in the air. Recognizing this public service crisis and doing something about it in order to prevent even greater crises in the decade ahead is definitely on the government's planning agenda. Whether it gets translated into the budgetary agenda is another question altogether. For in the end, all of these changes cost money, and the price tag will not be cheap. Like the nation's much neglected physical infrastructure, its neglected human infrastructure has much to be improved.

Indeed, the National Commission on the Public Service—also known as the Volcker Commission—in an urgent call for action has outlined numerous actions that should be taken to stem what appears to be an inevitable slide toward mediocrity and incompetence in the public service. The Commission's *Leadership For America: Rebuilding the Public Service* report, for example, gives us a glimpse of the major issues facing the public service as well as outlines possible changes taking place in the decade ahead. It provides a "big picture" of the past, present, and future from which to examine the details of getting a federal job. Possible solutions to the public service crisis include:

1. **Rebuild the public's trust in the public service.** Traditional public skepticism toward big government as well as perceptions of corruption, waste, and ineffectiveness in government have been exacerbated by more than a decade of political rhetoric denouncing the evils of government. Top leadership in government, from the President to members of Congress, should set the highest ethical standards as well as frequently emphasize the importance of the public service and public servants in an effort to develop a more positive and appealing image of public service.

2. **Efforts should be made to improve the presidential appointments process.** Each new President faces the problem of filling several hundred top government jobs within a few months after entering office. A new recruiting process should be instituted for quickly recruiting qualified appointees.

3. **More room should be made for top career executives at the very highest levels of government.** The continuing growth of presidential appointees should be reversed and cutback from the current level of 3,000 to no more than 2,000. While noncareer appointees are essential to the functioning of the public service, a greater use of top career talent is in order.

4. **Greater efforts should be made to decentralize government management.** Cabinet officers and agency heads should be given greater flexibility to administer agencies, including the power to hire and fire personnel. Greater emphasis should be placed on executive training of senior managers.

5. **The presidential/career partnership should be strengthened.** Presidential appointees and career executives need to work together in a relationship of mutual trust rather than an adversarial

"we/they" relationship of suspicion and mistrust. Therefore, all presidential appointees should receive adequate orientation to office, and cabinet secretaries and agency heads should participate more in choosing sub-cabinet officers.

6. **Major efforts should be made to rebuild student interest in the public service.** The future performance of the public service depends on its ability to attract some of the best and brightest entry-level talent to government. After more than a decade of eroding student interest in government, efforts should be made to rekindle the "public service" ethic at all educational levels, from increased civic education to expanding volunteer programs.

7. **Efforts need to be made to recruit the very best graduates.** Few top college graduates view the public sector as a place for developing meaningful, challenging, and rewarding careers. The President and Congress should establish a Presidential Public Service Scholarship Program for 1,000 college or college-bound students each year which would pay tuition and costs in return for several years of commitment to government service. Current college recruitment programs also need to be strengthened, such as expanding the Presidential Management Internship program from 400 to 1,000 positions each year.

8. **New channels of information need to be opened for recruiting individuals to government.** This includes the use of job fairs, electronic bulletin boards, computer software, and videos to inform college students about opportunities in government. OPM should establish a unified federal job bank to help students find openings in the public sector.

9. **OPM should simplify the recruiting process.** OPM should continue to decentralize hiring authority to departments and agencies. It should also experiment with new recruitment incentives for hard-to-recruit professions as well as experiment with on-the-spot hiring of both undergraduate and graduate students.

10. **Minorities should be increasingly represented in the public service.** The government should provide training, including high

school course work, for blacks and Hispanics upon entry into their government careers. Graduate schools of public affairs should develop more cooperative relationships with historically black and Hispanic colleges.

11. **More competitive pay needs to be provided at all levels in the public services.** The President and Congress must give higher budget priority to civil service compensation. Executive, judicial, and legislative salaries, especially at the senior levels, need to be adjusted to the 1969 levels of purchasing power in order to attract and retain talented public employees. Efforts should be made to institute a pay-setting system whereby federal employees in different cost-of-living settings (San Francisco versus Kansas City) receive differential compensation for the same jobs.

12. **Efforts should be made to strengthen the government's personnel agency—the Office of Personnel Management.** The weakening of OPM during the 1980s through a combination of budgetary and personnel cuts has left many agencies confused about the government's recruiting policies. This agency needs to be revitalized in efforts to develop more performance-oriented government personnel policies. Political appointees within OPM should be significantly reduced.

13. **Government productivity needs to be increased.** Annual bonuses should be given to senior executives to encourage competitiveness and productivity in the senior ranks. OPM should play a more important role in the performance appraisals and productivity improvement efforts of departments and agencies.

14. **Greater emphasis should be placed on training within the public sector.** OPM and the nation's public affairs schools should work together in defining the skills needed by today's public executives. OPM should help departments and agencies develop clearer career advancement programs as well as develop training programs or seek training assistance from other agencies or outside government. Closer collaboration between academics and practitioners is needed.

15. **The government work place needs to be improved.** More effort
     needs to be focused on improving working conditions.

Several of these recommendations are presently being acted upon,
especially in the areas of decentralization, productivity, recruitment, and
the pay system. Other recommendations may be implemented in some
revised form. And still others may never see the political light of day.
Some, such as minority representation, lack credibility when examining
the facts of federal personnel.

At the same time, Vice-President Al Gore's "Reinventing Government" initiative, also has focused on strengthening the public sector. In
contrast to previous government reform efforts, this initiative was
designed to downsize the federal government by 272,900 employers over
a four-year period (1993-1997). This has been one of the few reform
efforts that specifically attacked the growing size of the federal government. Also known as the National Performance Review (NPR), the basic
thrust of this reform effort has been to streamline the federal government
through the process of decentralization. When fully implemented, it
would mean fewer layers of management as well as fewer managers at all
levels of government. Agencies would be given greater authority to hire
and fire, and job seekers will face both a streamlined and decentralized
hiring system. Reinvented government essentially means a leaner and
more decentralized government. By 1998, these reform efforts actually
exceeded the goals in terms of downsizing federal employees. Today, the
government has 337,182 fewer employees (representing an overall 15
percent reduction) than when the reform efforts began in 1993.

The results of the historic congressional elections of November 1994,
which shifted political control of both houses from Democrats to
Republicans, appear to have accelerated the downsizing of the federal
government. Many departments and agencies, such as the Departments
of Education, Commerce, Energy, and Housing and Urban Development,
the Agency for International Development, the Equal Employment
Opportunity Commission, and the Small Business Administration, were
more endangered than ever before. Other departments, especially Justice
and Defense, seemed to have benefited under this new Congress. The
congressional temperament has been to cut the federal budget without
disturbing entitlements and defense expenditures. Given such thinking,
the political arithmetic has been simple: more agencies and personnel are
cut in the process of further downsizing the federal government; many

costly federal programs, especially welfare, were devolved to state and local governments. Fewer job opportunities were available with the federal government but more job opportunities were found with state and local governments. These governments have had to pay both the economic and political costs of this new "reinvented" federal government!

One thing appears certain in the decade ahead: the public service will undergo important changes in order to stem the tide toward mediocrity. As a result, greater emphasis will be placed on recruiting and retaining talented individuals. If these issues and problems can be converted into action, the next decade may well become one of the most significant restructuring periods for the public service. In the meantime, the public service faces numerous challenges from a political system that also is undergoing important changes. Major budgetary realignment is taking place as the Department of Defense downsizes and other agencies, such as the Department of Justice, become beneficiaries of new national priorities.

> **Reinvented government means leaner and more decentralized federal agencies—efforts that are supposed to stem the tide toward mediocrity.**

Keep in mind that most of this so-called crisis and recommended solutions relate to problems with the **system as a whole**. How it affects you, the individual, is another matter altogether. Regardless of these problems, many individuals still seek federal employment. Competition is very keen for many types of positions whereas hardly any competition exists for other types of positions.

One problem, however, remains for most individuals interested in federal employment: information on federal jobs and careers, agency operations, vacancy announcements, and how to get a federal job is not well communicated both inside and outside government circles. This information problem is partly responsible for much of today's public service crisis. Indeed, we see this as the single most important problem facing **both** the system and the individual.

A Different Approach

The following chapters are designed to help you target an effective federal job search as well as find your own career niche within the federal government. It begins with a simple premise concerning the role of information in the employment process:

> Most people lack accurate and useful information on finding a federal job and advancing within and beyond the federal system.

If they had more accurate and useful information, they would be more motivated to seek federal employment as well as understand the skills necessary for finding a federal job fast.

You will quickly discover that this is not your normal treatment of how to find a federal job. Most examinations of this subject primarily restate OPM's formal rules and regulations that define the federal hiring process; reprint forms; and get bogged down in minutia, much of which is irrelevant to finding a federal job. They often become preoccupied with the trees without presenting the importance of the larger forest. We include such formalistic rules and regulations as well as examine the **context** of federal employment and the **dynamics** of the hiring process. In so doing, we hope to bring to life what is often a dull and boring subject. We've attempted to show how the federal employment process operates in both theory and practice—from formal application procedures to informal networking and "wiring" practices. The result is a book that is a personal roadmap to discovering the many realities of federal employment that may or may not follow the formal rules and regulations. We believe we have presented **both** the forest and the trees within the framework of a practical, usable guide. At least that has been our goal.

We begin by examining many myths and motivations that often mislead as well as guide individuals into the federal employment arena. We then outline the structure and setting of the federal job market, including employment statistics for various growing and declining agencies. Shifting the focus from government as a whole (the "system") to the individual in search of employment (the "decision-maker"), the remainder of the book approaches the federal job search process from the perspective of the job seeker who must make several strategic decisions in order to find a federal job fast. The chapters outline the key steps involved in finding a federal job:

- Researching government agencies
- Identifying job alternatives

- Understanding the formal and informal hiring process
- Taking tests
- Locating vacancies
- Writing effective applications
- Submitting applications

The book also includes two chapters normally absent in most exa-minations of federal employment—the legislative and judicial branches of government (Chapter 9) and action planning (Chapter 10). It also includes three appendices: a list of all Federal Employment Information Sources, useful Internet addresses, and sample copies of the key federal application forms—the SF-171 and OF-612.

Choose the Right Resources

Each year millions of job hunters turn to career planning books for assistance. Normally they begin with a general book and next turn to resume and interview books. They may also find a few books, such as this one, that provide career information on specific employment fields.

If this book represents your first career planning book, you may want to supplement it with a few other key books. When we discuss the importance of networking and interviewing, for example, we recommend that you consult separate detailed volumes such as *Dynamite Networking For Dynamite Jobs, Interview For Success, Dynamite Tele-Search*, and *101 Dynamite Answers to Interview Questions* that show you how to effectively complete each of these job search steps. If you are looking for a directory of federal agencies—complete with descriptions of work and contact information—then we recommend our companion volume, *The Directory of Federal Jobs and Employers*. Several of our other books address various job search and advancement skills: *Change Your Job Change Your Life, Discover the Best Jobs For You, High Impact Resumes and Letters, Dynamite Resumes, Dynamite Cover Letters, 201 Dynamite Job Search Letters, Get a Raise in 7 Days*, and *Dynamite Salary Negotiations*. We also address particular job trends, career fields, and populations in the following books: *The Best Jobs For the 21st Century, The Complete Guide to Public Employment, The Complete Guide to International Jobs and Careers, International Jobs Directory, The Educator's Guide to Alternative Jobs and Careers, Jobs For People Who Love Travel, From Army Green to Corporate Gray, From*

Air Force Blue to Corporate Gray, and *From Navy Blue to Corporate Gray*. If you are transitioning from the military, be sure to take advantage of the career transition resources (job listings, resume database, employers, useful job search articles) on our affiliated military online service which can be accessed through two URLs: *www.greentogray.com* and *www.bluetogray.com*.

These and many other books are available in your local library and bookstore or they can be ordered directly from Impact Publications by completing the order form at the end of this book. You also may want to request a free copy of Impact's career brochure by sending a self-addressed stamped envelope (#10 business size) and it will be mailed to you:

IMPACT PUBLICATIONS
ATTN: Free Career Brochure
9104-N Manassas Drive
Manassas Park, VA 20111-5211

Nearly 2,000 career resources are available through Impact Publication's comprehensive "Career Superstore" on the World Wide Web:

www.impactpublications.com

Impact's site also includes new titles, specials, and job search tips for keeping you in touch with the latest in career information and resources.

We wish you well as you make your journey into the world of federal employment. If you follow the advice of this and subsequent chapters, you should be well on the way to quickly finding a federal job. While you may not find the ideal job, you will at least get your foot into an important door that can lead to a very rewarding career. You can open that door by putting your best foot forward with a powerful application that clearly communicates your qualifications to federal employers. In the meantime, don't neglect the importance of the federal government's information superhighway. For within the next few years, the watchwords for individuals interested in finding a federal job fast will be these:

You gotta get wired if you wanna get hired!

Your government and your next job may be only a few clicks away!

2

Myths, Realities, and Your Future

W here are the jobs? How do I get one? What's it like working for government? Underlying these frequently asked questions are certain assumptions about the federal job market and the work of public employees. While such questions may anticipate easy answers, the answers are much more complex when examining job opportunities amongst the multitude of agencies that define the federal job market.

Let's begin answering these initial questions by first examining several myths which could impede your job search within the federal government as well as affect your motivation for finding a federal job. These myths also focus on important employment issues affecting both job seekers and employers. Based on this discussion, you should be able to orient your job search in the right direction.

Muddlers and Their Myths

Most job seekers are unprepared and naive in approaching the federal job market; some might be best termed "job dumb." They muddle-through the process of finding a job with questionable perceptions about federal employment and how this job market works in both theory and practice.

Combining a few facts with numerous stereotypes, myths, and folk-lore—gained from a mixture of logic, experience, and advice from well-meaning friends and relatives—these perceptions lead job seekers down several unproductive paths. Such perceptions are often responsible for two beliefs which become self-fulfilling prophecies of unsuccessful job seekers: *"There are no jobs available for me"* and *"The system is closed to people with my educational background, interests, and skills."*

Overcoming Job Market Myths

Let's look at several myths that may dissuade you from taking effective action in today's job market. These myths are part of a general job search folklore that contributes to job search failure as well as numerous stereotypes that are the basis for perceptions about the nature of government work. Taken together, these myths prevent many people from becoming successful in today's job market. On the other hand, a set of corresponding realities dispel most of these myths as well as point you in the right direction for developing the necessary motivations and skills for achieving job search success.

> **Most job seekers muddle-through the job market with questionable perceptions of how it works.**

The first twelve myths are basic myths which often prevent individuals from being effective in finding a job. While they do not relate directly to government employment, they do so indirectly and thus form the foundation for several myths relevant to government:

MYTH 1:   Anyone can find a job; all you need to know is how to find a job.

REALITY: This "form versus substance" myth is often associated with career counselors who were raised on popular career planning exhortations of the 1970s and 1980s that stressed the importance of having positive attitudes and self-esteem, setting goals, dressing for success, and using interpersonal strategies for finding jobs. While such approaches may work well in an industrial society with low unemployment and for many sales positions, they constitute myths in a post-industrial, high-tech society which requires individuals to demonstrate both **intelligence and concrete work skills** as well as a **willingness to relocate** to new communities offering greater job opportunities. For example, many of today's displaced workers are highly skilled in the old technology of the industrial society, and they live and own homes in economically depressed communities. These people lack the necessary **skills and mobility** required for getting jobs in growing communities. Knowing job search skills alone will not help these people. Indeed, such advice and knowledge will most likely frustrate such highly motivated, unskilled, and immobile individuals.

MYTH 2: **The best way to find a job is to respond to classified ads, use employment agencies, submit applications to personnel offices, and surf the Internet for job vacancies.**

REALITY: Except for certain types of organizations and jobs, these formal application procedures are not the most effective ways of finding jobs. Such approaches assume the presence of an organized, coherent, and centralized job market. But no such thing exists. Although it exhibits some pockets of centralization, especially relating to online employment sites, for the most part the job market is highly decentralized, fragmented, and chaotic —a caricature of the overall American governmental system. Classified ads, employment agencies, and personnel offices tend to list low paying yet highly competitive jobs. Internet employment sites are often disappointing. Most of the best jobs—high level, excellent pay, least competitive—are neither listed nor advertised; they are most likely found through word-of-mouth or through headhunters. When seeking employment outside government, your most fruitful strategy will be to conduct research and informational interviews on what career counselors call the "hidden job market." In the case of government, you will need to supplement formal application procedures, such as responding to vacancy announcements with an effective SF-171, OF-612, or federal-style resume, by using informal approaches such as networking and informational interviews. Like the employment market in the private sector, government has both an "advertised" and a "hidden" job market. Chapter 8 outlines how you can best link the formal and informal approaches for developing a powerful job search within government.

MYTH 3: **Few jobs are available for me in today's competitive job market.**

REALITY: This may be true if you lack marketable skills and insist on applying for jobs listed in newspapers, employment agencies, or personnel offices. Competition in the advertised job market usually is high, especially for jobs requiring few skills. Numerous jobs with little competition are available on the hidden job market. Jobs requiring advanced technical skills often go begging. Little competition may occur during periods of high unemployment, because many people quit job hunting after a few disappointing weeks of working the advertised job market.

MYTH 4: **I know how to find a job, but opportunities are not available for me.**

REALITY: Most people don't know how to find a job, or they lack marketable job skills. They continue to use ineffective job search methods, such as submitting applications and waiting to hear from employers. Opportunities are readily available for individuals who understand the structure and operation of the job market, have appropriate work-content skills, and use job search methods designed for the hidden job market. Above all, the job market favors individuals who take action rather than those who engage in such paper or electronic rituals as submitting applications and waiting for employers to contact them by mail, email, or phone!

MYTH 5:   **Employers are in the driver's seat; they have the upper-hand with applicants.**

REALITY: Most often no one is in the driver's seat. Not knowing what they want, many employers make poor hiring decisions. They frequently let applicants define their hiring needs. If you can define employers' needs as your skills, you might end up in the driver's seat!

MYTH 6:   **Employers hire the best qualified candidates. Without a great deal of experience and numerous qualifications, I don't have a chance.**

REALITY: Employers hire people for all kinds of reasons. Most rank experience and qualifications third or fourth in their pecking order of hiring criteria. Employers seldom hire the best qualified candidate, because "qualifications" are difficult to define and measure. Employers normally seek people with the following characteristics: competent, intelligent, honest, and likable. "Likability" tends to be an overall concern of employers. Employers want **value** for their money. Therefore, you must communicate to employers that you are such a person. You must overcome employers' objections to any lack of experience or qualifications. But never volunteer your weaknesses. The best qualified person is the one who knows how to get the job—convinces employers that he or she is the **most** desirable for the job.

MYTH 7:   **It is best to go into a growing field where jobs are plentiful.**

REALITY: Be careful in following the masses to the "in" fields. First, many so-called growth fields can quickly become no-growth fields, such as aerospace engineering, nuclear energy, and defense contracting. Second, by the time you acquire the necessary skills, you may experience the "disappearing job" phenomenon: too many people did the same thing you did and consequently glut the job market. Third, since many people leave no-growth fields, new opportunities may arise for you. Fourth, if you go after a growth field, you will try to fit into a job rather than find a job fit for you. If you know what you do well and enjoy doing and what additional training you may need, you should look for a job or career conducive to your particular mix of skills, interests, and motivations. In the long-run you will be much happier and more productive finding a job fit for you.

MYTH 8: **People over 40 have difficulty finding a good job.**

REALITY: Yes, if they apply for youth jobs or lack current workplace skills. Age should be an insignificant barrier to employment if you have marketable skills, conduct a well organized job search, and are prepared to handle this potential negative with employers. Age should be a positive and must be communicated as such. After all, employers want experience, maturity, and stability. People over 40 generally possess these qualities. As the population ages and birth rates decline, older individuals should have a much easier time finding employment.

MYTH 9: **I must be aggressive in order to find a job.**

REALITY: Aggressive people tend to be offensive and obnoxious people. Try being purposeful, persistent, and pleasant in all of your job search efforts. Such behavior is well received by potential employers.

MYTH 10: **I should not change jobs and careers more than once or twice. Job-changers are discriminated against in hiring.**

REALITY: While this may have been generally true 30 years ago, it is no longer true today. America is a skills-based society: individuals market their skills to organizations in exchange for money and position. Furthermore, since most organizations are small businesses or units of government with limited advancement opportunities, careers within business and government tend to quickly plateau. For most people, the only way up is to get out and into another organization. Therefore, the best way to advance careers in a society of small businesses and government units is to change jobs frequently. Job-changing is okay as long as such changes demonstrate career advancement and don't take place too frequently. Recent changes in the federal retirement system (from CSRS to FERS) eliminate one of the major impediments—the lack of a portable retirement system—to making such job and career changes and thus should open up the system to greater mobility between the public and private sectors. Most individuals entering the job market today will undergo several career and job changes regardless of their initial desire for a one-job, one-career life plan.

MYTH 11:   **People get ahead by working hard and putting in long hours. If I work real hard, I should get promoted as well as improve my salary.**

REALITY: Success patterns differ. Many people who are honest, work hard, and put in long hours also get fired, have ulcers, and die young. Some people get ahead even though they are dishonest and lazy. Others simply have good luck or a helpful patron or mentor. Moderation in both work and play will probably get you just as far as the extremes. Chapter 3 outlines some realistic ways to become successful in addition to hard work and long hours.

MYTH 12:   **It's not a good idea to use connections in getting a job. I should apply through the front door like everyone else. If I'm the best qualified, I should get the job.**

REALITY: While you may wish to stand in line for tickets, bank deposits, and loans—because you have no clout—standing in line for a job is dumb. Every employer has a front door as well as a back door. Try using the back door if you can. It works in many cases.

Government Myths and Realities

While the twelve myths are relevant to the job market in general and should assist you in penetrating the public sector job market, another twelve myths are particularly relevant for government employment.

MYTH 13: **Government agencies are not hiring.**

REALITY: Government agencies always hire, even during the worst of times, such as the 1993-1997 period that witnessed a surprising 15 percent reduction of the federal workforce. Federal agencies have an average annual turnover rate of 10-14 percent. Furthermore, federal agencies hire nearly 1,000 people each day, or 300,000 each year. If they did not hire in response to natural attrition rates, they would lack the capacity to function. The fact they don't advertise widely is no reason to believe they are not hiring. Even during cutback periods, hiring takes place in most agencies; downsizing usually takes place through attrition rather than through firings. Your challenge is to learn how to get information on job vacancies and application requirements with federal agencies.

MYTH 14: **Working for the federal government means moving to Washington, DC.**

REALITY: Only 11.9 percent of the federal workforce is located in the Washington Metro area. The remaining 88.1 percent is spread throughout the country, with a particularly heavy concentration in California. Mainly centered around 10 regional cities, federal employees also work in small communities, remote areas, and abroad. The largest percentage of personnel concentrated in the

Washington Metro area are found in Congress and the legislative bureaucracy (100%), Supreme Court (100%), Smithsonian Institution (93.2%), National Regulatory Commission (76.6%), U.S. International Development Cooperation Agency (48.1%), Federal Emergency Management Agency (46.1%), U.S. Information Agency (43.3%), Office of Personnel Management (40.1%), General Services Administration (37.0%), and the Environmental Protection Agency (33.5%) as well as in the Departments of Education (69.1%), Commerce (52.1%), Energy (34.9%), Labor (34.3%), and State (28.6%). Agencies with the fewest number of employees in the Washington Metro area include the U.S. Courts (7.3 percent), Tennessee Valley Authority (0.1%), U.S. Postal Service (2.5%), Federal Deposit Insurance Corporation (12.3%), and the Departments of Veterans Affairs (2.6%), Defense (8.1%), Interior (11.8%), and Transportation (13.6%). In fact, you'll be lucky if you get to Washington!

MYTH 15: **Competition for government jobs is so great that I don't have a chance.**

REALITY: The same is probably true for jobs in the private sector. During difficult economic times, such as the recessions of 1981 and 1991, competition for federal jobs was increasingly keen as more and more individuals in the private sector turned to the federal government for what many perceived to be more secure employment opportunities than in the private sector. In addition, the annual turnover rate slowed considerably as fewer federal employees left government for jobs in the private sector. Their "wait and see" behavior contributed to the overall increase in competition for government positions. Accordingly, the quality of applicants increased dramatically during these recessionary periods. Many college graduates, who normally would not consider federal employment, were shocked to discover how keen competition was for entry-level administrative and professional positions.

While government employment is competitive, your chances of getting a federal job are much better if you know how to present yourself to agencies and you are persistent. Much of your competition is poorly organized for this job market even during hard economic times. Many give up within a few weeks after one or two application attempts, and few know how to write an effective SF-171, OF-612, or federal-style resume, uncover job leads, or follow-up applications. The key to success is targeting jobs for which you are qualified and learning how to best make your SF-171, OF-612, or federal-style resume stand above the crowd.

MYTH 16: **Government salaries are lower than those in the private sector.**

REALITY: The verdict on comparable pay still remains uncertain, although government studies periodically emphasize that inequities do indeed exist between public and private sector salaries with public salaries at a disadvantage. While some of these studies are self-serving, the major problem is always one of defining "comparability" and factoring in such noncomparable elements as "profit" and "risk-taking" versus "public service." In a culture that distrusts government and is skeptical of public employees, higher value is placed on movers and shakers in the private sector who are more oriented toward generating profits and taking risks than on those involved in consuming public funds. Salary inequities are evident in many cases, especially if you make $92,287 or $125,900 a year—the ceiling placed on many General Schedule and Senior Executive Services salaries respectively. Comparable private sector positions may pay $175,000 or more a year. However, government salaries are generous in the $32,000 to $70,000 annual salary ranges, especially for generalists. Comparable positions in the private sector tend to pay less. At the same time, highly skilled workers in this salary range may make 20 to 30 percent less than their counterparts in the private sector. Salary inequities are more a problem for individuals making at least $70,000 a year and whose careers have plateaued in the public sector. But many of these people are overpaid compared to similar work performed in the private sector. The federal government recently has made major efforts to end many obvious salary inequities, especially for individuals in high-demand positions and those residing in high-cost metropolitan areas. Public opinion still supports the existence of salary inequities between the public and private sectors, because public jobs are supported by taxpayers' funds and people choose public careers knowing full well that public salaries will not be the same nor more than salaries in the private sector. The real question is not if there are salary inequities but how much inequity should be tolerated before it becomes dysfunctional for the public sector.

MYTH 17:   **Government work is generally dull, boring, and full of red tape.**

REALITY: Work in general has its dull and boring moments. Regardless of how exciting we attempt to make work, only a small percentage of the workforce is fortunate to have jobs they really love eight hours a day. Government agencies have by no means cornered the market on dull and boring jobs and red tape. Large organizations and governmental agencies have similar organizational maladies normally associated with bureaucracy. Like many jobs in the private sector, many government jobs also are exciting, challenging, and devoid of red tape. The quality of the job depends on where you are in the organizational hierarchy and what you are doing.

MYTH 18:   **A great deal of incompetence and deadwood exists in government.**

REALITY: A great deal of incompetence and deadwood also exists in business and private industry. One major difference is that the private sector periodically cleans out its deadwood during recessions when the red ink requires cost-saving techniques. However, once recessions are over and businesses show profits, they again acquire and keep incompetence and deadwood. The real myth is that business and private industry are substantially more efficient and effective than government. After all, over 500,000 businesses fail each year; and many failures are due to mismanagement, incompetence, and deadwood. Government, on the other hand, is not allowed to fail, and thus it lacks a key imperative to clean its house. Moreover, with nearly 13 percent of the American workforce unionized, many organizations are constrained in making the necessary personnel decisions to get rid of their incompetence and deadwood.

> **The real myth is that business and private industry are substantially more efficient and effective than government.**

MYTH 19:   **Government tends to hire generalists and unskilled individuals.**

REALITY: Government tends to hire all types of individuals. It more and more hires qualified specialists who can demonstrate proficiency in particular skill areas. In general, it operates a very intelligent and skilled workforce. Few government jobs are available for the unskilled or dullards. In fact, most government jobs reflect general trends taking place elsewhere in the job market—they require more and more technical skills and regularly demonstrated competence.

MYTH 20:   **The best way to find a government job is to get a high score on an examination.**

REALITY: High scores on tests of skills are important, but they do not guarantee you a job. In addition, many government jobs do not require examinations. Depending on which position you apply for, application forms and resumes, along with recommendations and interviews, may be the only screening requirements. You will need to develop informal relationships with individuals in agencies, present yourself well in writing and in person, and follow-through the application process with personal contacts. The following chapters outline how to do this.

MYTH 21: **Political patronage and personal contacts are still important in getting a government job.**

REALITY: Political patronage still exists, but it is by no means widespread. Professional selection procedures and merit systems are firmly entrenched in most governmental agencies. Whom you know, however, can play an important and decisive role in the selection process, especially for high level positions. But the ubiquitous personal contact and the use of political pull have undergone a positive transformation: personal contacts tend to be professional contacts which help locate and screen qualified candidates. In this sense, personal contacts are both important and functional.

MYTH 22: **Once I work for government, I will have difficulty finding work in the private sector. Business doesn't want to hire former government employees.**

REALITY: Many government skills are directly transferable to business and industry. For example, firms doing business with government—especially contracting and consulting firms—readily hire former government employees. They need personnel who know the details of government. Indeed, a big revolving door exists between government and business. When you attempt to move from government to the private sector, your major problems will be in the areas of networking and communication. You must learn how to network outside government as well as present yourself in the language and style of business.

MYTH 23:   Government employees work eight-hour days, get generous benefits, and have a great deal of job security.

REALITY: This is true in many cases but not so in other cases. Many government employees, especially those in the Washington, DC Metro area, have reputations for hard work and workaholism. The federal government does offer some nice benefits, but these are by no means generous when compared to many benefits attached to jobs in the private sector. Job security is not what it used to be. The federal bureaucracy is being held more accountable for productivity, which affects work hours, salaries, benefits, and security.

> **Many government skills are directly transferable to business and industry.**

MYTH 24:   It's better to work for government than business—and vice versa.

REALITY: Yes, most people tend to "stand where they sit." "Being better" is a function of which side of the fence you sit on or where you think the grass is greener at any particular moment. Most jobs are not inherently exciting or rewarding. They are often what you make of them. Organizational charts and job descriptions merely give you a license to do a job. You and others will define the job, including its positives and negatives.

Major Realities

The facts of public employment are often quite different from the dominant image and myths guiding job searches. At the very least, you should be aware of these realities when preparing your job search:

- **The federal government hires almost every type of skilled worker.** The government's workforce includes approximately 150,000 engineers and architects, 120,000 accountants and budget specialists, 120,000 doctors and health specialists, 87,000 scientists, 45,000 social scientists, and 2,700 veterinarians.

- Regardless of government cutbacks, **public employment opportunities are numerous** and will remain so in the foreseeable future.

- Although the government hiring process is more formalized than hiring in business, **an informal hiring system also operates in government**. This informal system works similarly to the informal system, or "hidden job market," in the private sector. Networking is the key to making the informal system work to one's advantage.

- **A great deal of mystery and complexity seems to shroud the federal hiring process**; it dissuades many highly qualified candidates from entering the public sector.

- **It may take you longer to get a government job than a private sector job** because of more complex hiring procedures in government. On the other hand, some positions in government can be quickly filled—within a matter of minutes.

- **Government jobs are similar to other jobs**—rewarding and unrewarding, with advantages and disadvantages. Don't expect too much or too little from a government job.

- **Government salaries in general compare favorably to private sector salaries**. With benefits included, many government salaries are more generous than comparable positions in the private sector.

- **Government employees have more long-term job security than employees in business.** However, they pay a price for this security—limitations on salary and career mobility. The limitations reflect the fact that most government employees are not expected to be risk-takers, entrepreneurs, and product/profit producers. The system protects them from risks and failures.

- **Successful candidates know how to best get a job they are qualified to perform.** You will have a high probability of entering the public service if you develop the necessary skills and practice effective job search strategies as outlined in subsequent chapters.

You should now have a more realistic, though general, perspective from which to begin answering the three questions we posed at the beginning of this chapter: *"Where are the jobs? How do I get one? What's it like working for government?"* This chapter presented a basic orientation. Chapter 3 examines the advantages and disadvantages of government work as well as outlines some key factors contributing to success in the federal employment arena. The remaining chapters detail the important "where" and strategic "how" of finding a federal job fast.

3

Motivation For Success

S o you want to work for the Feds, America's single largest employer. What exactly motivates you to seek a government job? Do you have a long-term career plan in mind? Are your goals primarily policy, employer/institution, or self-centered? Do you, for example, mainly seek personal job security or are you looking for a satisfying job that enables you to serve the public or practice a particular policy-relevant skill? Do you have the necessary motivation and skills to make it in the public sector? Are you oriented toward success in the public sector or do you have unrealistic expectations of what it really takes to be a successful public employee? Are you prepared to adjust to the negatives of public employment such as limited career advancement, mobility, and financial rewards which may become more apparent 10 or 20 years from now?

Rules For Success

One of the first rules for successfully approaching government agencies is to **know yourself**. Why do you want to work for government? How realistic are your expectations in light of both government employment realities and your motivational pattern?

The second rule is to **know your audience**. What do you know about the particular government agency you wish to work for? Who are they? What do they do, where, how, and with what effects? How do they hire? What job search strategies and techniques are most appropriate for this particular agency?

The third rule is to **custom-design your job search** in response to what you learned from rules one and two. This includes developing a well-crafted application—the SF-171, OF-612, or a federal-style resume.

In the end, there is no substitute for acquiring both self-knowledge and knowledge of your audience and then linking this knowledge to an appropriate action plan designed for particular government agencies. If you do this, you should have no problem successfully navigating your job search through the chaos of government.

This chapter addresses the first rule for success. The remaining chapters of the book tackle rules two and three. Taken together, these rules and chapters should put you well on the road to job search success within the federal government.

Going Public

We believe **motivation** is an important determinant of how well you conduct your job search, communicate your qualifications to potential employers, and perform on the job. If you have clear, positive, and realistic goals, you are most likely to be successful in finding a job as well as in enjoying your work. However, if your goals are unclear—based on negatives concerning what you "don't like to do" and unrelated to the day-to-day realities of government—you may be headed for trouble with both your job search and your job in government.

> **Motivation is an important determinant of your job search success.**

Individuals who choose to work for government are motivated by a variety of positive and negative factors. Some confirm the general public expectation that government workers primarily seek security, good pay, excellent benefits, and an eight-hour work day. Others confirm our ideal of civic-minded and altruistic individuals doing the public's business—they want to serve their country and make meaningful differences in the lives of others. And still others seek government employment for negative reasons—they don't like working in the private sector where they must sell things and face the stress of performance quotas.

As with any job, government jobs have both positives and negatives. Therefore, let's take a general look at what it is like working for government. How does it differ from work in the private sector? Is it true what you hear about government jobs? These questions are difficult to answer given the diversity of government agencies and the dispersion of federal agencies throughout the United States and abroad. Such diversity and dispersion negate many generalizations about government agencies. For example, some agencies are very small and thus offer few high-level opportunities, slow advancement, limited mobility, and numerous responsibilities. Others, such as the Departments of Defense and Veterans Affairs and the U.S. Postal Service, are enormous and best approximate many of our negative notions of "bureaucracy" and "red tape" in government.

Overall, however, the federal government is a large organization with many employment advantages and disadvantages generally associated with large organizations: bureaucracy, red tape, loss of identity, mobility, career advancement, specialization, and good pay and benefits. While it's easy to stereotype government, stereotypes are not good predictors of individual situations.

Major Advantages

Many people seek government employment because they are motivated by various perceived advantages. Among these are:

1. **Salaries:** Government salaries are relatively good compared to similar positions in the private sector. This is especially true in the case of many federal employees and for lower level, basic skilled employees and generalists who are often overpaid for their level of skills and effort. However, as we will see shortly, this advantage becomes a disadvantage in many skilled areas and for individuals in high-level managerial positions. Salaries in these cases are not as competitive. But, in general, government salaries are good to excellent for comparable positions in the private sector.

2. **Benefits:** Government benefits are good to excellent, including health care and a generous pension plan. Federal workers with

30 years of service can retire at age 55. Those with 20 years service can retire at age 60. And even those with 5 years of experience can retire at age 62 and still receive benefits.

3. **Work hours and lifestyle:** Most government employees basically work an 8-hour day and a 40-hour week. Their evenings and weekends are normally free for other pursuits. Such a work situation enables most government employees to separate their personal from their professional lives. Their work need not be their life. Many private sector employees seek government jobs precisely because they are tired of working stressful 10 and 12 hour days, seven days a week.

4. **Working conditions:** Since government is not profit driven, the work is less stressful than many jobs in the private sector. While there are deadlines to meet and demands for productivity, and individual employees sometimes encounter incompetent superiors, much government work involves a great deal of on-going routines.

5. **Job satisfaction:** Many public employees are relatively satisfied with their jobs. They find the work interesting and rewarding in both monetary and personal terms. Far more employees are willing to make government a career than there are those who want to leave government for jobs in the private sector. Especially for jobs involving direct contact with the public, this intangible "opportunity to serve the public" is rewarding for many people.

6. **Security:** Most government jobs are secure. Few government employees lose their jobs due to budgetary cutbacks, elimination of their offices or jobs, or incompetence. Even in the worst of economic times, government employees will adapt to potential job loss by finding more secure government positions. Most agencies can easily downsize through innovative buyout schemes which monetarily reward individuals for leaving government voluntarily! To be fired in government is unusual, unless one is obviously incompetent, rebellious, or corrupt.

7. **Advancement and promotions:** Many public employees function within merit personnel systems which assure relative fairness in promotions and advancement. Well defined grievance procedures protect them from whimsical and capricious bosses. Especially in large government agencies, the promotion hierarchy tends to be well defined and open to performers.

8. **Future career investment:** Government jobs are a good investment for jobs and careers in the private sector with organizations on the periphery of government. Indeed, government experience is a prerequisite for many such jobs and careers. If you go into government with the idea of gaining valuable experience and skills for a future career in the private sector, your government experience will most likely be a very rewarding one. However, if you enter government with the idea

> **Government jobs are a good investment for jobs and careers in the private sector.**

of making this a life-long career, you may be in for some disappointments and frustrations in your later years as you receive fewer and fewer rewards in government service.

Distinct Disadvantages

Public employment also has several disadvantages which discourage individuals from seeking government employment as well as motivate others to leave government service for private sector employment. Many of these disadvantages are directly related to—indeed are the flip-side of—many of the so-called advantages:

1. **Salaries:** While government salaries in general are good to excellent, in certain cases they are not. Many skilled workers in high-demand occupations are underpaid when compared to their counterparts in the private sector. This is especially true in the case of medical, engineering, and computer personnel. High-level managers normally cannot exceed arbitrary salary ceilings set by Congress. Therefore, these individuals may experience few financial rewards for performing well in their

jobs. At the same time, federal salaries are often inadequate in high cost-of-living areas, especially in Washington, DC, New York City, Hawaii, Alaska, and several major metropolitan areas. The recently instituted "locality pay system," which provides differential pay in high cost-of-living areas, attempts to eliminate many of these pay inequities.

2. **Limited career mobility:** Especially in small government agencies, the advancement hierarchy may be limited. In larger agencies it may be difficult to move to other government positions because of a narrow skill specialty which is programmed for a particular office within an agency.

3. **Benefits:** Many of the traditional benefits of government, such as health care, have been gradually eroded with recent changes in the federal retirement system. As the federal retirement system is brought in closer alignment with private retirement systems, federal employees will be contributing financially more and more to their benefit plans.

4. **Few career options and the inability to change careers:** The nonportable nature of the federal retirement system has been such that many employees experience a federal form of "job lock"—they feel locked into their careers once they become vested in the retirement system. Many would like to change jobs or careers but they fear losing their retirement benefits. Indeed, thousands of dissatisfied federal employees are "doing time" in their present jobs because of this inflexible system. However, times are also changing in response to this serious problem. The shift from the nonportable CSRS to the more portable FERS retirement system should open up the bureaucracy to more job and career changers.

5. **Bureaucracy:** Government work in many agencies and units lacks challenges, involves a great deal of red tape, does not encourage initiative and creativity, and may involve working with deadwood. While these are characteristics of many large organizations, they may be more pronounced in government because many government agencies lack clearly defined and

measurable goals to achieve and measure performance. In addition, government employees are not expected to be creative risk-takers. One does not get rewarded for making mistakes!

6. **Politics, decision-making, and implementation:** Government is by nature political. But many politically naive people have a low tolerance for politics and thus find such environments frustrating and stressful. Good ideas often become compromised to the political interests of representatives, interest groups, and fellow bureaucrats. Decisions are seldom clear-cut, decisive, controllable, or final. Problems are seldom resolved—only acted upon in continuing cycles of decision-making that lead to other problems and issues. Implementation is inherently difficult given the political interests of parties involved who also affect the outcomes of implementation. Such a political environment frequently conflicts with individuals' professional values which stress finding and implementing the "one best solution" devoid of extraneous (i.e., political) considerations.

7. **Limited extra income opportunities:** Government employees have few opportunities to make additional income either on or off the job. Most "daylighting" and "moonlighting" commonly found in the private sector as well as among faculty in higher education are prohibited in the federal government. Therefore, most federal employees must learn to live within their salaries.

8. **Few perks:** Government employees receive few on-the-job perks normally associated with large organizations—car, expense accounts, and memberships. At best, government jobs come with a basic office—built by the lowest bidder and often windowless—equipped with a desk, chair, telephone, computer, secretarial assistance, and access to a copy machine.

9. **Status and public attitudes:** Most public employees are not held in high esteem, because they are not seen as "doers" who accomplish things of monetary value. Many individuals have negative attitudes toward public servants. They often view them as living off the public dole and being over-paid, underworked, and unproductive.

10. **Sense of powerlessness:** Much of government work is frustrating. Employees often find difficulty in deriving on-the-job satisfaction which is normally attendant with the nature of the work itself. A great deal of work gets processed, but concrete accomplishments are often difficult to identify and little satisfaction is derived. In large agencies, employees may feel like a cog in the wheel. They view their work as somewhat meaningless since it does not appear to accomplish anything of importance.

11. **Plateaued careers:** Many public employees find their careers plateau quickly in government due to a combination of limited career mobility, short advancement hierarchies, and arbitrary salary ceilings. A great many public employees in the age range of 38 to 45 suffer from what Marilyn Moats Kennedy identifies as the Killer Bs: Blockage, Boredom, and Burnout. They feel they have advanced as far as they can possibly go; many have lost interest in their work. They have job security and they are paid well, but they dislike their jobs because their government careers have essentially stalled in terms of promotions, salary increments, responsibilities, and rewards for performance. These are the career distressed who do not look forward to another 20 years in their present jobs and careers.

> **Many public employees find their careers plateau quickly in government.**

12. **Working conditions:** Given procurement regulations favoring the lowest bidders for government facilities, equipment, and supplies, many federal offices are dreadful places to work in— noisy, crowded, cluttered, ugly, and with few windows. Equipment is often outdated or difficult to integrate. Many private businesses would not tolerate such conditions that appear to be antithetical to worker productivity.

Weigh the Alternatives

Many observers may tell you the advantages of government service outweigh the disadvantages, and vice versa. Others will tell you government work is challenging and exciting—the best possible career to enter. Don't believe everything you hear. Few people are lucky enough to have challenging and exciting jobs they always love. Most jobs are a mixture of advantages and disadvantages, high points and low points. Try as we can to make work more challenging, exciting, and enjoyable, many jobs will remain dull and stressful. There simply is no objective way of determining the best alternatives for you. It largely depends on the individual and your motivation for work. You do the best you can in terms of self-assessment, research, and planning. Then you acquire work experience which may or may not fulfill your career aspirations.

In many respects, government work is very similar to work in other small, intermediate, or large organizations. If you work for a small private firm, you are less likely to use your specialized skills on a full-time basis. You must learn to be adaptive, do things you may not particularly enjoy or be skilled in doing, but these are things you must do in order to get the work done. Chances are you operate in a situation that is understaffed, stressful, and not conducive to innovation. You are always trying to get the basics done. For individuals who like to practice only

> **In many respects, government work is very similar to work in other small, intermediate, or large organizations.**

their specialty skills, such work environments are inherently frustrating and unstable. They tend to bring out one's weaknesses rather than enhance one's strengths.

On the other hand, such organizations tend to be less bureaucratic and more adaptive, creative, and responsive to their environment than many large organizations. Small organizations are preferred by individuals who enjoy the challenges which come with developing and doing different things, making and implementing decisions quickly, and receiving immediate feedback on performance. Indeed, many people thrive in such small and responsive organizations.

Large bureaucracies are found in both the public and private sectors. In this particular type of organization individuals tend to be conservative; they are more oriented toward maintaining existing patterns than with innovation, creativity, and risk-taking; and they play the games necessary to survive and advance within the hierarchy. Except for many employees within the covert service of the Central Intelligence Agency, many individuals—especially entrepreneurial types—are ill-suited for such work environments. They would enjoy and prosper more in settings which permitted them greater freedom and control over their work. In fact, entrepreneurial types who are oriented toward the public sector are probably better off working for a well-staffed small government organization or joining small and adaptive nongovernmental organizations.

Unfortunately, thousands of public employees are unhappy with their jobs precisely because their skills and motivational patterns are not conducive to the various work environments found in government. While at one time their jobs may have been exciting and challenging, their jobs today have changed, or they themselves have changed. As individuals acquire experience and their values, goals, and work situations change, many find themselves in different types of careers than they had previously enjoyed or anticipated for the future. These individuals might be happier in different jobs and careers if they were willing and able to make a career transition from government to the private sector. But good salaries, benefits, and security convince them to stick it out rather than change to jobs and careers which would be more appropriate for their particular mix of skills and motivations.

You can avoid becoming one of these career plateaued or displaced public employees if you do the proper self-assessment, gather information on alternative jobs and careers with different types of agencies, and realistically assess whether or not a particular public sector job is best for you. In the end, only you can determine what will fulfill your needs.

Comparable Worth and the Life-Long Government Career

Debates have gone on for years concerning whether public employees are overpaid or underpaid. Understandably, if you are a public employee, you may feel you are underpaid. After all, you know other people who make more money than you—and you feel you are just as hard a worker. Furthermore, many federal studies on comparable pay support your beliefs. On the other hand, if you work in the private sector, you may feel public employees are overpaid, especially if you owe additional taxes to the IRS in April! What do they produce given their seemingly generous salaries, benefits, and work environments? The stereotyped government employee may be the postal employee most citizens encounter on a regular basis or a faceless IRS worker who scrutinizes your taxes.

Needless to say, the old adage that most people "stand where they sit" operates when evaluating the relative worth of most peoples' work. Not surprising, most people think they work harder than others, and they are worth much more than they are paid at present.

Many governmental units regularly study comparable salaries in the private sector in order to bring government salaries in line with the competition. In addition, several studies have been commissioned to review data concerning the question of federal salaries. For example, the President's Advisory Committee on Federal Pay reported in November of 1980 that salaries of federal white-collar workers were 1 to 2 percentage points behind similar positions in the private sector. At the higher levels the salary gaps were considerable: salaries of top executives were on an average 7 percent behind comparable positions in the private sector; in some cases the lag was as much as 46 percent. Yet, government statistics showed the average federal white-collar worker earned $5,000 more than the private sector counterpart. However, skill requirements were higher for the federal employee. Other studies show federal employees receiving better pay and benefits than their private industry counterparts. A 1993 study of comparable pay again stressed the widening gap between government and private sector salaries, with government employees at a distinct disadvantage.

Given the inconclusive and contradictory conclusions of the various studies, it is difficult to conclude one way or the other how government salaries compare with private industry salaries. We can say with certainty how salaries for many technical positions, such as engineers and computer programmers, compare to one another in government and the private sector. We can also easily compare many entry-level secretarial and staff support positions. However, many other positions, especially higher level managerial positions, are difficult to compare because they lack comparable performance criteria.

Indeed, the problem with most comparable pay studies and debates is in establishing the criteria for comparability of positions. Studies often end up comparing apples to oranges. Many public employees possess specialized skills on the inner workings of government which are not directly transferable to the private sector. While these individuals may be white-collar workers earning $65,000 a year as a welfare analyst or grants specialist, in reality they would have difficulty finding a comparable level job in the private sector. In fact, one of the best indicators of comparable worth is what public employees actually do once they leave government for positions in the private sector. No studies have used actual career transitions as the basis for determining comparable worth. In the meantime, many government employees are convinced they are underpaid compared to the private sector.

Our experience with public employees tends to support the overpaid theory with major exceptions in the cases of technical personnel who are often underpaid. Even though many government officials feel they are underpaid, and some studies support this belief, most appear overpaid when they go job hunting in the private sector. When they begin marketing their public sector skills in private industry, many more individuals must take salary cuts than receive salary increases. Only after job hunting in the private sector do many public employees change their views about being underpaid. At the same time, this situation will vary with different types of positions. For example, teachers are generally underpaid; they can find better paying employment in the private sector —if they change their field of work. The same is true for many public safety positions. Individuals in these occupations must change careers in order to substantially increase their salaries in the private sector.

> **Salaries are not designed for individuals with life-long career aspirations in government.**

One of the major problems are the salaries of experienced managers and executives in government. Government salaries plateau at the upper levels because Congress puts pay caps on the top level positions. Consequently, a 50-year old official who reaches the top salary level is most likely to stay at that level the rest of his or her career regardless of their performance. While making $100,000 a year in government, this individual might be able to make $250,000 or more a year in the private sector in a comparable position entailing a similar level of responsibility.

But the real unspoken problem with government salaries is the career orientation of many employees. Many years ago young individuals entered government service for a few years of "public service" and then left for long-term careers in the private sector. This orientation has changed considerably during the past four decades. Today, many individuals enter government service with the idea of making it a life-long career. Only after ten or twenty years in government service do they realize that government salaries are not designed for individuals with life-long career aspirations within government. Regardless of all the comparable pay studies and the periodical laments of legislators and public employees about the "crisis of the public service," legislators simply will not advance the caps on government salaries much in the coming years. The public still views public employees earning $100,000 a year as a bit excessive when it comes out of their tax dollars.

A little more sacrifice and less preoccupation with making their government job a financially well rewarded career is probably in order. Consequently, when you reach the top in government, it's perhaps time to consider changing careers since you will never receive a salary comparable to what you feel you are truly worth. And helping open the ranks of government to newer and younger blood is probably not a bad idea after all.

In fact, you may do both yourself and government a favor by leaving government service after ten to fifteen years. Your government experience will most likely be rewarded in the private sector with a long-term career involving substantial financial rewards. And this is precisely what the thousands of "revolving door" players in government every year learn as they leave government positions for comparable "public sector" jobs with private organizations on the periphery of government—trade and professional associations, contractors and consultants, and nonprofit organizations. Their government experience was a necessary investment in a long-term and financially rewarding career in the private sector.

Know Yourself

We know that no one ideal motivational pattern is best suited for all jobs. Most people find jobs based upon a mixture of positive and negative motivations—they have certain things they both want and don't want in jobs. But individuals who primarily approach the job search from a positive orientation—stressing what they do well, enjoy doing, and what they really want to do—are most likely to enjoy their work and achieve career success. Their positive attitude contributes to their achievements.

Before examining the structure of federal employment, job alternatives, and appropriate job search strategies, we need to address a key consideration in getting the whole process underway—**knowing yourself** in relation to this job market and government jobs. Begin by asking these two questions about yourself:

- What is it I really want to do?

- What is my potential for successfully conducting a federal job search as well as for working in government?

Answers to these two questions will better prepare you for the analytical
and how-to chapters that follow.

Assess Your Capabilities

What do you do well and enjoy doing? What exactly do you want to do
in government today, tomorrow, next year, or five and ten years from
now? These questions focus on assessing your **strengths, values, and
goals**. Answers to these questions will help you better target your job
search around your major capabilities as well as clearly communicate
your qualifications to potential agencies and employers.

The process of assessing your strengths, values, and goals can be
extremely lengthy and time consuming. Indeed, some people spend
weeks generating such information on themselves. Others are able to do
so within a matter of minutes or a few hours. The longer you spend on
the assessment process, the more detailed and quality information you
should receive on yourself. The mechanisms for generating this information include self-directed exercises and tests. These are available in
numerous career planning and job search books or administered through
counselors and licensed psychologists. Several self-directed exercises are
outlined in two of our other books: *Discover the Best Jobs For You* and
The Complete Guide to Public Employment.

By no means thorough, a quick and easy way to initially assess your
strengths, values, and goals is to address these questions:

1. **What are your seven most significant achievements?** These
   consist of anything you enjoyed doing, believe you did well,
   and felt a sense of satisfaction, pride, or accomplishment in
   doing. Examine in detail each of these achievements. Try to
   identify common themes or patterns that emerge from these
   achievements. The end result should be a list of your major
   strengths, such as organize, lead, counsel, evaluate, supervise,
   manage, sell, persuade, communicate, implement, analyze,
   delegate, or inform.

2. **What are your major strengths?** Ask others who are familiar
   with your work to evaluate what they see to be your major
   strengths as well as your weaknesses. Also ask them what they
   think you need in a job or career to make you satisfied.

3. **What do you most enjoy about your work?** Your answer might include working with a team, competing with others, being creative, gaining recognition, helping others, solving problems, or taking risks. This question will help you identify your major work values.

4. **What are your major job frustrations and dissatisfactions?** This question also helps identify your major work values using a negative approach. When linked to the previous positive question, it gives you a comprehensive overview of what you like **and** dislike about work.

5. **What would you like to do before you die?** This question helps you identify some major goals you would like to achieve in life which may or may not be related to your job.

6. **What do you consider to be an ideal work week?** Identify the types of things you would like to do, including the types of people you prefer working with and the types of situations you would like to find yourself in.

Once you have identified your strengths and values, begin formulating them into a job and career objective that can be targeted toward potential agencies and employers. It should **link your strengths and values to the needs of employers**. In other words, this objective should be employer-centered rather than self-centered. For example, rather than state

> I would like a position that will lead to career advancement in government (a self-centered objective).

think in terms of an employer-centered objective that stresses your major skills, strengths, or accomplishments in reference to a specific agency, your work values, and the needs of employers. Now, let's restate this self-centered objective in more employer-oriented terms:

> I would like a position in the Department of Energy's **Office of Energy Research** (targeted agency) that will use my ability to **analyze and solve technical problems** (major skills or strengths) within a **team setting** (a major work value) that will contribute to **solving national energy problems** (employer-centered outcome).

The themes in this objective should appear in various sections of your SF-171, OF-612, or federal-style resume which detail your accomplishments in reference to a particular job—the subject of Chapter 7.

Know Your S.Q.G.

Just how successful are you likely to be in finding a federal job as well as in working for the federal government? You can begin answering this question by first assessing your potential for success. Let's start by completing and scoring the following Success Quotient for Government (S.Q.G.) test:

> Complete the following exercise by indicating your degree of agreement or disagreement with each statement. Circle the number to the right that best represents your response.
>
> SCALE: 1 = strongly agree
> 2 = agree
> 3 = maybe, not certain
> 4 = disagree
> 5 = strongly disagree

1. I know what I do well, enjoy doing, and
   what I want to do.   1 2 3 4 5

2. I can clearly communicate my goals and
   capabilities to employers.   1 2 3 4 5

3. I know what skills employers most seek
   in candidates.   1 2 3 4 5

4. I know how to write a powerful application.   1 2 3 4 5

5. I can quickly customize my application
   for different jobs.   1 2 3 4 5

6. I know where to send my application.   1 2 3 4 5

7. I know where to find federal job vacancies.   1 2 3 4 5

8. I know how to contact agency personnel
   who have the power to hire.   1 2 3 4 5

9. I can state why an employer should hire me.   1 2 3 4 5

10. I can develop a job referral network.   1 2 3 4 5

11. I can prospect for job leads.   1 2 3 4 5

12. I can follow-up on job interviews.   1 2 3 4 5

13. I know which questions most interviewers
are likely to ask me.   1 2 3 4 5

14. If asked to reveal my weaknesses, I know
how to turn the question around so it
stresses my strengths.   1 2 3 4 5

15. I know the various types of interviews I may
encounter and how to appropriately respond
to each situation.   1 2 3 4 5

16. I can easily approach strangers for job
information and advice.   1 2 3 4 5

17. I know where to find information on
government agencies that are most
interested in my skills.   1 2 3 4 5

18. I know how to go beyond vacancy announcements to locate job opportunities appropriate
for my qualifications.   1 2 3 4 5

19. I know how to interview appropriate people
for job information and advice.   1 2 3 4 5

20. I know many people who can refer me to
others for informational interviews.   1 2 3 4 5

21. I can uncover jobs on the nonadvertised,
hidden job market.   1 2 3 4 5

22. I know how to prepare and practice for the
critical job interview.   1 2 3 4 5

23. I know how to research the organization and
individuals who are likely to interview me.   1 2 3 4 5

24. I can telephone for job leads.   1 2 3 4 5

25. I'm prepared to conduct an effective
telephone interview.   1 2 3 4 5

26. I can nonverbally communicate my interest
and enthusiasm for the job.   1 2 3 4 5

27. I know how to follow-up the interview.   1 2 3 4 5

28. I can clearly explain to interviewers what
I like and dislike about particular jobs.   1 2 3 4 5

29. I can clearly explain to interviewers what
I want to be doing 5 or 10 years from now.   1 2 3 4 5

30. I can explain to interviewers why I made my
particular educational choices, including my
major and grade point average.   1 2 3 4 5

31. I know how to best dress for the interview.   1 2 3 4 5

32. I have a list of references that will speak
positive about me and my work abilities.   1 2 3 4 5

33. I can clearly state my job and career
objectives as both skills and outcomes.   1 2 3 4 5

34. I've set aside 20 hours a week to primarily
conduct informational interviews.   1 2 3 4 5

35. I know how to listen effectively.   1 2 3 4 5

36. I can explain why an employer should
hire me rather than someone else.   1 2 3 4 5

37. I can outline my major achievements
in my last three jobs and show how they
relate to the job I'm interviewing for.   1 2 3 4 5

38. I know what tests I need to take for the
job I want.   1 2 3 4 5

39. I know what the interviewer is looking
for when he asks about weaknesses.   1 2 3 4 5

40. I know what foods and drinks are best to
select when being interviewed during
lunch or dinner.   1 2 3 4 5

41. I enjoy working with others in a cooperative environment.   1 2 3 4 5

42. I don't need a plush office nor job perks.   1 2 3 4 5

43. I'm prepared for work situations that may
be ambiguous and involve many levels of
decision-making.   1 2 3 4 5

44. Money, power, prestige, and public esteem
are not important to me in a job.   1 2 3 4 5

45. I can tolerate being supervised by
individuals less competent than me.   1 2 3 4 5

46. I know what job and career alternatives
are available for me outside government.   1 2 3 4 5

47. I'm prepared for a career that may offer
me little career advancement and small
salary increments after several years
of service.   1 2 3 4 5

48. I'm willing to work with others even
though I may disagree with their goals
and decisions.   1 2 3 4 5

49. I enjoy working with the public.   1 2 3 4 5

50. I'm prepared to have my performance
regularly evaluated and be promoted
according to merit rather than seniority.   1 2 3 4 5

TOTAL S.Q.G.   [   ]

Once you have completed this exercise, add up your total score to get your composite S.Q.G. If your score is below 100, you may be well prepared to successfully handle the federal job search as well as work in government. If your score is between 100 and 150, you are heading in the right direction, and this book will help you increase your job search competencies.

However, if your score falls between 151 and 250, you have a great deal of work to do. This book will quickly help you achieve a significant increase in your S.Q.G. The chapters that follow address many of the above statements either directly or indirectly as they show you how to find a federal job fast.

4

Winners, Losers, and the Future

What is the public sector? How does it relate to the private sector? What are the major trends for the public sector in the decade ahead? What type of jobs are available in the public sector? How many jobs are there? Where are the jobs? How do I go about finding a government job? What are some of the major alternatives to working for government? If I leave government, what could I do? How can I become most effective in acquiring a federal job and advancing my career?

Prerequisites For Effectiveness

Many job seekers want answers to these and other employment questions. Encountering numerous agencies and personnel offices, they seek advice on how to simplify the job finding process. While the answers to these questions are anything but simple, this chapter outlines a useful concept of public employment which should help clarify understanding of this process. Furthermore, this concept is the basis for developing the "how-to" strategies and tactics for taking effective job search action as outlined in subsequent chapters of this book.

The next few chapters address these and other key questions. They focus on two major "how-to" prerequisites for effectiveness in today's public sector job market:

- **You must understand how the public sector operates as well as know the realities of public employment before committing your time and energy to this employment arena.** We examine the structure of government and the hiring process in order to go beyond the myths in Chapter 2.

- **You must use job search strategies appropriately designed for the public sector.** This requires developing and implementing a job search that is responsive to both the formal and informal employment arenas operating inside and outside government.

The following chapters simplify the overall complexity of federal employment by placing it within the larger context of job trends, networks, and alternatives in order to better understand:

- public employment trends

- public sector networks and networking

- alternative job markets relating to public employment

One word of caution is in order before you begin the chapters that follow. It is one thing to **understand** government and another to **apply** how-to strategies to your particular situation. The trends we outline are based upon large amounts of data which hold true for government **as a whole**. They do not necessarily apply to you **as the individual**. Indeed, subsequent chapters are specifically designed to equip you with the necessary knowledge and skills to get what you want in spite of these and other general trends.

The bottom line is for you to set goals and be persistent—indeed tenacious—in following through with strategies to get what you want. Statistics and trends outlined in these chapters merely provide an important **context** within which you will develop **your own** effective federal job search strategies.

The Public Sector Context

The public sector consists of a relatively stable and predictable set of organizations which affects the way government conducts business. Well integrated into the private sector, the public sector also is a highly decentralized, fragmented, and chaotic system.

The public sector encompasses all organizations and institutions directly or indirectly related to the business of governing communities, states, and nations. These are represented in the following figure:

It includes government organizations as well as peripheral organizations primarily oriented toward and dependent upon government. Involving numerous types of institutions and organizations, the **primary peripheral organizations** consist of:

- Trade and professional associations involved in influencing public policy formulation in government.

- Contracting and consulting firms which primarily receive government contracts.

- Nonprofit organizations performing public service functions.

- Foundations providing resources to other peripheral groups.

- Research organizations engaged in policy-related research.

- Public support groups, lobbyists, and law firms influencing both the formulation and implementation of public policy.

While this is not the usual definition of the public sector, it is very useful for our purposes. As you will see throughout this book, government is one of many institutions—albeit the most significant given its substantial monopoly of financial resources and scope of decision-making—involved in governing communities and influencing the specific direction and content of public policies. For job seekers, governments and their peripheral institutions comprise an **interrelated network** of public sector job and career opportunities. These institutions offer thousands of job vacancies each day. By familiarizing yourself with this network, as well as each institution within this network, you will be better able to identify job opportunities and advance your public sector career. A complete discussion, including job search techniques appropriate for each major institutional complex defining the public sector, is found in our expanded volume, *The Complete Guide to Public Employment*.

The Government Complex

Government is the single largest employer in the United States. One in seven civilian employees, or nearly 20 million individuals, work for government organizations. Millions of other nongovernment jobs depend on providing services to government agencies. Of these, approximately eight million jobs in the private sector are paid through federal government contracts. In fact, the U.S. Department of Defense alone, which spends over $250 billion each year on contractors, is responsible for generating nearly 3.5 million jobs in private industry. Another 10 to 20 million private sector jobs are dependent upon contractual relationships with state and local governments, especially the more than 100,000 educational institutions and 7.5 million educators that define America's public educational complex.

The civilian government complex consists of numerous units of government and public employees distributed in a variety of functional areas as outlined in the charts on page 61. While loosely related to one another, each unit of government manages its own personnel and engages in different hiring practices.

> **One in seven civilian employees, or nearly 20 million individuals, work for government organizations.**

Even within a single unit of government, several hiring systems will operate for different types of employees and different government units. For example, each agency in the federal government has its own personnel system, and many offices within agencies also operate their own systems which include separate hiring programs and practices. Consequently, viewed as a "government job market," this system is highly decentralized and fragmented—both within and between governmental units. It continues to become even more decentralized and fragmented as the federal government engages in new decentralized reform efforts, and local governments, especially special districts which increased by 3,599 units since 1987, continue to proliferate.

The largest single category of government employees—and also the fastest growing—is educators (8.1 million), which comprises 52 percent of the government workforce at the state and local levels. Educational positions also have been primarily responsible for recent major growth and decline trends in public employment.

Federal government employment constitutes 15 percent of all public employment. Nearly 98 percent of all federal employees work for 110 executive agencies. Three agencies—Defense, Postal Service, and Veterans Affairs—employ nearly 7 of every 10 federal workers. Despite recent cutbacks in the Department of Defense personnel, this department still employs 3 out of every 10 federal workers. As indicated on page 62, the six largest agencies employ 79.9 percent of all federal civilian employees.

Government employment does not stop with 18.5 million employees

GOVERNMENT UNITS AND EMPLOYEES, 1995

Level	Units	Employees
TOTAL	**86,743**	**19,521,000**
Federal	1	2,895,000
State	50	4,719,000
Local	86,692	11,906,000
▪ Counties	3,043	2,514,000
▪ School Districts	14,556	5,774,000
▪ Townships/Towns	16,666	475,000
▪ Municipalities	19,296	2,442,000
▪ Special Districts	33,131	701,000

SOURCE: U.S. Bureau of Census
* 1992 is the latest year for complete statistics on all levels of government. In 1995, total employees was 19,521,000.

GOVERNMENT PAYROLL BY FUNCTION, 1992
(in millions of dollars)

	Total	Federal[1]	State	Local
TOTAL	41,237	9,687	9,437	22,113
▪ National defense[2]	3,294	3,294	(X)	(X)
▪ Postal Service	2,359	2,359	(X)	(X)
▪ Space research and technology	109	109	(X)	(X)
▪ Education	15,724	41	3,551	12,132
▪ Highways	1,238	18	613	607
▪ Health and hospitals	4,048	876	1,584	1,587
▪ Public welfare	982	34	464	485
▪ Police protection	2,253	304	250	1,699
▪ Fire protection				
▪ Sanitation	771	(X)	(X)	771
and sewerage	518	(X)	7	510
▪ Parks and recreation	489	66	69	353
▪ Nature resources	1,150	732	349	70
▪ Financial administration	1,119	400	343	376
▪ Other government administration	646	95	126	424
▪ Judicial and legal	952	172	338	442
▪ Other	5,585	1,187	1,743	2,657

X = Not applicable   [1] Includes employees outside US   [2] Includes international relations
SOURCE: U.S. Bureau of the Census

LARGEST FEDERAL AGENCIES BY
CIVILIAN EMPLOYEES, 1998

Agency	Employees	Percent
TOTAL FEDERAL EMPLOYMENT	**2,779,406**	**100.0**
▪ Executive Branch	2,717,569	97.8
▪ Judicial Branch	31,092	1.1
▪ Legislative Branch	30,745	1.1
SIX LARGEST AGENCIES	**2,353,385**	**79.9**
▪ Postal Service	858,066	30.9
▪ Department of Defense	726,690	26.1
▪ Veterans Affairs	242,534	8.7
▪ Department of Treasury	153,729	5.5
▪ Department of Justice	120,104	4.3
▪ Department of Agriculture	100,161	3.6

SOURCE: U.S. Office of Personnel Management, Office of Workforce Information, May 1998

attached to executive branch bureaucracies. Another 500,000 individuals occupy elected and appointed legislative and judicial positions at the federal, state, and local levels. The government complex also includes the District of Columbia and five territorial governments. Furthermore, 2.1 million individuals are employed in the armed forces. Overall, government employment is over 22 million.

The concentration of government employees varies by geographical area. For every 1,000 citizens, for example, there are 57.9 state and local employees, ranging from a high of 82 per 1,000 in Alaska to a low of 38 per 1,000 in Pennsylvania. California alone has nearly 1.5 million state and local employees whereas Vermont has fewer than 30,000. Federal government concentration averages 10 employees for every 1000 citizens, or 1 percent of the total population or 2 percent of the working population.

The federal civilian workforce is widely distributed throughout the country as well as abroad. Nearly 88 percent of federal employees are located outside the Washington, DC Metro area. About 150,000 civilian employees work overseas, although only 83,000 are U.S. citizens. The State of California alone has nearly as many federal employees as the Washington Metro area—over 300,000. Since the federal government is divided into 10 administrative regions, the regional centers of New York, Philadelphia, Boston, Chicago, Atlanta, Kansas City, Dallas, Denver, San Francisco, and Seattle have a disproportionate concentration of federal workers, employing 36.9 percent of all federal civilian employees.

As the chart on pages 64-65 indicates, federal employees work in all 50 states. Most of them work in major metropolitan areas or in smaller communities with military bases, research facilities, and Department of Energy installations. The largest percentage of civilian federal employees work for the Department of Defense and U.S. Postal Service.

While over 90 percent of government employees work for executive agencies, numerous job opportunities also are available in the bureaucracies of the legislative and judicial branches of government. For example, within the federal government the legislative branch employs 30,745 individuals; the judicial branch employs 31,092. Although less visible to the public, agencies within the legislative branch grew rapidly during the 1970s and 1980s but began declining during the past five years in response to the overall downsizing of government; the increase has been 18.5 percent since 1965 (from 25,947 to 30,745). Employment within the judicial branch, however, has steadily increased since 1965, more than quadrupling (426%) in the past 23 years (from 5,904 to 31,092).

The work of the federal government encompasses a wide range of functions, from collecting taxes and conducting scientific research to promoting employment and foreign policy. While public safety is largely considered a local and state government function, the federal government also performs numerous public safety functions that go beyond such high visibility agencies as the FBI (Federal Bureau of Investigation) and the DEA (Drug Enforcement Administration). Indeed, the federal government employs over 100,000 law enforcement officials who primarily operate from 17 different agencies. If you are interested in law enforcement work, you need not look only at local or state police departments. Consider some of the many federal agencies identified on page 65 as possible law enforcement employers.

Growth, Decline, and Stability

As illustrated in the table on page 66, the number of government units actually declined by 50 percent—from 155,116 to 78,269 units—during the period 1942-1972. Between 1972 and 1992 government units increased by nearly 11 percent, primarily driven by the continuing proliferation of small special districts.

Despite the decline in the number of government units—primarily precipitated by the consolidation of thousands of school districts during

CIVILIAN FEDERAL EMPLOYEES BY STATE

State	Total Employees* (1,000)	Percent Defense
TOTAL	2,906	31.4
Northeast	**481**	**26.3**
CT	24	20.7
MA	60	19.5
ME	124	26.6
NH	17	58.8
NJ	75	34.6
NY	152	11.8
PA	129	38.1
RI	10	41.8
VT	5	12.5
Midwest	**492**	**24.7**
IA	18	8.0
IL	104	19.4
IN	41	37.0
KS	25	27.3
MI	56	20.1
MM	32	9.0
MO	66	28.9
ND	8	25.8
NE	15	26.7
SD	9	15.3
WI	27	11.5
South	**1,254**	**33.9**
AL	57	44.5
AR	19	25.6
DC	212	8.1
DE	5	32.7
FL	112	29.4
GA	88	41.2
KY	35	35.4
LA	34	25.7
MD	133	31.0
MS	24	43.6
NC	46	33.0
OK	45	50.2
SC	32	59.0
TN	56	13.9
TX	177	33.9
WV	15	11.0
VA	161	66.2
West	**642**	**37.4**
AK	15	32.2

AZ	39	26.0
CA	315	39.5
CO	53	26.0
HI	25	75.6
ID	10	13.5
MT	11	11.6
NM	26	36.5
NV	11	18.9
OR	29	10.2
UT	36	57.9
WA	65	43.8
WY	6	17.0

* Excludes members and employees of Congress, Central Intelligence Agency, Defense Intelligence Agency, employees overseas, temporary census enumerators, seasonal and on-call employees, temporary Christmas help of the U.S. Postal Service, and National Security Agency)

SOURCE: U.S. Office of Personnel Management and U.S. Bureau of the Census

FEDERAL LAW ENFORCEMENT AGENCIES
Federal Agencies Employing 500 or More Full-Time Officers With Authority to Carry Firearms and Make Arrests

Agency	Relevant Employees
TOTAL	**68,825**
▪ U.S. Customs Service	10,120
▪ Federal Bureau of Investigation (FBI)	10,075
▪ Federal Bureau of Prisons	9,984
▪ Immigration and Naturalization Service	9,466
▪ Administrative Office of U.S. Courts	3,763
▪ Internal Revenue Service (IRS)	3,621
▪ U.S. Postal Inspection Service	3,567
▪ Drug Enforcement Administration	2,813
▪ U.S. Secret Service	2,186
▪ National Park Service	2,160
▪ U.S. Marshals Service	2,153
▪ Bureau of Alcohol, Tobacco, and Firearms	1,959
▪ U.S. Capitol Police	1,080
▪ Tennessee Valley Authority (TVA)	740
▪ U.S. Forest Service	732
▪ GSA–Federal Protective Services	732
▪ U.S. Fish and Wildlife Service	620

SOURCE: U.S. Bureau of Justice Statistics, Federal Law Enforcement Officers, December 1993

EVOLUTION OF GOVERNMENT UNITS, 1942-1992

Government Level	1942	1952	1962	1972	1982	1992
TOTAL	**155,116**	**116,743**	**91,237**	**78,269**	**82,341**	**86,743**
U.S. Government	1	1	1	1	1	1
States	48	48	50	50	50	50
Local Govts.	155,067	116,694	91,186	78,218	82,290	86,692
Counties	3,050	3,049	3,043	3,044	3,041	3,043
Municipalities	16,220	16,778	18,000	18,517	19,076	19,296
Townships/Towns	18,919	17,202	17,142	16,991	16,734	16,666
School District	108,579	67,346	34,678	15,781	14,851	14,556
Special Districts	8,299	12,319	18,323	23,885	28,588	33,131

SOURCE: U.S. Bureau of the Census

the 1940s, 1950s, and 1960s—the number of government employees nearly tripled from 1950 to 1990. Following general population growth and labor participation trends, the long-term pattern for government employment is toward growth. However, the annual growth in government employment has been slower than the nation's annual population increases and employment increases in other sectors of the economy.

While government employment more than doubled during the past three decades, most of this growth took place at the state and local levels during the 1960s and 1970s. For the period 1950 to 1990, for example, state government employment increased by 243 percent and local government employment grew by 217 percent. The following table summarizes the growth in public employment from 1950 to 1990.

CHANGING GOVERNMENT EMPLOYMENT, 1950-1990

Level of Government	1950	1960	1970	1980	1990
EMPLOYEES (1,000s)	**6,503**	**8,808**	**13,028**	**16,213**	**17,638**
■ Federal (civilian)	2,117	2,421	2,881	2,898	3,167
■ State and Local	4,285	6,387	10,147	13,315	14,671
(Percent of total)	66.9	72.5	77.9	82.1	83.2
■ State	1,057	1,527	2,755	3,753	4,231
■ Local	3,228	4,860	7,392	9,562	10,240
AVERAGE ANNUAL PERCENT CHANGE					
■ Employees (Total)	+.5	+3.5	+4.2	+1.5	+.8
■ Federal	-8.9	+.4	+2.2	+1.0	+.9
■ State	(NA)	(NA)	+6.3	+1.5	+1.3
■ Local	(NA)	(NA)	+4.4	+1.7	+.7

The most rapidly growing units of government have been special districts. Between 1970 and 1983, employment with special districts increased an average of 5 percent each year—a rate 2 to 10 times higher than all other forms of government combined. By 1987 the largest number of special district governments dealt with natural resources (6,360 units), fire protection (5,070 units), and housing and community development (3,464 units). While the number of township governments and school districts continued to decline, special districts continued to increase in number during the 1980s and 1990s as illustrated on page 61.

Increases and decreases in the number of governmental units has had relatively little effect on public employment. Special districts, for example, are usually small and employ few officials. Overall, a 1 to 2 percent annual growth rate in government employment at all levels is more a reflection of the general population growth rate than increases in the number of governmental units. In fact, the growth in government employment is lower than the overall rate of population growth.

CHANGING UNITS OF LOCAL GOVERNMENT, 1982-1992

Unit of Government	1982	1992	Percent Change
▪ Counties	3,041	3,043	+.0006
▪ School Districts	14,851	14,556	-.0198
▪ Township/Towns	16,734	16,666	-.0040
▪ Municipalities	19,076	19,296	+.0115
▪ Special Districts	28,588	33,131	+.1589

SOURCE: U.S. Bureau of the Census

Most public employment increases during the past three decades responded to three general changes in society:

- Post-World War II population increases requiring extensive expansion of educational facilities, highways, and other local infrastructure and services.

- The increased demand for more community and social services in response to a generally more affluent and aging population.

- Revitalized and more liberal state legislatures and bureaucracies which played increased social advocacy roles.

Federal employment trends differed from state and local patterns. From 1950 to 1990, federal employment increased by only 49 percent, at an incremental annual rate of 0.5 to 1.5 percent. Most of this growth took place during the period 1950 to 1970. The period 1970 to 1981 actually witnessed a 1.0 percent decline in federal employment. Yet, the federal budget increased by over 1200 percent (from $40 billion to $526 billion) during the same period.

Why did federal employment fail to grow as dramatically as state and local bureaucracies, especially given major budgetary capabilities to do so? The answer to this question relates to two general trends off-setting the need to increase federal personnel in direct proportion to budgetary increases. First, much of the budgetary increase was in the form of transfer payments to states and localities: categorical and block grants and revenue sharing funds. From 1960 to 1981, federal aid to state and local governments increased 1200 percent, from $7.0 billion to $86 billion; by 1986 federal aid had increased another 31 percent to $113 billion. And by 1994 it had increased another 61 percent to $182 billion. In 1992 the majority (89 percent) of aid was targeted for health ($71 billion or 39 percent), welfare ($44 billion or 24 percent), education ($29 billion or 15 percent), and transportation ($21 billion or 11 percent).

> A "hidden bureaucracy" of contracting and consulting firms was well entrenched in relation to the federal government.

One of the major impacts of federal aid was to stimulate the growth of state and local bureaucracies—especially in the areas of health, welfare, education, and transportation—rather than enlarge the federal bureaucracy. State and local bureaucracies had to increase their staffs to handle the influx of federal funds.

Second, private contractors and consultants played a greater role in providing federal government services. Contracting-out government services and employment increased significantly during the 1960s and 1970s as federal agencies shifted from providing direct services to obligating funds and managing contracts. Procurement became a major growth industry in the federal government. Contractors not only provided goods and services to agencies, many also supplied contract workers to staff agencies. In the most extreme case, over 80 percent of the employees in the Department of Energy are contract workers hired by private contractors to operate Department of Energy facilities. By the early 1980s a "hidden bureaucracy" of contracting and consulting firms was well entrenched in relation to the federal government. The Washington metropolitan area alone—where they are frequently referred to as "Beltway Bandits" or "Suburban Consultants"—has over 3,000 such firms doing business with the bureaucracy.

While many contracting and consulting firms specialize in defense contracting, others provide services to numerous agencies, ranging from project design to delivering specific services to agency clientele. Similar firms do business with state and local governments.

An overall employment pattern in government is evident: state and local governments tend to increase personnel in response to budgetary increases; federal budgetary increases tend to stimulate the growth of state and local bureaucracies as well as the increased involvement of contracting and consulting firms specializing in public services.

Cutbacks

Since the early 1980s, the pattern of growth in state and local bureaucracies has been altered somewhat. Recessions combined with taxpayers' revolts resulted in public employment declining for the first time since the immediate post-World War II period.

Major declines in public employment began in 1980. The sharpest declines took place at the state and local levels. Between 1980 and 1981, employment in municipalities declined by 3.6 percent; counties by 2.4 percent; townships by 2.0 percent; and school districts by 1.1 percent. Only special districts registered an increase in employment—1.7 percent. Declines were evident in all functional areas except police protection. Education experienced the greatest cutbacks; highway departments registered the largest percentage decrease in employees. Indeed, by 1981 there were 245,000 fewer government employees, representing a 1.8 percent decline at the state and local levels.

Although not as dramatic as declines in state and local governments, the federal bureaucracy also experienced personnel declines during the 1980s. Shortly after taking office, President Reagan did what new presidents only talk about—trim the federal bureaucracy. Reduction-in-force (RIF) procedures went into effect, frightening and demoralizing thousands of federal employees from Hawaii to Maine who began thinking the unthinkable—possible job loss and insecurity. During the

1980s there were several winners and losers as public policy priorities were reordered among agencies, as evidenced in the figures on page 64.

While cutbacks in most agencies resulted in temporarily downsizing the total number of full-time employees, they disguised increases in part-time employees and the increased use of contractors and consultants. An extreme case is the Department of Energy. By 1990 more than 85 percent of the employees in Department of Energy offices were private contractors rather than full-time federal employees! Indeed, a 1994 GAO report concluded that these contractors cost the Department of Energy 40 to 55 percent more than permanent government employees, although other analysts might challenge these figures.

While full-time personnel declined in many agencies, budgets continued to increase and peripheral organizations participated more in the day-to-day operations of agencies. Furthermore, despite RIFs and other downsizing efforts, the federal bureaucracy actually grew by 237,000 jobs or a relatively incremental rate of 0.8 percent during the Reagan administration. Major employment increases took place in the Department of Defense during this period.

Certain "downsizing" patterns emerged during the Reagan years which continue today under the new "reinventing" government philosophy. While nearly 60,000 federal employees lost their jobs by 1984, the federal government continued to hire approximately 1,000 new employees each day. In most months it hired about 20,000 new workers, but in some months it hired as many as 50,000. Instead of substantially shrinking the federal bureaucracy, the Reagan administration actually slowed the rate of job growth by reordering personnel priorities among and within agencies as well as between grades of officials. It tinkered with a few politically vulnerable programs. For example, the Department of Health and Human Services (HHS) lost a disproportionate number of employees in weak service programs; HHS employees in GS-11 to GS-15 positions—classifications which grew dramatically during the 1970s—were more vulnerable to the personnel cuts than employees in lower grades. For many government employees, such reform efforts appeared to be another shell game for public employment.

The New Revolution in Government

But it took the Clinton administration, which came to power in 1994, to dramatically decrease federal employment as part of its goal to overhaul the federal bureaucracy. Led by Vice President Gore, this new reform movement sent shock waves through many government quarters, especially public unions, with its ambitious plan to eliminate more than 272,000 jobs, or over 10 percent of the federal workforce, during a five-year period. Middle management, personnel, procurement, and administrative staffs would be especially hard hit by the planned cutbacks. The big losers would be the Office of Personnel Management and the Department of Defense. A trendy new reform philosophy, backed up with concrete proposals to streamline bureaucracy—"reinventing government"—influenced these efforts. Efforts to eliminate unnecessary regulations, reorganize regional field operations, and downsize personnel took center stage in these reforms. A new round of hiring freezes, early retirements, buyouts, and reductions-in-force were initiated, repeating the perennial effort to make government both look and feel more efficient and effective. With the press preoccupied with short-term partisan political battles and scandals, some of the most significant long-term reforms in government took place with little public interest or awareness.

> **From 1994-1998, some of the most significant long-term reforms in government took place with little public interest or awareness.**

The verdict is still out on the results of these reforms, especially whether the government operates better than before. A recent Brookings Institution report by Donald F. Kettl ("Reinventing Government: A Fifth-Year Report Card"), however, gave these efforts an overall grade of 'B'. Here's what he found:

Category	Grade	Analysis/Conclusion
➤ Downsizing	B	Accomplished goal but weak workforce planning
➤ Identifying government objectives	D	1995 focus on what government should do evaporated as GOP budget threats faded
➤ Procurement reform	A	Purchasing system operates more efficient than ever
➤ Customer service	B+	Good progress in some agencies but failures in others

➤ Disaster avoidance	B+	IRS remains problematic; FEMA experienced turnaround
➤ Political leadership	C+	Strong at top but inconsistant below
➤ Performance improvements	C+	On sidelines in shaping agency plans
➤ High-impact agencies	Incomplete	On sidelines in shaping agency plans
➤ Service coordination	Incomplete	Still in initial stages
➤ Relations with Congress	D	Weak efforts to develop legislative support
➤ Trust in government	C	Improving but probably due to a healthy economy
➤ Use of other reform models	B-	Grab-bag approach rather than careful analysis
➤ Effort	A+	Sustained, high-level attention invested in management reform
➤ **OVERALL**	**B**	**Substantial progress made in five year but more work lies ahead**

SOURCE: Based on Washington Post summary, September 4, 1998, A23

But one thing is certain—the federal government in 1998 is a very different government than in 1994. Indeed, a quiet revolution has taken place within the federal government during the past five years. Major reforms have been implemented and the most obvious result is that this is a much smaller government than before. The Clinton adminstration actually exceeded what many people thought were unrealistic downsizing goals: by August 1998, the federal government had eliminated 337,182 jobs which represented a 15 percent decrease in personnel over a five year period! Most of the decrease took place through attrition—early retirements, buyout schemes, and hiring freezes. In fact, only 36,661 people were laid off during this period. At the same time, major increases in personnel took place in the U.S. Postal Service and the Department of Justice.

Implications and Outcomes

The implications of such post-1994 radical downsizing have been at least three-fold:

1. **Many agencies were not hiring.** While the federal government was restructuring its application process to make it easier and faster to get hired, in reality job applicants found much of the federal government simply closed to new hires because of a combination of hiring freezes and the government's relocation program for displaced workers which gave current employees preference for jobs in other agencies. How long this situation will continue is uncertain. In 1998, the Department of Defense, continued to encourage early retirement with buyouts. Hiring freezes continued in many agencies that were still in the process of "reinventing" themselves.

2. **Morale declined significantly in downsized agencies.** In order to reach employment targets, employees were being told to do more with less personnel. Not surprising, morale in many agencies took a big hit. Despite Vice-President Gore's attempts to put a "happy face" on this new downsized government, there were few happy faces in the downsized agencies; many employees developed attitude problems. This was not a fun time to be a federal employee. If you were lucky enough to land a federal job, there was a good chance you would be working with the working wounded who were operating in a survival mode.

> There were few happy faces in the downsized agencies; many employees developed attitude problems. This was not a fun time to be a federal employee.

3. **Many agency personnel offices were overworked and understaffed.** One of the great ironies of downsizing was that agency personnel offices were often the first to get

downsized, but they also were supposed to handle much of the additional workload attendant with downsizing initiatives, such as handling early retirements and buyouts. Despite new approaches and technology, personnel offices were majoring in their own problem—too few personnel to handle downsizing agency personnel!

While the end result of these reforms was to halt the incremental growth of federal employment, the changes might also increase procurement activities: agencies may need to hire more contractors and consultants to make up for new personnel shortfalls created by these latest reforms. Ironically, one of the major goals of these reforms was to downsize agency procurement offices—the very ones that were supposed to help prevent waste, fraud, and abuse in government!

Another trend emerged during this cutback era and continues today: government budgets continue to increase but at a slower rate than in previous decades. Some government employees will be cut from the public payroll, but fewer new employees will be hired in general. However, the "hidden government" of contracting and consulting firms will continue to do business as usual with agencies. Many will increase their employees in direct proportion to declines in government employment. Except in defense, contracting and consulting should continue to be growth industries in the decade ahead.

FEDERAL GOVERNMENT WINNERS AND LOSERS, 1980-1998

EXECUTIVE AGENCIES	Employment 1980	1998	Increase/ Decrease	Percent Change
THE WINNERS				
▪ Federal Deposit Insurance Corp.	3,587	7,762	+4,175	+116.4
▪ U.S. Courts	14,404	30,709	+16,305	+113.2
▪ Justice	57,041	120,104	+63,063	+110.6
▪ U.S. Postal Service	666,228	858,066	+191,838	+28.8
▪ Treasury	131,713	153,729	+20,016	+16.7
▪ State	23,791	24,618	+827	+3.5
▪ Veterans Affairs	239,625	242,532	+2,907	+1.2

THE LOSERS

▪ Commerce	196,544	40,365	-155,179	-79.5
▪ Tennessee Valley Authority	51,531	13,898	-37,633	-73.0
▪ Health and Human Services*	163,921	59,462	-104,459	-63.7
▪ General Services Administration	38,620	14,196	-24,424	-63.2
▪ Office of Personnel Management	8,564	3,573	-4,991	-58.3
▪ U.S. International Development Agency	6,271	2,874	-3,397	-54.2
▪ Government Printing Office	6,949	3,443	-3,506	-50.5
▪ Federal Trade Commission	1,896	1,032	-864	-45.6
▪ Housing and Urban Development	17,413	9,852	-7,561	-43.3
▪ Labor	24,482	15,786	-8,696	-35.5
▪ Education	7,167	4,801	-2,366	-33.0
▪ Agriculture	144,124	100,161	-43,963	-30.5
▪ Energy	21,680	16,246	-5,434	-25.1
▪ Defense	967,890	726,690	-241,200	-24.9
▪ Small Business Administration	5,891	4,474	-1,417	-24.1
▪ Interior	88,924	71,803	-17,121	-19.3
▪ Transportation	74,368	64,046	-10,322	-13.9

* Downsizing reflects the fact that the Social Security Administration within HHS became an Iindependent agency with a total workforce of 65,857 in May 1998.
SOURCE: U.S. Office of Personnel Management., May 1998

Indeed, in 1994 public employee unions finally began to turn their attention to the hidden government of contractors and consultants in criticizing the Clinton administration's reinventing government initiatives. In its simplest form, the criticism went like this: why should contractors and consultants be exempt from reinventing government? Shouldn't they, too, be required to engage in cost-cutting efforts just like government agencies? Many public employees felt they were unfairly being singled out for reform efforts, which actually translated into reductions-in-force, when studies showed it was more cost-effective to hire full-time bureaucrats rather than consultants. Had contractors and consultants, who largely operate outside public view and political criticism, become sacred cows immune to government reform efforts? The answer seemed clear: of course. How else can you expect to run a complex government affected by over-zealous politicians and administrators who constantly seek the limelight by beating up on a politically weak bureaucracy? Ironically, contractors and consultants could provide continuity within government while government agencies went on their periodical "reform" journeys to look more efficient and effective.

As we move into the 21st century with a restructured world order that has witnessed a substantial decline in "Cold War" military hardware and personnel throughout the 1990s, cutbacks continue to take place within the Department of Defense (DOD) as well as amongst defense contractors—key beneficiaries of the reordered pro-military budgetary and personnel priorities during the 1980-1987 period. Depending on the extent of these cutbacks, they could have a major negative impact on defense contractors who got fat and happy during the post-World War II Cold War era. Indeed, in 1994 two of the nation's largest defense contractors symbolized the financial and employment realities of this new downsizing era. On March 7, 1994, Martin Marietta Corporation and Grumman Corporation—which in 1993 had combined revenues of $12.6 billion and employed 109,000 people—agreed to a $1.93 billion merger. Northrop Corporation muddied the waters by countering this offer and finally winning the bidding war on April 4, 1994 with a price tag of $2.17 billion. This merger would guarantee the continuing existence of Grumman Corporation, a well established and highly respected defense contractor specializing in military aircraft, defense electronics, computer software, reconnaissance, intelligence, and space, which faced a daunting future of trying to cope with its declining fortunes in the post-Cold War era. While Northrop won this major merger battle, Martin Marietta will most likely emerge as the world's largest defense electronics firm and retain its position as the nation's largest defense and aerospace contractor. The outcomes for other defense contractors—both prime contractors and subcontractors—also appeared certain: less business, fewer employees, and more attempts at mergers with other defense contractors.

Similar mergers, buyouts, and downsizings took place in 1993 and 1994 within the defense industry as contractors scrambled to adjust to this new era of uncertain but substantially lower military spending. In 1993, for example, Martin Marietta acquired GE Aerospace from General Electric for $3 billion. In 1994 Martin Marietta announced the future acquisition of General Dynamics Corporation's rocket division for $208 million, and Loral Corporation finalized plans to acquire IBM's Federal Systems Division for $1.5 billion. As one Grumman executive summarized the realities of this new defense contracting era, "You acquire somebody, get acquired, or go out of business" (*Washington Post,* March 8, 1994). And Raytheon Corporation, a major defense contractor best known for producing the popular Patriot Missile, announced the closing of several plants and the layoff of 4,400 workers. Consequently, job and career opportunities with defense and aerospace contractors throughout the 1990s were unpredictable as "Cold War careers" either came to an end or were transformed into "post-Cold War careers." As many defense contracts negotiated in the late 1980s were scheduled to terminate in 1994 and 1995, defense contractors quickly moved to diversify their businesses. Many restructured their businesses away from producing military aircraft and other defense and aerospace related hardware and moved toward producing electronics and computers for the civilian market. Much of the remaining business within defense contracting shifted from manufacturing military hardware to producing defense electronics and engaging in research, development, and testing activities.

> The Department of Defense as well as defense contractors took the biggest hits during the 1990s in response to major cutbacks in defense spending, personnel, and bases.

Whether such cutbacks result in substantially reducing the national deficit as well as reallocating resources to other government agencies and contractors is one of the most interesting questions facing the public sector—a sector not noted for making radical shifts in budgetary priorities. Our best guess follows our "Law for Downsized Public Spending": money will flow to those areas experiencing high political support and low resistance—to "Mom and Apple Pie" issues. We put our bets on reallocating resources to the high profile policy areas of health, education, and public safety—the great government growth industries for the next decade. The health, education, and criminal justice bureaucracies of federal, state, and local governments, as well as amongst peripheral institutions—contractors, consultants, nonprofit organizations, foundations, associations, research groups—should expand accordingly.

At the same time, we expect the U.S. Postal Service will continue to modernize and grow. In fact, the U.S. Postal Service has undergone a major transformation during the past five years which make this independent agency an increasingly attractive place to work. We also expect a turnaround with the Department of Defense. It may soon conclude its cutbacks have been too extreme for its new international roles.

Finding Your Best Place to Work

All agencies are not equal in the federal government. Like many organizations in the private sector, some are outstanding, most are okay, and some are dreadful places to work. Finding the best place to work in the federal government will require some effort on your part in discovering which agencies are best suited for your particular mix of interests, skills, and abilities. You'll have to conduct research on different agencies to learn about their missions, internal operations, personnel, accomplishments, problems, and opportunities. In other words, which ones are an excellent "fit" for both you and the agency?

Fortunately, some studies have been conducted to assist you in identifying what are **reputed** to be some of the best and the worst federal agencies. A survey conducted by *Fortune Magazine* of former government executives, who are members of the Council for Excellence in Government, asked them to rate federal agencies according to four criteria:

- quality of the management
- quality of the work force
- quality of service
- return on the tax dollar

The results of the survey identified the following as the most and least respected federal agencies:

Most Respected:

1. National Security Council
2. Federal Reserve
3. National Institutes of Health
4. Council on Economic Affairs
5. Office of the Treasury Secretary
6. Office of Special Trade Representative
7. Defense Advanced Research Projects Agency
8. Federal Bureau of Investigation
9. Central Intelligence Agency
10. Securities and Exchange Commission

Least Respected:

1. Bureau of Indian Affairs
2. Small Business Administration
3. Indian Health Service
4. Department of Education
5. Office of Thrift Supervision
6. Commission on Civil Rights
7. Department of Housing and Urban Development
8. Equal Employment Opportunity Commission
9. Consumer Product Safety Commission
10. Employment and Training Administration

Some observers might add the IRS (Internal Revenue Service) to this "Least Respected" list. The IRS's inability to fundamentally reform itself, especially its notorious management problems, during the "reinventing government" period raises questions about its attractiveness as a workplace for job seekers.

> The most highly regarded agencies tend to be older agencies that have high visibility, a political consensus concerning their missions, stable leadership, and high quality political appointees.

Not surprising, the most highly regarded agencies tend to be older agencies that have high visibility, a political consensus concerning their missions, stable leadership, and high quality political appointees. The lowest regarded agencies tend to be newer, lack a clear political consensus about their missions, and experience funding cuts and personnel cutbacks.

You may want to consider this information when you begin targeting the agencies identified in the remainder of this book. The best places to work are most likely to be the ones identified in the top ten as well as those experiencing personnel growth rather than decline.

Predicting the Future

Given past patterns of growth, stability, and decline in government employment, what can we expect in the future? Certain trends are evident based on knowledge of future demographic changes, basic public service needs, and a significant restructuring of public policy priorities. We see several broad trends during the past few years that argue for some major departures for the public sector in the decade ahead. We see thirteen important changes for the federal government and the public sector in general:

1. **A changing world order attendant with new regimes in Eastern Europe and the former Soviet republics, worldwide economic dislocations, continuing poverty and political turmoil in Third and Fourth World countries, and the expansion of international drug wars and terrorism will result in new public policy initiatives and hiring emphases within the federal government as well as amongst consultants, contractors, nonprofit organizations, and research groups.**

These trends have important implications for the future shape of the public sector. The break-up of communist regimes in Eastern Europe, the restructuring of Russian politics and economics, the re-emergence of communist regimes in failed market economies, continuing political turmoil in the Middle East and Asia, and the changing roles of China, Japan and other major Asian economies could have far reaching consequences for the public sector in the United States. An extremely downsized U.S. Department of Defense and intelligence agencies in disarray, such as the CIA, will once again begin to expand their personnel and operations in response to new dangers in the international environment. At the same time, the State Department, Peace Corps, the Agency for International Development, and international-related agencies in the Departments of Commerce, Agriculture, Transportation, Treasury, and Health and Human Services will expand their operations in response to new worldwide economic crises.

However, given the volatility of such changes, as well as the incremental nature of the federal budgetary process, dramatic changes will be slow in coming. By the year 2000 Russia will likely re-emerge as a significant military force affecting international political developments. Ironically, Department of Defense adjustments to the changing world order will most likely lag by one to two years given constraints inherent in the annual budgetary process. Disappointing economic opportunities in Europe, failed economies in Asia, and a stronger U.S. dollar abroad will result in refocusing attention on managing international trade and monetary relations. Problems with poverty and political turmoil in Third and Fourth World countries will place greater emphasis on improving the U.S. presence abroad through the activities of the State Department, Peace Corps, and the Agency for International Development. Continuing problems with drug wars and terrorism will mean increased employment within the Defense, State, and Justice departments. Indeed, the role of the military may be transformed in the next decade to better deal with the problems of terrorism and drugs.

2. **A highly downsized Department of Defense creates greater competition for federal jobs.**

Competition for federal jobs continues to be keen in part due to the fact that many downsized Department of Defense employees seek jobs with other federal agencies. Large numbers of deactivated non-commissioned officers turn to the federal government for civilian employment. More and more retired officers, who normally avoid federal employment because of retirement pay restrictions, look to the federal government for employment; many of their traditional post-military job opportunities in the private sector with defense contractors disappear within the rapidly shrinking defense establishment. Individuals seeking federal jobs without veterans preference face increased difficulty competing in this highly competitive environment.

3. **Continuing public safety problems attendant with drug problems, unemployment, and poverty require increased government expenditures and hiring to contain public safety problems.**

Expect steady increases in employment within the criminal justice system—police, courts, and prisons as well as among peripheral organizations involved with criminal justice issues. The judiciary at all levels will continue to grow in response to public safety and criminal justice problems. Lawyers and paralegals can expect more and more job opportunities within this troubled criminal justice system. Prisons continue as a major growth industry in the decade ahead. Federal involvement with prisons also will increase.

4. **Public health becomes a major public policy issue in the decade ahead. Health care delivery requirements result in increased public spending on health care.**

Despite public debates to the contrary, federal, state, and local health care bureaucracies experience significant growth as do associations, nonprofit organizations, and consultants and contractors specializing in health care issues. Public employment opportunities abound for individuals with health care expertise.

5. **Education takes on renewed importance because of the growing gap between the "have's" and "have not's" in America's new talent-driven economy.**

The federal government initiates new programs to deliver more short-term, skills-intensive training for individuals who are not prepared for the jobs of today and in the decade ahead. These jobs require high-tech skills that can be best delivered outside traditional educational classrooms and programs. More and more attention is given to promoting apprenticeship programs as well as three- to six-month training programs.

6. **Energy and environmental problems take center stage in public policy debates and capture a larger share of the federal budgets. Greater emphasis will focus on handling toxic waste dumps that endanger the well-being of communities.**

Governments at all levels will attempt to solve energy and environmental problems by contracting-out both policy-making and implementation to private consultants and contractors. Communities near military bases will receive considerable attention since many of the adjacent bases are literally aging toxic waste dumps endangering community health. The Department of Energy will become the model of a highly "privatized" public agency; contractors and consultants largely run this agency from top to bottom. Expect employment opportunities for environmental specialists to increase accordingly both within government and amongst businesses, nonprofit organizations, and associations involved with these issues.

7. The decade ahead will witness greater employment mobility between the public and private sectors.

Given changes in the federal application and retirement systems and the portability of federal pension funds, more and more federal employees will move back and forth between the public and private sectors. As part of the federal government's continuing decentralization of personnel matters to agencies, the U.S. Office of Personnel Management no longer requires the unpopular Standard Form 171 (SF-171) and thereby permits agencies to accept SF-171s along with other application forms—OF-612s and federal-style resumes. More individuals will apply for federal positions under this new application system which may create chaos in some agencies which are not equipped to handle resumes and other types of applications. Expect changes in the retirement system to help revitalize the public sector.

8. Downsizing will continue in several agencies but to a much lesser extent than during the 1994-1998 period.

The whole downsizing movement in the federal government will largely plateau. Agency personnel levels should remain relatively stable in the coming decade, returning to a more normal fluctuating growth rate of 0 to 1.0 percent each year.

9. The federal government will probably continue to replace personnel at the present no-growth rate of approximately 1,000 new employees each day.

The Departments of Justice, State, and Veterans Affairs, the Environmental Protection Agency, and the U.S. Postal Service will continue to increase in size due to public policy priorities to expand in these areas. The number of positions related to the procurement process will increase in all agencies except Defense due to an expanding government contracting role and continuing problems with the government procurement process. As the federal budget grows and government employment plateaus, non-military private contracting and consulting firms will probably expand their business with federal, state, and local government agencies.

10. **A quiet revolution continues to take place in government due to the "reinventing government" initiatives of the mid-1990s. A new and highly competitive public service emerges as a result of transformations in personnel taking place in the early 1990s.**

Recessions tend to bring out the best of people, at least for government employment. The tight and restructured job market of the early 1990s saw more and more people leaving the private sector for government jobs. Indeed, for many people facing a recessionary job market, government employment seemed to be a relatively open, secure, and well paying alternative to the declining number of private sector jobs which also were increasingly becoming low paying jobs. The overall education, skill, and experience levels of these government employees is high—much higher than many current employees who joined government five or ten years earlier.

12. **Government personnel procedures today are more apolitical and professional than ever before. They will continue to be so in the future.**

Except for a few ambassadorships and the frequent use of the General Services Administration and a few other agencies as dumping grounds for the politically well-connected, gone are the good-ole-boy days when politicians dumped incompetents into government agencies and political connections could get you a job with little or no demonstrated skills or experience. Patronage systems have given way to merit systems based upon systematic recruitment, selection, and promotion procedures. While the ubiquitous "connection" is still important for getting a government job—indeed, essential for you to use—it tends to be professional in nature. The name of the game today is "profe-

> The name of the game today is "professional networking" rather than using "political pull"—a significant shift in how the game is played.

ssional networking" rather than using "political pull"—a significant shift in how the game is played.

13. **Public sector jobs continue to require more technical skills and competition remains high for a limited number of vacancies available in most agencies.**

Once largely a job market for generalists, the public sector today engages in highly technical activities requiring substantial educational and technical skills. Given the relatively good pay and security of government employment, not surprisingly many people want to work for government. Thus, you can expect to encounter competition from numerous candidates who possess relatively strong educational and technical backgrounds. Competition will be especially keen during recessionary periods when more individuals apply for federal jobs and fewer federal employees decide to leave the government for jobs in the private sector. The quality of candidates also will increase substantially during such periods.

Knowing these trends, your task should be to identify how you can best link your skills and abilities to job vacancies in the federal government. Because of no-growth and limited-growth job situations in government, it is very important to plan and target your job search on particular agencies with growth potential. The evidence is clear: numerous and exciting job opportunities are available, but only for those who prepare well for an increasingly competitive, professional, and technical federal government where careers tend to plateau within a short period of time.

5

Agencies, Positions, and Pay

Many people want to work for the federal government. For them, this is where the action is. Regardless of what others may say to the contrary, pay is good and benefits are excellent. Despite occasional downsizing, job security is virtually guaranteed. Many jobs are exciting, and more status, prestige, and financial rewards go to federal government employees than to state and local officials.

Understanding the System and Process

But getting a job with the federal government is another matter. This level of government appears complex, confusing, and difficult to enter. Competition is fierce, applications are complex, and the hiring process takes time. Hiring procedures are not uniform. The legislative, judicial, and executive branches, for example, each have their own hiring systems. Within the executive branch, the U.S. Postal Service, CIA, FBI, and Foreign Service hire differently from many other agencies. And certain agencies and positions are exempted from standard personnel regulations. Information on federal job vacancies used to be updated weekly, printed as vacancy announcements, and made available through Federal Job

Information Centers and agency bulletin boards. Now it's updated daily and made accessible electronically over the Internet 24-hours a day.

The effective job seeker first needs to understand the government complex and the hiring process and then begin targeting individual agencies with job search strategies designed for the peculiarities of different agencies and positions. That's our task in the next five chapters —make sure you have an adequate understanding of the realities of government hiring as well as equip you with job search strategies that will work with the agencies you wish to target.

Agencies and Employers

The federal government employs nearly 2.8 million civilians and 1.8 million military personnel who move more than $2.5 trillion each year (literally spends $7.6 billion a day) into more than 83,000 state and local governments, 160 countries, and an enormous private sector of vendors, contractors, and nongovernmental organizations. The business of this government is incredible. It staffs and manages whole communities, such as the Pentagon and military bases at home and abroad. It is literally a cradle to the grave government: delivering babies; providing day care services; extracting taxes; educating, hiring, and retiring individuals; providing social security and health care; and burying the dead.

> **The business of government is incredible. It is literally a cradle to the grave government.**

Federal employees work for 136 different agencies in the three branches of government. The executive branch is divided into three major types of agencies:

- The Executive Office of the President (13 offices with 1,605 employees)
- The Departments (14 departments with 1,650,197 employees)
- Independent Agencies (95 agencies with 1,065,767 employees)

The federal government also consists of numerous corporations, government-sponsored enterprises, boards, committees, commissions, and quasi-official agencies which employ hundreds of additional people.

Office of Personnel Management (OPM)

The Office of Personnel Management is the federal government's central personnel or civil service agency in charge of administering a merit system. However, it is not as centralized as one might expect nor is it a hiring agency. Many job seekers still misunderstand OPM's role in the application, screening, and selection processes. The reason for this is OPM's past role which was highly centralized. Indeed, OPM used to collect and screen applications and test applicants for most agencies. Applicants would receive OPM "ratings" which would then qualify them for particular agency positions. This old system has been abolished in favor of a highly decentralized and flexible hiring system that primarily operates at the agency level.

> **Many job seekers still misunderstand OPM's role in the application, screening, and selection processes.**

While each agency has its own personnel office, the Office of Personnel Management (OPM), an independent executive agency, stands at the apex of the federal personnel system. Until the late 1980s, OPM played an important role in directly recruiting and screening applicants for many types of positions and for certain agencies. However, as key personnel functions, such as issuing vacancy announcements, rating applicants, and training, were increasingly decentralized to individual agencies in the 1980s, today OPM plays a more supportive role in helping agencies meet their personnel needs. This office is responsible for:

- issuing government-wide personnel regulations
- establishing basic qualification standards for all occupations
- providing employment information for competitive service positions
- certifying agency delegated examining units to conduct their own examinations
- providing support services to agencies
- managing some application, testing, and screening processes
- providing policy direction and guidance on promotions, reassignments, appointments in the excepted and competitive services, reinstatements, temporary and term employment, veterans

preference, workforce restructuring, career transition, and other staffing provisions
- administering the Senior Executive Service program and other merit-based executive personnel systems
- coordinating temporary assignment of employees
- providing limited training services
- assisting agencies in meeting their personnel needs
- extending benefits to employees and government retirees

OPM's primary responsibilities relate to competitive positions in the federal civil service which encompass General Schedule grades 1 through 15 and Federal Wage system positions. Together, these positions include 1,404,987 jobs or 50.5 percent of all federal government jobs.

During the past few years OPM has undergone a major transformation as it increasingly decentralized many of its functions to other agencies as well as became a major participant in the "reinventing government" movement. The end result has been to significantly downsize the agency, from 8,564 employees in 1980 to 5,184 employees in 1994 and then further reduced to 3,573 employees in 1998—a 31 percent reduction in personnel in just five years! At the same time, OPM has been responsible for reforming the federal application and hiring processes as well as for putting in place a comprehensive automated information system that can be conveniently accessed via the Internet, telephone, and touch screen computers. If you are interested in learning about how to apply for a federal job, just click on to the Internet and go directly to OPM's online Federal Employment Information System (USAJOBS) for all the details, including vacancy announcements and applications forms:

www.usajobs.opm.gov

This system also can be accessed through these three alternative communication mediums:

➤ **Electronic Bulletin Board:** Tel. 912/757-3100 or Telnet: *fjob.opm.gov*

➤ **Automated Telephone System:** Dial either 912/757-3000 or TDD 912/744-2299

➤ **Touch Screen Computer Kiosks:** located in all OPM offices
   and in many federal office buildings (see Appendix A)

If you are interested in learning more about the federal personnel system
in general—including information on salaries, benefits, and rules and
regulations—go to directly to OPM's main Web site where you can
access a wealth of information 24-hours a day:

www.opm.gov

Whatever you do, don't forget to make contact with OPM. This
agency functions as the most important government-wide gateway to
information on federal government employment and the federal merit
system. Savvy federal job seekers initially explore OPM's Web site for
information on how to best apply for a federal job. Make sure you're one
of the savvy job seekers!

Employment Levels

The table on pages 92-93 summarizes employment distribution by
government branches, major agencies, and geographic dispersion of
agency personnel.

The total federal government workforce represents 18 percent of all
public employees. Eighty-eight percent of federal employees work
outside the Washington, DC Metro area, including 103,403 who work
abroad (63,879 U.S. citizens; 39,524 non U.S. citizens) primarily for 10
agencies that have a major overseas presence: Agency for International
Development; Peace Corps; U.S. Information Agency; and the Departments of Agriculture, Commerce, Defense, Air Force, Army, Navy, and
State. The three largest civilian employers are the U.S. Postal Service and
the Departments of Defense and Veterans Affairs, which employ 30.9,
26.1, and 8.7 percent of the total federal workforce respectively.

Federal employment has been relatively stable over the past 25 years.
Between 1960 and 1980 federal employment increased by 22.9 percent,
for an average annual increase of 1.1 percent. In 1981 federal employment actually decreased by 67,000 and by another 39,000 in 1982. As
indicated in the statistical table on pages 74-75 of Chapter 4, agencies
experiencing major cutbacks in the 1980s and 1990s were the Tennessee
Valley Authority, General Services Administration, Office of Personnel

FEDERAL CIVILIAN EMPLOYMENT
BY MAJOR AGENCIES, 1998

AGENCY	Total Employees	Percent in Washington Metro area
TOTAL	2,779,408	11.6
Legislative Branch	**30,745**	**94.1**
–Congress	17,215	100.0
▪ U.S. Senate	6,412	100.0
▪ U.S. House of Representatives	10,788	100.0
–Architect of the Capitol	1,744	100.0
–Botanic Garden	43	100.0
–Congressional Budget Office	220	100.0
–General Accounting Office	3,283	65.4
–Government Printing Office	3,443	88.4
–Library of Congress	4,369	99.4
–U.S. Court of Veterans Appeals	79	100.0
–U.S. Tax Court	280	98.4
Judicial Branch	**31,092**	**7.2**
–Supreme Court	383	100.0
–U.S. Courts	30,709	5.7
Executive Branch	**2,717,569**	**11.5**
–Executive Office of the President	**1,605**	**99.4**
▪ Executive Residence at White House	84	100.0
▪ National Security Council	42	100.0
▪ Office of Administration	173	100.0
▪ Office of Economic Advisors	31	100.0
▪ Office of Environmental Quality	19	100.0
▪ Office of Management & Budget	502	100.0
▪ Office of National Drug Control Policy	114	100.0
▪ Office of Policy Development	28	100.0
▪ Office of Science & Technology Policy	31	100.0
▪ Office of U.S. Trade Representative	162	95.5
▪ White House Office	399	100.0
–Executive Departments	**1,650,197**	**13.1**
▪ Agriculture	109,454	11.5
▪ Commerce	37,416	53.9
▪ Defense	726.690	9.5
▪ Education	4,801	69.2
▪ Energy	16,246	38.3
▪ Health & Human Services	59,462	23.7
▪ Housing & Urban Development	9,852	26.0
▪ Interior	71,803	12.6
▪ Justice	120,104	21.9
▪ Labor	15,786	37.9
▪ State	24,618	34.0
▪ Transportation	64,046	15.3
▪ Treasury	153,729	15.7
▪ Veterans Affairs	242,534	2.9

–Independent Agencies	1,065,767	8.2
▪ Environmental Protection Agency	18,307	32.9
▪ Equal Employment Opportunity Commission	2,586	25.5
▪ Federal Communications Commission	2,027	82.7
▪ Federal Deposit Insurance Corporation	7,762	18.5
▪ Federal Emergency Management Agency	5,294	26.3
▪ Federal Reserve Board of Governors	1,675	100.0
▪ Federal Trade Commission	1,032	82.7
▪ General Services Administration	14,196	32.8
▪ National Aeronautics and Space Administration	18,985	22.8
▪ National Archives and Records Administration	2,667	41.2
▪ National Labor Relations Board	1,904	28.9
▪ Nuclear Regulatory Commission	3,040	66.8
▪ Office of Personnel Management	3,573	42.8
▪ Panama Canal Commission	9,656	00.1
▪ Securities and Exchange Commission	2,810	67.1
▪ Small Business Administration	4,474	18.4
▪ Smithsonian Institution	5,211	90.3
▪ Social Security Administration	65,857	2.4
▪ Tennessee Valley Authority	13,898	0.1
▪ U.S. Information Agency	6,373	49.5
▪ U.S. International Development Cooperation Agency	2,876	53.6
▪ U.S. Postal Service	858,066	2.7

SOURCE: U.S. Office of Personnel Management, Office of Workforce Information, Statistical Analysis and Services Division, May 1998. These figures include all full-time permanent (2,330,678 or 83.9%), intermittent (137,347 or 4.9%), full-time temporary (131,877 or 4.7%) and part-time (179,504 or 6.5%) positions. These figures do not include the key intelligence agencies which are excepted by law from reporting employment statistics: Central Intelligence Agency, National Security Agency, Defense Intelligence Agency, and the National Imagery and Mapping Agency. We estimate the CIA has 25,000-30,000 employees; the other intelligence agencies may employ another 30,000 people.

Management, U.S. International Development Cooperation Agency, Government Printing Office, Small Business Administration, and the Departments of Education, Commerce, Housing and Urban Development, Labor, Energy, Health and Human Services, Transportation, and Agriculture. On the other hand, several agencies experienced major increases in personnel throughout the 1980s and 1990s: Federal Deposit Insurance Corporation, U.S. Postal Service, and the Departments of Justice, Treasury, Defense, Veterans Affairs, and State. Despite major cutbacks in some agencies, federal government employment actually increased by 8.8 percent between 1980 and 1990, representing an average annual increase of just under 1 percent. In fact, until 1994, federal government employment tended to increase incrementally at the rate of .5 to 1.5 percent a year. Such incremental growth came to a sudden halt in 1994 when the federal government proceeded on a deliberate downsizing path that resulted in reducing overall federal employment by 15 percent over a five year period, for an unprecedented average annual reduction of 3 percent!

Regardless of the recent declines in federal employment, there are plenty of job opportunities available even during lean hiring years. After all, given an average annual turnover rate of nearly 14 percent, nearly 400,000 job opportunities are available with the federal government each year. If you have appropriate skills, know where to find openings, produce and distribute a well organized SF-171, OF-612, or federal-style resume, target agencies, and use effective job search skills, you should be able to quickly land a federal job.

> **Regardless of the recent declines in federal employment, there are plenty of job opportunities available even during lean hiring years.**

Competitive and Exempted Services

The federal government does not have a single, unified personnel system. Its 2.8 million employees are classified into different services and positions. The federal civil service, for example, classifies positions into competitive or exempted services. Surprisingly, barely a majority, or 50.5 percent (1,404,987 jobs), of all federal government positions are in the **competitive service** (the U.S. Postal Service with its 858,066 employees represents the largest exempted service). Competitive service positions fall under the civil service regulations, codified in the Civil Service Reform Act of 1978, which are administered by the Office of Personnel Management. Such positions must adhere to the "merit principles" of openness, fairness, and nondiscrimination. These positions come under Presidential authority, are subject to periodic reductions-in-force regulations and hiring freezes, and follow internal seniority rules.

At the same time, Congress, the judiciary, and several agency positions are exempted from these regulations. These positions lie outside the authority of OPM and are subject to individual agency personnel regulations. Individuals in these positions do not accumulate civil service seniority which would apply to other positions in the competitive service. Executive agencies classified in the **exempted services** include:

- Central Intelligence Agency
- Defense Intelligence Agency
- Executive Protective Service (Secret Service—Uniformed Branch)
- Federal Bureau of Investigation
- Federal Reserve System, Board of Governors
- General Accounting Office
- U.S. International Development Cooperation Agency
- National Imagery and Mapping Agency
- National Science Foundation (only scientific, engineering, and a few high-level managerial positions are exempted)
- National Security Agency
- U.S. Nuclear Regulatory Commission
- Postal Rates Commission
- U.S. Postal Service
- U.S. Department of State (skilled specialists and experienced secretaries only; all others take the foreign service exam)
- Tennessee Valley Authority
- U. S. Mission to the United Nations
- Veterans Affairs, Department of Medicine and Surgery

These agencies have their own set of personnel procedures for hiring and managing personnel, which may include special applications that go beyond the SF-171, OF-612, or federal-style resumes. Therefore, individuals should contact these agencies directly for information on special application procedures and required documents.

Exempted Positions and Appointments

Exempted positions, which comprise 49.5 percent of all positions, are not subject to OPM standards. Such positions are exempted because they are difficult to fill through normal recruitment channels. They include:

- Professional and Administrative Careers—GS-5 thru GS-7
- Teachers in the Department of Defense's overseas dependent schools
- Attorneys
- Doctors, dentists, and nurses with the Department of Veterans Affairs

- Scientists and engineers with the National Science Foundation
- Chaplains with the Veterans Affairs and Justice Departments
- Drug enforcement agents

Certain individuals can also qualify for exempted **appointments** which involve entry into the competitive service through special procedures. These appointments are primarily for the severely physically handicapped and Vietnam era veterans. If you think you qualify for such an appointment, contact OPM (*www.opm.gov*) or an agency personnel office for information on specific application procedures.

Temporary and Term Appointments

The federal government has special provisions for hiring both temporary and term employees. Agencies use these hiring categories to fill positions for which they have a temporary need. Since these are not permanent appointments, employees in these positions do not receive competitive status nor reinstatement eligibility, and their benefits are limited. In addition, such employees cannot apply for permanent appointments through agency internal merit promotion procedures since they do not have "status" which is a requirement for such positions. Individuals in temporary or term positions should be able to gain important qualifying experience as well as information on upcoming vacancies and hiring practices. They also should be acquiring valuable networking experience that can later be leveraged for finding a permanent federal job. But temporary and term appointments in no way guarantee success in getting a permanent position. While they are not stepping-stones, they do help individuals better prepare themselves for other positions.

> Individuals in temporary or term positions should be able to gain important qualifying experience as well as information on upcoming vacancies and hiring practices.

A **temporary appointment** is for one year or less and it includes an expiration date. These appointments are used to fill a short-term position, meet a special employment need, or fill positions involving intermittent or seasonal work schedules. Individuals in these positions do not serve a probationary period and they are not eligible for promotion, reassignment, or transfer to other jobs. Most of these positions are filled through open competitive examinations but some may be noncompetitive. Temporary employees earn leave and qualify for Social Security and unemployment compensation. However, they do not receive other fringe benefits extended to career civil servants. Temporary employees can purchase health insurance after one year of temporary service.

A **term appointment** is designed for project work that lasts more than one year but not more than four years. Such appointments are frequently used for special projects, extraordinary workloads, abolishing a position, reorganization, funding uncertainty, or contracting out of a function. Most term vacancies are filled through open competitive examination procedures, although some are filled noncompetitively. Term employees earn leave and have many of the same benefits of permanent employees, including heath and life insurance, within-grade increases, and Federal Employees Retirement System and Thrift Savings Plan coverage.

For Information on vacancies that are specified as "temporary" or "term" appointments, see current vacancy announcements available through OPM's Federal Employment Information System (USAJOBS) or through agency personnel offices.

Classifications and Compensation

The total federal workforce is divided into two major classification systems. White-collar professional, administrative, scientific, clerical, and technical employees are paid according to the **General Schedule** (GS), which is graded from GS-1 to GS-15 and uniformly applied throughout the federal government. The table on page 97 summarizes the base pay rates on the General Schedule.

These salary rates encompass most white-collar positions in the competitive service. Exceptions include higher salary rates for employees in 31 major metropolitan areas. Employees in these areas receive locality pay adjustments, which are based on a percentage increase, due to the higher costs of living in these areas. OPM issues separate rate charts for each of these metropolitan areas. For example, locality pay adjustments in 1998 were 5.6 to 12 percent higher in the continental U.S. and 10 to 25 percent higher outside the continental U.S. The New York City, Los Angeles, Detroit, Chicago, and Hartford metropolitan areas receive the highest locality pay adjustments. Higher starting salaries also are given

GENERAL SCHEDULE OF FEDERAL
SALARY RATES BY GRADE, 1998
(excludes locality payments)

Within-Grade Step Increases

Grade Levels	ONE	TWO	THREE	FOUR	FIVE	SIX	SEVEN	EIGHT	NINE	TEN
GS-1	12,960	13,392	13,823	14,252	14,685	14,938	15,362	15,791	15,809	16,214
GS-2	14,571	14,918	15,401	15,809	15,985	16,455	16,925	17,395	17,865	18,335
GS-3	15,899	16,429	16,959	17,489	18,019	18,549	19,079	19,609	20,139	20,669
GS-4	17,848	18,443	19,038	19,633	20,228	20,823	21,418	22,013	22,608	23,203
GS-5	19,969	20,635	21,301	21,967	22,633	23,299	23,965	24,631	25,297	25,963
GS-6	22,258	23,000	23,742	24,484	25,226	25,968	26,710	27,452	28,194	28,936
GS-7	24,734	25,558	26,382	27,206	28,030	28,854	29,678	30,502	31,326	32,150
GS-8	27,393	28,306	29,219	30,132	31,045	31,958	32,871	33,784	34,697	35,610
GS-9	30,257	31,266	32,275	33,284	34,293	35,302	36,311	37,320	38,329	39,338
GS-10	33,320	34,431	35,542	36,653	37,764	38,875	39,986	41,097	42,208	43,319
GS-11	36,609	37,829	39,049	40,269	41,489	42,709	43,929	45,149	46,369	47,589
GS-12	43,876	45,339	46,802	48,265	49,728	51,191	52,654	54,117	55,580	57,043
GS-13	52,176	53,915	55,654	57,393	59,132	60,871	62,610	64,349	66,088	67,827
GS-14	61,656	63,711	65,766	67,821	69,876	71,931	73,986	76,041	78,096	80,151
GS-15	72,525	74,943	77,361	79,779	82,197	84,615	87,033	89,451	91,869	94,287

to certain hard-to-fill positions, especially in the scientific, technical, and medical fields. Each vacancy announcement will specify exact pay information, including any pay differentials.

Pay rates for the Senior Executive Service (SES)—senior management and executive positions that used to be classified as GS-16 to GS-18 positions but now have their own elite service representing .04 percent of all federal employees—are higher than for individuals working under the General Schedule. In 1998, SES pay levels were as follows:

ES-1	$99,200
ES-2	$103,900
ES-3	$108,600
ES-4	$104,500
ES-5	$118,400
ES-6	$118,400

Locality pay adjustments for SES members ranged from a high of $109,428 for an ES-1 in Los Angeles metropolitan area to a low of $104,577 for an ES-1 in Orlando, Florida. The highest pay any permanent federal employee could receive in 1998 was $125,900, which represented Senior Executive Service members at the ES-4 to ES-6 levels. In fact, individuals in ES-4, ES-5, and ES-6 positions in Los Angeles made the same annual salary—$125,900.

Trade, labor, and other blue-collar workers—70 percent of whom are employed by the Departments of Army, Navy, and Air Force—are paid on the **Federal Wage System** (WG). Grades range from WG-1 to WG-15 and the pay in each grade varies for each of 137 geographical areas. Over 400,000 employees are classified as WG.

Other pay systems operate for the U.S. Postal Service, the Foreign Service, law enforcement officials, and a few other positions. Again, each vacancy announcement will include details on pay rates and the relevant pay systems.

Representativeness

The total federal workforce is relatively representative of the distribution of males and females in the general population: 56.7 percent of all federal employees are female. However, a disproportionate number of males occupy the senior levels (GS 13-15 and SES) of the civil service—74 percent.

Contrary to what many people may believe, minorities are extremely well represented at all levels in the federal government. Indeed, the federal workforce employs a disproportionate number of minorities in comparison to their general distribution in the population. Blacks in particular are over-represented in the U.S. Postal Service (20.8 percent of postal work force versus 10.3 percent in national labor force). Blacks, Hispanics, and other minorities occupy 26 percent of all positions in the federal government, including 12 percent of all GS 13-15 and SES positions. They are disproportionately represented at the GS 1-4 levels (38.5 percent) and within the blue-collar Wage Grade system (33 percent). For many minorities—especially Blacks—the federal government is an attractive and exceedingly open employment arena. Periodic attempts to improve the "representativeness" of women and minorities in the federal government increasingly focus on the meaning of this concept in relationship to higher level managerial positions.

Job Types and Alternatives

The federal government hires individuals in five categories of jobs (PATCO) which consist of the following:

- **Professional Occupations (23%):** These require knowledge of science or specialized education and training at a level equal to a bachelor's degree or higher. Examples include engineers, accountants, biologists, and chemists. Engineers (95,000) and nurses (40,000) are the largest professional groups with the federal government.

- **Administrative Occupations (26%):** Require increasingly responsible experience or a general college education. Examples include Personnel Specialists and Administrative Officers.

- **Technical Occupations (19%):** These are associated with a professional or administrative field, but they are nonroutine in nature. Examples include Computer and Electronic Technicians.

- **Clerical Occupations (14%):** These involve work which supports office, business, or fiscal operations. Examples include Clerk-Typist, Mail and File Clerk.

- **Other Occupations (2%):** All other occupations not classified as professional, administrative, technical, or clerical. Includes many blue-collar and trade occupations, such as painters, carpenters, and laborers.

The federal government has as many different types of positions as the private sector. Since a complete list of positions would take up the remainder of this book, we examine the major classifications as well as identify those positions which employ the largest number of individuals.

The Office of Personnel Management, using a numerical code, classifies all General Schedule positions (also considered white-collar occupations) into over 400 different occupations organized into 22 groups and families. These include the following classification codes, occupational groups, and total number of employees per group:

CODE	TITLES	EMPLOYEES
GS-000	Miscellaneous Occupations	65,662
GS-100	Social Science, Psychology, and Welfare	65,740
GS-200	Personnel Management and Industrial Relations	41,895
GS-300	Administrative, Clerical, and Office Services	369,009

GS-400	Biological Sciences	58,003
GS-500	Accounting and Budget	128,142
GS-600	Medical, Hospital, Dental, and Public Health	141,555
GS-700	Veterinary Medical Science	2,188
GS-800	Engineering and Architecture	132,466
GS-900	Legal and Kindred	78,755
GS-1000	Information and Arts	18,639
GS-1100	Business and Industry	92,231
GS-1200	Copyright, Patent, and Trade-Mark	2,961
GS-1300	Physical Sciences	34,272
GS-1400	Library and Archives	8,412
GS-1500	Mathematics and Statistics	13,337
GS-1600	Equipment, Facilities, and Service	13,646
GS-1700	Education	33,127
GS-1800	Investigation	88,415
GS-1900	Quality Assurance, Inspection, and Grading	11,009
GS-2000	Supply	34,402
GS-2100	Transportation	45,265

GRAND TOTAL ------------------------------------- **1,479,448**

Wage System occupations (considered blue-collar) are also classified into 400 different occupations that are organized into 37 job family groups. These consist of the following classification codes, occupational groups, and total number of employees per family group:

CODE	TITLES	EMPLOYEES
WG-2500	Wire Communications Equipment Installation and Maintenance	756
WG-2600	Electronic Equipment Installation and Maintenance	15,868
WG-2800	Electrical Installation and Maintenance	12,939
WG-3100	Fabric and Leather Work	1,556
WG-3300	Instrument Work	1,915
WG-3400	Machine Tool Work	6,344
WG-3500	General Services and Support Work	18,672
WG-3600	Structural and Finishing Work	2,114
WG-3700	Metal Processing	5,107
WG-3800	Metal Work	10,423

WG-3900	Motion Picture, Radio, Television, and Sound Equipment Operating	238
WG-4000	Lens and Crystal Work	45
WG-4100	Painting and Paper Hanging	4,471
WG-4200	Plumbing and Pipefitting	6,170
WG-4300	Pliable Materials Work	644
WG-4400	Printing	2,643
WG-4600	Wood Work	4,740
WG-4700	General Maintenance and Operations Work	17,722
WG-4800	General Equipment Maintenance	2,257
WG-5000	Plant and Animal Work	2,590
WG-5200	Miscellaneous Occupations	2,429
WG-5300	Industrial Equipment Maintenance	11,635
WG-5400	Industrial Equipment Operation	10,404
WG-5700	Transportation/Mobile Equipment Operation	15,523
WG-5800	Transportation/Mobile Equipment Maintenance	17,081
WG-6500	Ammunition, Explosives, & Toxic Materials Work	2,041
WG-6600	Armament Work	3,473
WG-6900	Warehousing and Stock Handling	25,453
WG-7000	Packing and Processing	2,900
WG-7300	Laundry, Dry Cleaning, and Pressing	1,626
WG-7400	Food Preparation and Serving	12,607
WG-7600	Personal Services	355
WG-8200	Fluid Systems Maintenance	3,175
WG-8600	Engine Overhaul	4,334
WG-8800	Aircraft Overhaul	14,036
WG-9000	Film Processing	15
WG-9900	Vessel Jobs Excluded From Federal Wage System	3,372

GRAND TOTAL -------------------------------------- **248,739**

White-collar GS positions employing the largest number of individuals (10,000 or more) consist of:

- Secretary (GS-0318)   64,484
- Miscellaneous Clerk and Assistant (GS-0303)   61,845
- Computer Specialist (GS-0334)   55,301
- Miscellaneous Administration and Program (GS-0301)   50,515
- Nurse (GS-0610)   40,165
- Management and Program Analysis (GS-0343)   39,492
- Criminal Investigating (GS-1812)   34,576
- Contracting (GS-1102)   28,210

- General Attorney (GS-0905)   25,385
- Social Insurance Administration (GS-0105)   25,323
- Air Traffic Control (GS-2152)   23,781
- Electronics Engineering (GS-0855)   23,566
- General Business and Industry (GS-1101)   20,082
- Tax Examining (GS-0592)   19,453
- General Engineering (GS-0801)   18,997
- Engineering Technician (GS-0802)   18,797
- Accounting Technician (GS-0525)   17,865
- Supply Clerical and Technician (GS-2005)   17,026
- Internal Revenue Agent (GS-0512)   14,609
- Forestry Technician (GS-0462)   13,393
- Budget Analysis (GS-0560)   12,887
- Mail and File (GS-0305)   12,837
- Accounting (GS-510)   12,741
- Correctional Officer (GS-0007)   12,601
- Civil Engineering (GS-0810)   12,390
- Auditing (GS-0511)   12,247
- Nursing Assistant (GS-0621)   11,439
- Practical Nurse (GS-0620)   11,366
- Logistics Management (GS-0346)   11,266
- Personnel Management (GS-0201)   10,978
- Electronics Technician (GS-0856)   10,934
- Medical Officer (GS-0602)   10,760
- General Education and Training (GS-1701)   10,594
- Mechanical Engineering (GS-0830)   10,243
- Medical Clerk (GS-0679)   10,176

Blue-collar occupations under the WG system which employ the largest number of individuals (5,000+) include:

- Materials Handling (WG-6907)   15,539
- Maintenance Mechanic (WG-4749)   12,124
- Custodial Working (WG-3566)   11,942
- Aircraft Mechanic (WG-8852)   11,907
- Heavy Mobile Equipment Mechanic (WG-5703)   10,199
- Electronics Mechanic (WG-2604)   8,064
- Motor Vehicle Operating (WG-5703)   7,317
- Sheet Metal Mechanic (WG-3806)   7,254
- Food Service Working (WG-7408)   7,052
- Electrician (WG-2805)   6,016
- Automotive Mechanic (WG-5823)   5,817

If you are interested in detailed information on each of these occupational groups, including the minimum qualifications as well as the typical duties and responsibilities for each position, you should examine copies of the federal government's standard personnel reference materials which are found in the following books: *Operating Manual for Qualification Standards for Positions Under the General Schedule* (formerly known, and still referred to, as *Handbook X-118: Qualification Standards for Positions Under the General Schedule*) and *Position-Classification Standards*. Both books are available through OPM, federal personnel offices, and agency libraries. These are essential documents any serious federal job seeker should review prior to completing a SF-171, OF-612, or federal-style resume. These documents give the details, including the proper language for communicating qualifications, of positions that agency personnel must adhere to when evaluating applications.

> The federal government's standard personnel reference materials provide a wealth of information on positions and the critical KSAs you must include in your application.

For example, the KSAs (job elements consisting of Knowledge, Skills, Abilities, and other characteristics) you include on your application in reference to a specific vacancy announcement are critical in the evaluation process. Since you can find some of the language of KSAs in the *Handbook X-118* (but be sure to examine the vacancy announcement carefully since it will specify KSA requirements), you should consult this book before presenting your qualifications on your application in reference to the KSAs. The Federal Research Service also publishes two useful books for developing the KSA language—*The KSA Workbook* and *The KSA Sampler*. Consequently, the closer you bring your application in line with the requirements of positions and the language of evaluators, the more effective you will be in landing a job.

The Department of Labor's *Dictionary of Occupational Titles* and *Occupational Outlook Handbook*, Russ Smith's *Federal Applications That Get Results*, Neale Baxter's *Opportunities in Federal Government Careers*, and several publications and handouts issued by the Office of Personnel Management and personnel offices of individual agencies also include information on these positions. Be sure to familiarize yourself with the requirements specified for particular positions.

The Typical Federal Employee

Federal employees are often stereotyped in terms of characteristics. In 1998, the average federal employee made $46,056 per year and was 45.3 years old and male (57.2 percent). Nearly 40 percent had at least a bachelor's degree. Approximately 17% were black and 39.4 percent belonged to a union. The average employee had worked with government for over 15 years. Nearly 27 percent were veterans; over 4 percent were retired military of which nearly 85 percent had been enlisted personnel.

Strategies

Successful federal job applicants know how to cut through the sometimes confusing and frustrating hiring process. What separates them from unsuccessful candidates is their:

- Knowledge of the details of individual agencies, personnel procedures, and job vacancies.

- Skill in developing and marketing a good application (SF-171, OF-612, or federal-style resume) that clearly communicates their experience, qualifications, and strengths to agencies and hiring officials, with special emphasis on the language of KSAs.

- Patience, persistence, and drive in seeing the process through to the end.

You should begin your job search with a thorough understanding of both the formal and informal hiring processes in the federal government. While you can get a job by only following the formal system of responding to vacancy announcements, taking tests, and completing application forms, your odds will improve considerably if you also pursue jobs in the informal system of prospecting, networking, informational interviews, and referrals. Your success will depend on how well you **relate** the formal and informal systems to one another. The next three chapters will outline how you can best do this by responding to vacancy announcements, writing an outstanding application, and using effective job search strategies.

6

Job Listings, Tests, Applications, and Scams to Avoid

inding a federal job fast requires a basic understanding of where you can find job vacancies and what entrance tests and applications are required. And this critical part of the job finding process has recently undergone several changes. Within the past five years, the federal government has made some dramatic changes in the way it announces vacancies, accepts applications, and screens candidates. While vacancy announcements used to be available only in printed form and through OPM or an agency personnel office, now they are also available via telephone, fax, and the Internet. If you have a computer modem, you can easily browse vacancy announcements online. The federal government has also changed its application process. Declared obsolete, the old Standard Form 171 (SF-171) is no longer required. Agencies can now accept alternative applications such as the OF-612 and federal-style resumes.

Job Listings

Since you can only apply for specific jobs announced by federal agencies, it's important to know which agencies you are interested in working for and then monitor their vacancy announcements. At the same time, you can survey job openings throughout the federal government by acquiring a listing of current vacancies.

Welcome to the brave new digital world of electronic information and applications. If ever there was a good example of a "reinvented" government, the so-called confusing and complex federal employment process would be it. Despite all the talk about waste and abuse in government, the federal government has been investing wisely in the future by developing alternative print, telephone, fax, computer, and Internet systems to quickly dispense information on agency vacancies and the application process. In fact, if you can get all the electronic pieces to come together, you may be only a click away from your next job!

> **The federal government has been investing wisely in the future by developing alternative print, telephone, fax, computer, and Internet systems to quickly dispense information on vacancies and the application process.**

All federal agencies must send information on nonstatus job vacancies to the Office of Personnel Management. OPM, in turn, makes employment information available through several user-friendly print and electronic mediums. Its Federal Employment Information System can be accessed by doing the following:

1. **Call OPM's *Career America Connection:*** Tel. 912/757-3000, TDD Service at 912/744-2299. Available 7 days a week, 24-hours a day, this telephone-based system provides information about current employment and career opportunities worldwide; special programs for students, veterans, and people with disabilities; the Presidential Management Intern Program; salaries and benefits; special messages; and much more. You can record a message requesting that application packages, forms, and other employment related literature be mailed or faxed to you. Request Federal Employment Info Line Factsheet EI-42, "Federal Employment Information Sources," for a complete listing of local telephone numbers or start with Appendix A (page 212) for current listings. Materials requested by telephone are normally sent within 24-hours.

2. **Contact OPM's** *Federal Job Opportunities "Bulletin"*
   Board. Tel. 912/757-3100, 7 days a week, 24-hours a day.
   Since this is a computer-based bulletin board system, you need
   a personal computer equipped with a modem and communications software, as well as a telephone line. This system allows
   you to access a great deal of federal employment information,
   including vacancy announcements, salaries and pay rates, and
   specific employment details. Best of all, you can conveniently
   view current open examination and vacancy announcements
   worldwide while you are online or download them to your
   computer. Many of the jobs announced on the FJOB have
   complete text announcements attached. You can also leave
   your name and address to have application packages and
   forms mailed to you. You also can contact this bulletin board
   on the Internet: *fjob.opm.gov* for Telnet or *ftp.fjob.opm.gov*
   for File Transfer Protocol. Information about obtaining federal
   job announcement files via Internet mail should be directed to
   this email address: *info@fjob.opm.gov*

3. **Surf OPM's Worldwide Web site**—*www.usajobs.opm.gov*
   This site provides access to the Federal Jobs Data Base of
   worldwide opportunities; full text job announcements; answers to frequently asked federal employment questions via
   delivery of Employment Info Line fact sheets; and access to
   electronic and hard copy application forms. The system has
   a terrific search engine that enables users to specify agencies
   and locations and then identify positions that fit one's preferences. If you use only one medium for accessing federal
   employment information, make sure it's this powerful Web
   site: *www.usajobs.opm.gov*

4. **Use a Federal Job Information "Touch Screen" Computer.** This computer-based system uses touch screen technology. Consisting of hundreds of kiosks found in OPM
   offices, Federal Office Buildings, and many other locations
   throughout the country, the kiosks are generally available
   Monday through Friday during normal business hours. Just
   follow the user-friendly touch screen directions and you can
   access current worldwide federal job opportunities, online

information, and more. The system also allows you to leave a message requesting that application packages, forms, and other employment related literature be mailed to you. Request Federal Employment Info Line Factsheet EI-42, "Federal Employment Information Sources," for a complete listing of locations that have Touch Screen Computers. We also include information on these locations in Appendix A.

5. **Contact the "FedFax" system.** You can easily request that employment information and forms be faxed to you 24-hours a day, 7 days a week by using your touch-tone telephone or fax machine. The system will not fax vacancy announcements or job listings. You can access FedFax at these numbers:

Atlanta	404/331-5267
Denver	303/969-7764
Detroit	313/226-2593
San Francisco	415/744-7002
Washington, DC	202/606-2600

6. **Visit your local State Employment Service Office.** All State employment offices will have information on federal employment. Depending on the organization and resources of the office, it may have this information in print form, on microfiche, or on computer. Many of these offices are linked to OPM's Federal Employment Information System.

Since OPM's Federal Jobs Data Base (part of the Federal Employment Information System) is updated daily, you should check it frequently for new job listings. Most vacancy announcements specify closing dates which can be soon after the announcement appears. The sooner you learn about a vacancy, the more time you will have to submit a first-class application. In addition to dispensing important employment information and forms, you'll find full text vacancy announcements on the FJOB, USAJOBS Web site, and Touch Screen Kiosks. In some cases, especially for hard-to-fill positions or those requiring a major recruitment effort, (i.e., Border Patrol Agents for the Immigration and Naturalization Service) you can even apply for a job online by completing a questionnaire and then submit it electronically to an agency's personnel office. Although, as we will see in the next chapter, you really should put more effort into your application, especially how you will present your KSAs in reference to a particular vacancy announcement.

If you are looking for a printed listing of all vacancies available throughout the federal government, including both status and nonstatus positions, it's best to subscribe to a private listing service. The most comprehensive such listings are the *Federal Career Opportunities* published by the Federal Research Service and the *Federal Jobs Digest* published by Breakthrough Publications. Chapter 8 includes order information on these publications.

Deadlines and Open Continuous Positions

When you get ready to apply for a position, make sure you do so within the designated opening dates. Some positions may be open for applications for only ten days whereas others are open for thirty days. Some are open indefinitely, indicating the federal government is continuously hiring individuals for those positions ("open continuous positions"). In most cases you must contact the agency hiring authority for complete information on application procedures. They should provide you with a detailed vacancy announcement that outlines the requirements for the position. It will tell you if you need to take any tests, outline the duties and responsibilities, specify the salary, and note which documents you must submit to be considered for the position.

> "Open continuous positions" are ones that have no application deadlines—an agency continually recruits for the particular position.

If you are accessing job listings via the Internet, you should be able to locate all the necessary information electronically. Most detailed vacancy announcements can now be accessed online. If you don't use the Internet, you'll have to find the telephone number of the agency and call the personnel office directly for vacancy information. Alternatively, you can use OPM's telephone and fax options, which we outlined earlier, to request application information. Once you receive the application details, you are well advised to carefully read the vacancy announcement and rework your SF-171, OF-612, or federal-style resume to best respond to the requirements of the position.

Tests

Contrary to what many people believe, there is no longer a Civil Service Examination. This does not mean you don't need to take some type of examination. In some cases, especially for positions that require demonstrated skill proficiency, a test may be required. Indeed, you can be assured most clerical positions involve such a proficiency test. Other positions, such as Foreign Service Officer with the State Department, require a written and oral Foreign Service Examination which normally is given once a year; sometimes it is suspended, depending on recruitment needs. Many jobs with the U.S. Postal Service also require written examinations. If you are interested in the U.S. Postal Service, you should acquire Veltisezar Bautista's *The Book of U.S. Postal Exams*.

Whether or not a test is required depends on the particular position. Each vacancy announcement will indicate whether or not a specific examination is required. In most cases, applicants will not need to take an examination. They only submit a SF-171, OF-612, resume, or complete a questionnaire in response to the detailed application requirements outlined in the vacancy announcement. Using a "case examining" approach to screening candidates, agency personnel review and rate each application in reference to the qualifications (especially the KSAs) specified for the position. They then interview their top candidates in their final stages of making a selection.

College Graduates and the Case Examining Approach

Entry-level programs designed specifically for recruiting college graduates have had an off-and-on history. For years the Professional and Administrative Careers Program (PACE) was the main program for recruiting college graduates. Individuals took a PACE examination, were rated, and then placed on central registries from which agencies would select qualified candidates for entry-level professional and administrative positions in the GS-5 to GS-7 range. Criticized for years, the program was suspended in the early 1980s and finally replaced by the Administrative Careers With America (ACWA) program in 1990. This program reintroduced examinations, but the examinations covered six different occupational groups and were designed to test for reasoning and analytic skills rather than knowledge of job-specific subject matters. The program was hailed as an improvement over the old PACE program and hopefully would result in recruiting a whole new generation of college graduates into the public service.

Lasting only four years, the Administrative Careers With America (ACWA) program is now history. The program was abolished as of November 19, 1994. Originally designed and implemented in 1990 to replace the long suspended PACE program, the ACWA program was designed for recruiting recent college graduates into entry-level GS-5 to GS-7 positions. Written tests under the ACWA program covered entry-level positions for six different occupational groups.

The ACWA program was abolished because of the changing structure of hiring within the federal government and because of the very limited hiring taking place for these positions. Under the ACWA program, individuals meeting certain academic or experience requirements qualified for GS-5 through GS-7 professional and administrative positions by taking an examination in their appropriate occupational area. Their score on the examination, in turn, determined their eligibility for a whole class of entry-level positions. Using a "central inventory" system, OPM placed individuals on "central inventories" from which agencies could then select "qualified candidates."

> **Agencies now use a "case examining" approach to screening candidates— evaluate elements in each application package.**

While such a centralized examining and ranking system appeared fair and competitive, it was a tremendous waste of time and money for everyone involved. In fact, given the recession of the early 1990s, coupled with political pressures to downsize and "reinvent" government, few agencies hired for such entry-level positions. Many agencies, instead, were preoccupied with managing their current personnel levels by recruiting within the government and by devising strategies for reducing in-house personnel. Hiring through the ACWA program did not make sense for agencies engaged in realigning and shedding their personnel. In addition, many candidates qualifying under the ACWA program were not interested in many of the positions, because of location and salary considerations, or they had found other employment in the meantime. As a result, the government spent a great deal of time and money administering the ACWA program, and students taking the ACWA examination waited and waited and waited to hear from agencies that ostensibly were using the central inventories to hire college graduates for entry-level professional and administrative positions. While few individuals were hired under this program, many people were justifiably unhappy with this centralized hiring process.

As the federal government continued to decentralize its personnel functions, the whole concept of "central inventories" came under attack. OPM's approach was to replace central inventories with a "case examining." approach. It worked like this. OPM announced a specific position when an agency was ready to recruit. Job seekers who wanted to be considered for the specific position applied to OPM. OPM scored all the applications it received and issued a list of eligible candidates, in rank order, to the agency for its consideration.

Students and others who once qualified for the ACWA programs must now respond to individually announced job vacancies. These vacancies are issued by individual agencies and can be accessed through OPM's Federal Employment Information System. Each announcement outlines application procedures. Using the Internet, you can download an application form or go the more traditional route by requesting by phone or fax that an application form be mailed to you. After answering the questions about your experience and education, return the form to the agency personnel office. Your qualifications are then assessed in reference to the hiring criteria for the position and as specified in the vacancy announcement.

The case examining approach to hiring within the federal government costs less and is more effective for both agencies and applicants. Similar to applying for a job in the private sector, you submit an application for a specific position. Your application, in turn, is assessed in reference to that position. Using this approach, agencies can hire quickly, and applicants can quickly learn about the status of their applications.

Physically Handicapped

The federal government offers a variety of services to applicants with disabilities. These include special test media, assistance in the examination room, and special examination criteria. Most personnel offices of each agency have someone designated as a selective placement coordinator to assist handicapped applicants in finding and applying for positions. OPM also has granted a special examining authority to federal agencies allowing them to appoint physically handicapped applicants to positions on a trial basis. If the employee proves successful, the appointment may become permanent. To meet the requirements for consideration under the physically handicapped authority, you must be certified as eligible by your State Vocational Rehabilitation or VA Vocational Rehabilitation office.

Veterans' Preferences

If you served on active duty in the U.S. military and were separated under honorable conditions, you may be eligible for veterans' preference. To receive preference if your service began after October 15, 1976, you must have a Campaign Badge, Expeditionary Medal, or a service-connected disability. For further details, call OPM at 912-757-3000. Select "Federal Employment Topics" and then "Veterans." Or, dial OPM's electronic bulletin board at 912/757-3100. Veterans' preference does not affect Senior Executive Service jobs or when competition is limited to status candidates (current or former federal career or career-conditional employees).

Veterans can claim a 5 or 10-point preference. To claim a 5-point veterans' preference, you must attach a copy of your DD-214, *Certificate of Release or Discharge from Active Duty,* or other proof of eligibility. To claim a 10-point veterans' preference, attach an SF 15, *Application for 10-Point Veterans' Preference,* plus the proof required by that form.

Registers

For years OPM has maintained registers, or the "central lists" of applicants who were qualified to fill entry-level positions. When an agency had such vacancies, OPM would refer qualified candidates to the agency which, in turn, invited them to interviews. As of November 20, 1994, these registers have been abolished. Applicants now apply directly to agencies in response to specific job openings rather than in response to broad occupational groups.

Applications

The federal application process has changed considerably during the past year as agencies have been given more application options. No longer is the SF-171 required as an application form. Indeed, individuals applying for some positions, such as nurses and border patrol officers, can now apply over the telephone using the telephone key pad to answer a series of qualifying questions or via the Internet. Many applicants also complete computer-scannable questionnaires detailing their qualifications and job-related experience. OPM scores the questionnaire responses to determine the most highly qualified candidates. Hiring agencies then receive from OPM a list of the best qualified applicants for the job.

As noted earlier, the federal hiring process is oriented toward specific **positions**. You must become familiar with positions and agencies rather than a general rating process. Once you learn about a vacancy, contact the individual and office in charge of issuing the vacancy announcement for complete information on application procedures. In most cases the vacancy announcement will ask for a completed SF-171, OF-612, or federal-style resume. This one to two-page announcement will outline the duties and responsibilities of the position, indicate the level of experience sought, and specify all documents required to be submitted with your application package. It will also specify a particular deadline for receipt of applications, unless it is an open continuous position. Read the vacancy announcement very carefully for key words relating to the knowledge, skills, abilities, and other requirements for the job. You must demonstrate these in the "Experience" descriptions of your SF-171, OF-612, or federal-style resume. Failure to do so will eliminate you from consideration or result in a low rating. For more information on how to best interpret and respond to today's federal vacancy announcements, including numerous examples of such announcements, you may want to acquire copies of *Using Today's Reinvented Vacancy Announcement*, *Reinvented Federal Job Application Forms Kit*, *The KSA Workbook*, and *The KSA Sampler*. All four booklets are published by the Federal Research Service and are available directly from Impact Publications (see order form at the end of this book).

Scams to Avoid

OPM warns applicants to be wary of scam artists who attempt to sell unnecessary information on federal job opportunities. Many scam artists place classified ads in newspapers, magazines, and periodicals saying they can help you find a federal job—for a fee. They often use official sounding names, such as the "U.S. Agency for Career Advancement" or "Postal Employment Service." Many of them claim to have access to a "hidden" or unadvertised federal job market as well as jobs that require no experience but pay extremely well. A disproportionate number of these operations focus on postal jobs, claiming they offer sample test questions and applications. They frequently have a toll-free telephone number through which an operator attempts to sell a booklet or refer the caller to a pay-per-call number for more information.

The truth is that none of these operations can find you a federal job nor do they provide any better information than is available free of charge through government agencies. The postal jobs scam artists merely sell you the same, or much worse (inaccurate and dated), information than is available through the U.S. Postal Service. In the case of postal jobs, few full-time permanent positions are available, and hiring takes place through 85 district offices. Through your local district post office you can get an application form and any other necessary information free of charge. The same is true for all other federal jobs—everything is available free from the hiring agency. Better still, most of it is available online at no charge through OPM's gateway site: *www.usajobs.opm.gov*

If you pay someone to help you find a federal job, chances are you've made a big and costly mistake on what may well be a very frustrating experience with your government. If you suspect an employment advertisement or a company that offers federal employment services may be fraudulent, contact the following organizations:

Federal Trade Commission: Tel. 202/326-3128

Postal Crime Hotline: U.S. Postal Inspection Service, Tel. 1-800-654-8896 (open 24 hours a day)

National Fraud Information Center (part of the National Consumers League): Tel. 1-800-876-7060. Available weekdays, 9am to 5pm, Eastern Standard Time, or on the Internet at *www.fraud.org*

Your State Attorney General or local Better Business Bureau

The key to getting a federal job fast is a powerful SF-171, OF-612, or federal-style resume. As we will see in the next chapter, these applications need to be completed with great care. Like a well-crafted resume used in the private sector, the SF-171, OF-612, or federal-style resume is your ticket to opening the doors to federal employers. You must do your application right if you want it to stand out from many other applications being submitted for the same position. With an expertly written SF-171, OF-612, or federal-style resume, your chances of getting a federal job fast should be greatly enhanced.

7

Vacancies and Application Options

As part of the federal government's continuing attempts to "reinvent" itself, on January 1, 1995 it declared the traditional application form obsolete. No longer could agencies require the unpopular Standard Form 171 (SF-171) as the only acceptable application form. They now accept several different types of applications, from SF-171s and OF-612s to federal-style resumes and other written formats (see OF-510). For some positions, such as nurses and border patrol officers, applications are accepted over the telephone or online by completing an electronic questionnaire. Each agency specifies in its vacancy announcement acceptable application forms. You need to become familiar with each of these in order to choose which application best works for you.

New Options, Old Requirements

When OPM decided to eliminate the SF-171 requirement, it did so for the ostensible purpose of streamlining the application process for both applicants and agencies. While applicants used to complete a lengthy and detailed SF-171, and could use it to apply for many different positions, the new application changes now mean applicants must complete different applications for different positions and agencies. Consequently, this new application process is more complicated for individuals who must now apply for different positions with different agencies that have different application requirements.

All vacancy announcements will specify acceptable types of applications. The typical announcement includes a blanket application form statement under an "Application Procedures" section such as this:

> "Candidates should submit a resume, Standard Form 171, or OF-612, or some other format, as long as the following information is included: name, address, day/evening telephone numbers with area code; Social Security number; country of citizenship; name, city, state, and zip code of high school and college or university attended; type and year of degree received (with copy of transcript, if available); work experience, which includes job titles, employer's name and address, supervisor's names and phone number, starting and ending dates, hours worked per week, salary, and duties and accomplishments. You may also include additional training courses completed, special skills, certificates and licenses, honors, awards and/or special accomplishments, etc. Also include a copy of your most recent performance appraisal, and information pertaining to the rating factors listed above."

Not surprising, such "application" requirements involve generating a great deal of information that is normally captured in a well structured form, such as the SF-171 or OF-612. If you venture beyond these forms, you do so at your own risk! But that is your choice.

Today's federal application options encompass the following:

1. SF-171: This is the green Standard Form 171, or "Standard Application for Federal Employment," which has been used for years in applying for federal positions. All agencies still accept the SF-171. Despite widespread dissatisfaction with this form—a kind of love/hate relationship—most personnel specialists within each agency understand it and know how to evaluate candidates accordingly. Since OPM no longer produces this form nor the software, it may be difficult to find an SF-171 to complete. However, it is still well and alive if you visit the FedWorld Information Network (operated by the National Technical Information Service Technology Adminis-

> **Even though the SF-171 is an older form, completing one will not be held against you.**

tration of the U.S. Department of Commerce) at the following URL: *www.fedworld.gov*. This site allows you to download the SF-171 and the OF-612. Even though the SF-171 is an older form, completing one will not be held against you. In many respects, the old SF-171 is superior to the newer options. We include a sample copy of this form in Appendix C.

2. **OF-612:** The OF-612, "Optional Application for Federal Employment," is the new optional application form designed to replace the SF-171 as well as simplify the application process. Since it is an optional form, it is not required by agencies. Applicants can choose to use it in lieu of an SF-171 or a federal-style resume. This so-called new form is very similar to the SF-171. You can download a copy of the OF-612 visiting OPM's site (*www.usajobs.opm.gov*) or the FedWorld Information Network (*www.fedworld.gov*). We include a sample copy in Appendix C.

3. **Federal-style resume:** This is another option available for applicants who choose not to complete an SF-171 or OF-612. However, it is not the same as a resume you might prepare for a job in the private sector. At best, this represents a "resume with peculiar federal characteristics." OPM specifies in OF-510, "Applying for a Federal Job," what must be included on this type of resume. You must include certain

> **A federal-style resume is not the same as a resume you might prepare for a job in the private sector.**

types of information on this resume, much of which is not found on resumes in general

4. **Other options:** Agencies may elect to use other types of applications. Indeed, OPM has experimented with various types of automated applications, from scannable questionnaires to electronic applications using telephone key pads and touch screen technology. However, many of these applications are initial screening devices. Few may yield the quality of information found on a well written SF-171 or OF-612.

OF-306

All agencies, at various stages in the application process, require applicants to complete a "Declaration For Federal Employment" (OF-306) to determine their suitability for federal employment and to authorize a background investigation. This form (see example in Appendix C) includes questions relating to background matters, such as military service, previous federal employment, violations of law, convictions, federal debt delinquency, and federal employment of relatives. By completing and signing this form, you certify the accuracy of all information on your application. Any false statements can disqualify you from employment or are grounds for being fired or prosecuted and jailed.

SF-171

Much of the following discussion on writing principles also applies to the OF-612 and federal-style resumes. To fully benefit from this discussion, you may wan to have a copy of the SF-171 in front of you. We include a copy of the form in Appendix C. Several resources mentioned at the end of this chapter also include working copies of the SF-171.

The Document

The SF-171 can be intimidating and less than revealing of your qualifications—but only if you let it become so. Criticized for being too long and not particularly informative, the basic SF-171 lives on nonetheless. In fact, the Library of Congress still requires the SF-171 (being a congressional agency, it doesn't have to give application "options"). The SF-171 remains the application of choice for many individuals.

Despite numerous criticisms aimed at this form, you need to turn what is potentially a negative situation into a positive one by restructuring the form to clearly communicate your qualifications. It should perform the same central function as a resume—advertise you for a position and communicate your qualifications to employers. If you complete the SF-171 according to our advice, you will overcome one of the major obstacles to acquiring federal employment.

The SF-171 is a four-page application form. It appears deceptively simple to complete, but it is an extremely complex document for those who know its value. Many people pay $100 or more to have professionals assist them in completing the SF-171. Others are able to complete the form in less than an hour by filling in the blanks in long hand. Those who know the importance of the SF-171 should spend hours—indeed a few days—in putting together an effective SF-171.

> **Those who know the importance of the SF-171 should spend hours putting together an effective SF-171.**

The SF-171 is more than just a statement of your qualifications. It is the basis for determining several important outcomes in the federal hiring process:

1. **It is the basis for determining your eligibility for specific positions:** The SF-171 is examined and given a point rating by examining authorities (OPM or agency personnel) in reference to specific vacancy announcements. The rating is then matched with the minimum ratings required for the position.

2. **If you want to be considered for federal employment, it must accompany your application for positions with specific agencies:** In addition to OPM examiners, agency evaluation panels carefully examine the SF-171 when ranking eligible candidates.

3. **It determines if you will be called for an interview:** Like a resume, the SF-171 advertises your qualifications to potential employers. It is one of the most important calling cards for getting a job interview.

4. **It determines your pay level if you are hired:** Since the SF-171 determines your rating, it also determines in which grade step you will be placed on the salary scale.

Each job vacancy announcement will specify what application forms need to be submitted to the agency. In the case of Wage Grade jobs, applicants complete a job interest card or a special application form rather than the SF-171. However, most government positions accept the SF-171. Even though not required, many agencies prefer reviewing this document because its well organized categories provide them with essential information for evaluation—information that may be missing on the typical resume.

Key Principles

When completing your SF-171, keep in mind that you are potentially writing to four different audiences which have four separate goals:

Audiences	**Goals**
1. OPM evaluators	■ Set eligibility rating
2. Agency evaluators	■ Rank candidates
3. Hiring officials	■ Select candidate for an interview
4. Personnel officials	■ Determine salary grade/step

Unlike a conventional resume, which is aimed at getting the interview, your SF-171 must fulfill all the other requirements before having its final impact—a job interview and, if hired, determine your pay level.

How, then do you write an effective SF-171 which will satisfy all audiences? Several basic principles should be followed when completing this document:

1. **Read the instructions carefully:** A simple and obvious principle, but many people forget the simple and obvious and end up making costly mistakes.

2. **Type or computer generate the form:** A typed or computer generated form communicates a certain degree of profes-sionalism. Be sure your typing is neat, clean, and error free. Agencies also accept computer generated SF-171s. Several private firms sell computer software that enables users to generate the form on dot matrix, letter quality, and laser printers. The software enables you to achieve the greatest degree of flexibility in custom designing your SF-171 in response to different positions.

3. **Draft your SF-171:** Develop work sheets for each section. Only after condensing your database from these sheets should you complete a final copy.

4. **Develop a master copy:** Leave items 1, 11, 12, 48, and 49 blank. You will complete these items when you actually submit a copy of your SF-171 for a particular position. Never date and sign your original copy (Items 48 and 49).

5. **Complete all blanks:** Unanswered blanks mean incomplete applications and raise negative questions. If a question does not pertain to you, write in "N/A" (Not Applicable) rather than leave it blank.

6. **Customize several items by attaching continuation or add-on sheets:** Especially customize the most important items—24 and 32 on "Work Experience" and "Special Qualifications."

7. **Emphasize your KSAs throughout the SF-171:** Your KSAs consist of your Knowledge, Skills, Abilities, and other (personal) characteristics. These are the most important job elements evaluators concentrate on when reviewing SF-171s. Information on KSAs, including the proper language to use when writing the various sections, is included in the vacancy announcement as well as in the OPM "bible" for personnel managers—*Handbook X-118, Qualification Standards for Positions Under the General Schedule* (recently revised and retitled as the *Operating Manual for Qualification Standards for General Schedule Positions* but still popularly known as the *Handbook X-118*). For assistance in writing your KSAs, we recommend the two publications by the Federal Research Service: *The KSA Workbook* and *The KSA Sampler*.

8. **Examine the vacancy announcement carefully and respond to it specifically by customizing your qualifications around the specifics of the announcement:** Qualifications for jobs tend to be spelled out in detail on the vacancy announcements. Read the announcements carefully and underline those things that appear to be important qualifications for the position in question. Try to customize your SF-171 as much as possible around the qualifications spelled out in the particular vacancy announcement. A SF-171 designed to be used for any position simply is not good enough. It

misses the specific details required for positions. Agencies and evaluators look for the details on qualifications—not your goals or interests. Especially focus on the details of your knowledge, skills, abilities, and other characteristics (KSAs). The more you can elaborate on these job elements, the better you should be positioned to receive a high rating that leads to a job interview.

9. **Be concise and well organized:** A well organized SF-171 should not run more than 10 pages—but preferably 6 to 8 pages. Edit your writing so that each word counts.

10. **Use a good writing style:** Similar to writing resumes, use the active voice and action verbs to describe your skills, abilities, and accomplishments. Your descriptions should be easy and interesting to read.

11. **Focus on your accomplishments when describing your work experience:** Formal duties and responsibilities are normally found in position descriptions and they are important to rating your SF-171. However, you should also go one step further by stating specific accomplishments that go beyond the formal duties and responsibilities.

12. **Include relevant volunteer experience:** If this experience relates to the job you are applying for, include it in a separate experience block (Item 24).

13. **Check your spelling, grammar, and neatness:** Your SF-171 should be perfect in every way possible. Spelling and grammatical mistakes communicate negative messages.

14. **Emphasize the most important information:** You can emphasize by putting the most important information first, underline, capitalize, or bullet items. Avoid excessive use of such emphasizing devices.

There are two keys to developing an effective SF-171. First, you should *customize* the SF-171 beyond its standard four-page format.

Second, you should *use a functional-skills vocabulary* to describe your experience which relates to relevant KSAs.

There are two ways to **customize your SF-171**. One method is to expand the length of each section (experience, honors, special qualifications) in order to provide more detailed information. You do this by completing the short continuation sheet attached to the SF-171; develop your own more lengthy customized sections by clipping and pasting the section headings to separate sheets of paper; purchase customized forms; or use a computerized SF-171 writing program which generates a completed form. Complete these expanded sections in as much detail as possible. The "Experience" section is the most critical, and it requires a great deal of time and effort.

Another way to customize your SF-171 is to rewrite the "Experience" sections to respond specifically to the qualifications outlined in a particular job vacancy announcement. Read each announcement carefully and then use similar skills terminology in your SF-171. If you customize your SF-171 in this manner, you must retype the "Experience" sections for each vacancy announcement. While this is a time consuming process, it is the most effective approach for addressing the exact qualifications for a particular position. Remember, federal evaluators and hiring officials are always looking for "the details" or specifics relevant to their particular agency and vacancies. Generalities commonly associated with functional resumes and transferable skills used by career changers in the private sector do not particularly enhance your qualifications in the eyes of federal evaluators and hiring officials. They want to see "the beef" in candidates' experience statements.

> **Be sure to customize your SF-171 beyond its standard four-page format.**

Complete the Form

Let's critically examine each item on the SF-171. Please refer to the sample SF-171 in the Appendix. We will start at the top and work through each item, including how to customize various sections.

1. **Kind of position you are filing for.**

    Leave this item blank on your original form. Complete it with the appropriate announcement number and job title when you submit a copy of your form in response to an announcement.

2-6. **Social security, birth date and place, name, address.**

    Self-explanatory. Use your current address or one which is your most permanent or predictable one for receiving mail. Use a street address—no P.O. Box numbers. If you change your address after submitting the SF-171, make sure you give your new address to the agency.

7. **Other names ever used.**

    Self-explanatory.

8-9. **Home and work phone.**

    Self-explanatory. While you may not wish to be contacted at work, most people in personnel are discrete when contacting individuals with their present employers. Include both numbers. A simple rule to follow is "don't play hard to get."

10. **Previous federal government civilian employment.**

    Self-explanatory. It asks for your highest grade, classification series, job title, and inclusive dates. Be sure to include all information. For example: GS-470-11, Soil Scientist. When in doubt, contact your former agency personnel office for the details. If no previous federal experience, enter "N/A."

11. **Availability or starting date.**

    Leave blank on your original but specify a date—month and year—on the copies you submit to agencies.

12. **Lowest pay or grade you will accept.**

Leave this item blank on your original. Include this information on the copy you submit to the agency. Information on the pay and grade levels will be included on the vacancy announcements of agencies.

13. **Location of employment.**

This is up to you, although the vacancy announcement will most likely specify the work location for the position. The more open you are to options, the more you will be considered for jobs in different locations. However, if you only want to work in the Washington Metro area or in Hawaii, specify these locations in the appropriate blank and boxes.

14. **Hours of work.**

Self-explanatory. Indicate how many hours per week you are willing to work, including intermittent work and work on weekends and in shifts.

15. **Temporary employment.**

You must decide if you are willing to take temporary employment. You do not receive the same benefits as full-time, permanent employees. However, many federal employees got their foot in the door by stating "Yes" to this question. You can always say "Yes" and then change your mind when you see exactly what "Temporary" means for a specific position. This is not a commitment to temporary employment. Rather, it is an indication of your willingness to be flexible. You can always say no if offered a temporary position you do not want.

16. **Willingness to travel overnight.**

This is up to you. Some government jobs require travel. Specify the degree to which you are willing to travel.

17-22. Military service and veteran preference.

Nearly 27 percent of all federal employees are former veterans who receive a 5 to 10 point advantage in their eligibility ratings. Spouses, widows(ers), and mothers of veterans also receive preference under this category. Be sure to complete the requested information if you are eligible for this preference. If you claim a 10-point preference, you will need to complete and attach Standard Form 15 and other required documentation as specified in this form.

23. Permission to contact present employer.

Self-explanatory. Use your own judgment. You may want to answer "No" to this if you don't want your present employer to know that you are applying for a federal job or if your relationship will not enhance your application.

24. Experience.

This is the most important section on the SF-171. At this point you need to customize the form around your KSAs (**K**nowledge, **S**kills, **A**bilities, and other characteristics). While examiners will carefully examine each section of Item 24, the form allows you to describe two positions (A and B) and provides only 2¾ inches of space to describe your duties, responsibilities, and accomplishments for each position. If you provide this information using only the space allotted, you will do poorly on your rating.

It is perfectly acceptable—indeed expected at the agency and program level—for you to re-work this section of the SF-171.

Customizing involves two types of activities, one physical, another analytical. The physical part requires clipping and pasting the original form onto continuation sheets or purchasing customized forms available through private sources identified in the resource section of this chapter. If you have a computerized SF-171 program, customizing will be much easier. Your general rule of thumb should be to expand your most recent position (A) to a full one to two-page customized form. Your second most recent position should be put on a one-half to full-page customized form. All other positions should be described in at least one-half page. Positions of more than 15 years ago can be summarized under a single category using no more than one-half page. Insert these continuation sheets between pages 2 and 3 of the SF-171. Make sure that this customizing does not result in an SF-171 of more than 10 pages!

The second customizing activity involves tailoring your work experience descriptions to the specific announcements and position descriptions. The two most important sources for doing this are:

- **OPM's *Handbook X-118 (Operating Manual for Qualification Standards for General Schedule Positions)*.** Available through OPM and other agency personnel offices, this book details the experience required for various positions. Examiners use this book and thus relate well to its language. You should look at this book to get the proper language to use in describing your work experience.

- **Vacancy announcements.** These listings detail the experience and skills required. Examine them carefully and try to pull as much as possible from your past work experience that directly relates to the requested qualifications. The more you can write your descriptions around the exact specifications for the position, the better your chances of receiving a high rating and ranking.

This is not the time and place to engage in creative writing or throw functional skills language into this section in hope that you can cover your lack of experience and skills. Examiners and hiring officials want to see the details and content—not the fluff that often appears on functional resumes. Use powerful action verbs and skills language, but do so around specific duties, responsibilities, and accomplishments. In the end, this section of your SF-171 should approximate an improved chronological resume. If you don't have the requisite experience and skills, don't waste your time and others' by applying for a position beyond your level of experience. A "can do" attitude is okay and should be encouraged, but it runs into the hard reality of evaluation criteria which is specified in terms of duties, responsibilities, accomplishments, and salaries. For example, a general responsibility may be "supervised division reports." This can mean anything from "typed and filed two 10-page reports each month" to "supervised a staff of 20 researchers and writers in producing five 100-page reports each month." There is a difference especially when the one individual's salary was $20,000 a year and the other's was $60,000 a year, even though both supervisory jobs sound the same at a highly generalized level. Remember, evaluators and hiring officials want to know the **details** of your experience and how they might relate to the "uniqueness" of their agency and programs.

The actual writing of this section should follow the same basic advice normally given for writing combination and improved chronological resumes (see our *High Impact Resumes and Letters* and *Dynamite Resumes* for major writing principles and useful examples). However, a few adjustments are necessary:

- **Start with your most recent job and work in reverse chronological order.** You should include work relevant to the position for which you are submitting an application.

- **Give inclusive employment dates.** Account for any periods of unemployment exceeding three months. Hopefully, you were doing something relevant to your knowledge and skills.

- **Provide as much salary data as possible.** This is one of the most important pieces of data on your form. The more you can report, the better your rating. The figure you state can be above your base salary. Annualize special fees or commissions. If your most recent experience was as a teacher or a Peace Corps Volunteer, you need to do some creative thinking on how to get your salary figure up to a level more commensurate with your abilities. If not, the federal rating system will discriminate against you. You can avoid some discrimination by engaging in creative arithmetic. For example, you may have made $30,000 a year as an educator, but your skill level should be $55,000 with the federal government. If you put down $30,000 as your last salary, you will probably be considered for a $35,000 level federal job, at best. Try to annualize your teaching salary by including other income, such as a $500 a day consulting fee you earned, to get a more accurate picture of your worth. Your salary figure will be held against you if you don't do something about it. But be sure you can document these figures.

- **Give an appropriate reason for leaving.** In the "Your reason for leaving" box, follow a general rule for all aspects of your job search: be honest but not stupid. If you had trouble on your last job, were fired, or resigned because you hated the job, put in a positive statement such as "further career advancement." That is most likely true and it doesn't raise unnecessary questions about your abilities at this point. But be ready to address the question in an honest but positive way if asked about it in an interview.

- **Provide a positive position title.** You can be creative in this box. Many positions do not have formal titles or the titles are somewhat negative or misleading. If this is your case, create a title which most accurately reflects your work in a positive manner. If you were a housewife, you may want to include this as a position title or change it to "Volunteer" if you were heavily involved in volunteer work. In your "Description of work" section, be sure to identify the details of your volunteer work, especially those duties, responsibilities, and accomplishments that directly relate to the position you seek. Always avoid stating "unemployed." This signifies doing nothing when, in fact, you were doing a great deal during a period of unemployment. "Homemaker," "house husband," or "volunteer" are more preferable position titles than "unemployed."

25-31. Education.

This section is self-explanatory in terms of specifying schools attended, majors, credit hours, and degrees received. However, be as thorough as possible since education does count a great deal in the evaluation process. You may want to attach a continuation sheet or complete OPM Form 1170/17 in lieu of completing this cramped section. But be sure to refer the reader to the attachment with a statement such as "See continuation sheet 2.3" or "See attached Form 1170/17."

You should include in Item 31 ("other courses or training related to the kind of jobs you are applying for") all types of educational experience besides those already listed. Include workshops, correspondence courses, military training, and other types of training experiences which relate to your qualifications and skills for the job you seek. Avoid educational experiences unrelated to your goals. Be sure to include names, dates, places, hours, certifications, and other pertinent information.

32-35. Special skills, accomplishments, and awards.

This category stresses your initiative, creativity, leadership, and communication skills. You may also wish to use continuation sheets for Item 32 ("Give the title and year of any honors, awards or fellowships you have received. List your special qualifications, skills or accomplishments that may help you get a job.") since this section provides less than one inch of space for presenting this information. You should include the following data in this section:

- **Special skills:** What other things can you do that did not appear in the job descriptions of Item 24? If you have computer, typing, or special communication skills, include these since they are useful in most work settings.

- **Patents and inventions:** Include creations that would qualify as inventions or were patented.

- **Publications:** List complete bibliographic information on your most important publications, publishing activities, or writing experience. This category enables you to specify your written communication abilities—a highly sought after skill in many organizations.

- **Public speaking experience:** List what you have done, with whom, where, and when. If your list is extremely long, summarize the speeches into categories.

- **Membership in professional or scientific societies:** Give names or organizations as well as the dates and extent of your participation, especially if you played significant leadership and management roles.

- **Hobbies:** Include only serious, job related hobbies. Revealing that you play handball does not strengthen your SF-171 or your image!

- **Other:** Anything you can think of that will strengthen your qualifications. It should be a skill or product outcome. Remember, communication and analytic skills are some of the most important ones you can emphasize.

This section also asks you to include any typing or dictation authority (Item 33), special job-related licenses or certifications you received (Item 34), along with the dates and licensing authority, and foreign language proficiency (Item 35)—items which are self-explanatory.

36. References.

List three references, including their addresses, phone numbers and occupations. References who can speak of your work skills and accomplishments are ideal choices. Be selective by choosing only those who can speak highly of you and who are aware that you are applying for a job. It would be good to first call them, inform them of your plans, and ask for their permission before including their names in this section.

37-44. Citizenship, convictions, termination, and retirement benefits.

Self-explanatory. Check the "Yes" or "No" box depending on which is true in your case. Similar information is requested on the new OF-306 ("Declaration for Federal Employment"), which is an expanded version of this section on the SF-171.

45. Detailed answers.

Include details on any previous items requiring clarification. Avoid using negative language here. Try to turn what may appear to be a negative into a positive. For example, if you were fired because you refused to falsify an employer's records, do not just state you were fired because you did not get along with your employer. Instead, state the firing in positive terms (truthful) for you, emphasizing your integrity: "Left employment for refusing to falsify employer's tax records as instructed to do by supervisor. Employer subsequently indicted for fraud and tax evasion. Case pending."

48-49. Signature and date.

While you are instructed to sign and date the SF-171 at the end of page 4, do not sign and date your original copy. When you submit a copy of your form, you must provide an original signature—not a photocopy. Consequently, only sign and date **copies** of the form when you submit your application in response to a specific position.

Once you have finished drafting each section of the form, try to condense it as much as possible without sacrificing content and appearance. Use bullets, caps, and underlining for emphasis—but don't overdo these devices. Neatly type each section—single-spaced with eye-pleasing margins and subheadings.

> **Failure to observe any of the rules may result in lowering your rating as well as delaying your application.**

The "Continuation Sheets" must be inserted between pages 2 and 3 of the form. Make sure you refer to the appropriate continuation sheet for each item requiring this additional information. In addition, the continuation sheets must be the size of the original form or in an 8½ x 11" size. At the top of each continuation sheet include your name, birth date, and announcement number or position title. Put page numbers in the bottom left hand corner starting with 2.1 and running them sequentially to 2.5 or 2.6. But no more than a total of 10 pages of which six would be continuation sheets.

Pay particular attention to the details of completing this form. Failure to observe any of the rules may result in lowering your rating as well as delaying your application. Forgetting simple things, like dating the form, signing it in ink, or putting your name on the continuation sheets, can negate what is otherwise an outstanding SF-171.

OF-612

The "Optional Application for Federal Employment" (OF-612) is similar in many respects to the SF-171. An example appears in the Appendix. In fact, many of the questions appearing on the OF-612 also appear on the SF-171. When completed with the OF-306 "Declaration for Federal Employment," these two documents look very similar to the complete SF-171!

We recommend completing a master OF-612. Leave questions 1, 2, 3, and 18 blank. Make copies of your master, and complete these questions when you apply for a specific position.

1. Job title in announcement

Self explanatory. Leave this item blank on your master copy. Fill it in with the appropriate job title appearing on the vacancy announcement when submitting it to an agency.

2. Grade(s) applying for

Complete this item with the grade level specified in the agency vacancy announcement. For example, "GS-1412-11/12" means the position is for a Technical Information Specialist at the GS-11 or GS-12 levels.

3. Announcement number

Be sure to include the announcement number. This number is found at the upper right hand corner of the vacancy announcement. It may look something like this: Announcement 95-031.

4. Last, first and middle names

Self explanatory.

5. Social Security Number

Self explanatory.

6. Mailing address

Give your complete mailing address. Use a street address rather than a post office box. Street addresses make you look more permanent than post office box numbers.

7. Phone numbers

Include numbers where you can be reached both during the day and in the evening or where a message can be left for you.

8. Work Experience

This is the most important section of the OF-612. How you describe your experience will largely determine your rating. Follow the same writing principles we identified for completing the experience section on the SF-171.

9. May we contact your current supervisor?

Be prepared to answer "yes" or give a good reason why you say "no."

10-12. Education

Self explanatory.

13. Other Qualifications

This is an extremely important section in which you may want to use continuation sheets to expand the section. Here you outline job-related training, skills, accomplishments, and recognition. Keep in mind that this section asks for "job-related" items. Avoid including a laundry list of irrelevant experiences.

14-18. Miscellaneous questions

Self explanatory.

Be sure to sign and date the copy of the OF-612 that you submit to the agency. Make sure your signature is an original rather than a photocopy.

Federal-Style Resumes

Agencies now accept resumes in lieu of a SF-171 or OF-612. However, the resume you submit must follow strict guidelines for creating a federal-style resume as outlined in OPM's flier on "Applying For a Federal Job" (OF-510). This resume, in effect, is a SF-171 or OF-612 written in a resume format. Your federal-style resume must include the following information in addition to specific information requested in the job vacancy announcement:

Job Information:

- Announcement number, and title and grade(s) of the job for which you are applying

Personal Information:

- Full name, mailing address (with ZIP Code) and day and evening phone numbers (with area code)
- Social Security Number
- Country of citizenship (Most federal jobs require U.S. citizenship)
- Veterans' preference
- Reinstatement eligibility (If required, attach SF-50 proof of your career or career-conditional status.)

Education:

- High School
  - Name, City, and State (ZIP Code if known)
  - Date of diploma or GED
- College and universities
  - Name, City, and State (ZIP Code if known)
  - Majors
  - Type and year of any degrees received (If no degree, show total credits earned and indicate whether semester or quarter hours)
- Send a copy of your college transcript only if the job vacancy announcement requests it.

Work Experience:

- Give the following information for your paid and nonpaid work experience related to the job for which you are applying. (Do not send job descriptions.)
  - Job title (include series and grade if federal job)
  - Duties and accomplishments
  - Employer's name and address
  - Supervisor's name and phone number
  - Starting and ending dates (month and year)
  - Hours per week
  - Salary
- Indicate if we may contact your current supervisor.

Other Qualifications:

- Job-related training courses (title and year)
- Job-related skills, for example, other languages, computer software/hardware, tools, machinery, typing speed
- Job-related certificates and licenses (current only)
- Job-related honors, awards, and special accomplishments, for example, publications, memberships in professional or honor societies, leadership activities, public speaking, and performance awards (Give dates but do not send documents unless requested)

Given all the specific federal government-relevant information requested on such a resume, you may want to just complete the SF-171 or OF-612! You can now create a federal-style resume by using USAJOBS online resume builder. This Internet site (*www.usajobs.opm.gov/access.asp*) allows users to create, edit, and save a resume to be electronically submitted to federal agencies that advertise opportunities in OPM's jobs database. However, keep in mind that the most effective federal-style resumes are those that represent a major investment of time and effort in describing work experience and other qualifications in the language of KSAs. The resume should be part of a larger application package.

Distributing Your Applications Right

Now that you have created an excellent SF-171, OF-612, or federal-style resume, what do you do next? You must get it into the proper hands for evaluation, rating, and screening. Hopefully your application will be your ticket to job interviews and a job offer.

Your application should be targeted toward four major audiences that may or may not get involved at various stages of the evaluation process:

- **OPM evaluators:** Depending on which positions you apply for, OPM may be involved in evaluating your application at some point in the hiring process. For some positions, OPM gets involved initially. For other positions, OPM may examine the application after the agency has completed its evaluation work. When OPM evaluates your application, it does so to determine if you are qualified for the level of position being applied for. However, OPM rarely gets involved in evaluating applications these days because most of this work has been decentralized to agency personnel offices.

- **Agency evaluators:** They receive your application as well as other required materials as requested in the vacancy announcement. The personnel office then evaluates your application package to determine your eligibility. When you send your application to an agency, you must complete all items, such as the position title, number, availability, and salary, most of which appear on the vacancy announcement. Without this information, agency evaluators cannot process your application.

- **Program office:** The program office receives the application packages and selects those who should be contacted for interviews. Normally at least three top candidates will be interviewed. The program office may request a particular candidate by name if the application was properly submitted and meets the criteria for eligibility.

- **Agency personnel office:** Depending on the agency, other officials in the personnel office may determine your salary step/grade level once you are hired.

Distribution of your application in the federal government follows a similar pattern as in the private sector when using a resume—you send it in response to specific vacancy announcements. Each vacancy announcement will specify the proper procedures for submitting your application and any other supporting materials as well as the level of qualifications that should be represented in your application. While most vacancy announcements will specify opening and closing dates for submitting applications, some positions are termed "Open Continuous Positions." This is one category of positions that constitutes one of the few remaining registers in the federal government.

Open Continuous Positions are those which require the continuous recruitment of personnel. They are usually hard-to-fill positions or ones which experience high turnover of personnel, such as clerical and certain engineering and high-tech positions. Since these positions do not have opening and closing dates specified, you can submit your application at anytime for these particular positions. Once an agency receives your application, they will evaluate it and let you know if you will be invited for an interview. The position stays "open" until it is filled.

When you submit your application in response to a vacancy, send it in a 9 x 12" envelope rather than in a No. 10 business envelope. A nice flat application is always preferable to one that has been folded.

Evaluate Your Product

Once you have completed your application and are ready to distribute it, you should evaluate it. Look over your application in reference to the evaluation criteria on pages 142-143.

Useful Resources

Several private firms provide training seminars on how to write effective applications. In the Washington Metro area, for example, most of these seminars are listed in the Monday business supplement of the *Washington Post* under the weekly career section of the business calendar.

The Federal Research Service publishes a useful application kit—*The Federal Job Application Forms Kit*—which includes sample forms and advice for completing each section of various application forms.

A few self-directed books also outline the mechanics of completing an effective application. Impact Publications publishes a separate book entitled *Federal Applications That Get Results: From SF-171s to Federal-Style Resumes* (Dr. Russ Smith) which provides step-by-step guidance on completing federal applications. Also, look for Patricia Wood's *Applying For a Federal Job* (Bookhaven) and Kathryn K. Troutman's *The Federal Resume Guidebook* (JIST Works).

DataTech produces a popular computer software program designed for writing and producing the SF-171, OF-612, and federal-style resumes: *Quick & Easy Federal Application Kit*. This program is available in four different versions: Personal (Single—$49.95), Family (2 users—$59.95), Office Pack (8 users—$129.95), and Professional (office—$399.95).

All of these resources are available through Impact Publications by completing the order form at the end of this book or by visiting the government section of their online bookstore:

www.impactpublications.com

EVALUATION OF FEDERAL APPLICATION
PRODUCTION AND DISTRIBUTION

CHARACTERISTIC	Presence Yes	No	Actions Needed

Overall Appearance

1. Neat
2. Easy to read
3. Looks professional
4. Typed
5. Reproduced as clean, clear, and straight copies.

Continuation Sheets

1. In proper order between pages 2 and 3
2. Name, birth date, and position at top
3. Page numbers at bottom left
4. Referenced in appropriate items

Individual Items

1. Items 1, 11, 12, signature, and date left blank on original SF-171
2. All other items completed in detail
3. Not more than 10 pages in length (preferably five pages in the case of the OF-612)

Writing Style

1. Concise
2. Uses subheadings
3. Emphasizes most important information
4. Incorporates KSAs as required in vacancy announcement
5. Uses active voice and action verbs
6. Stresses skills and accomplishments

6. Free from grammatical,
   spelling, and
   punctuation errors.   ___   ___   _____

Distribution

1. Items 1, 11, 12, signature,
   and date completed for
   SF-171; items 1, 2, 3,
   signature, and date
   completed for OF-612   ___   ___   _____
2. All requested application
   materials compiled and
   sent with the SF-171,
   OF-612, or federal-style
   resume   ___   ___   _____
3. Cover letter enclosed   ___   ___   _____
4. Mailed flat in a 9 x 12"
   envelope   ___   ___   _____

8

Beyond Vacancies and Applications: Effective Job Search Strategies

How will you approach the federal job market that is embedded within a highly decentralized, fragmented, and chaotic governmental system? This is a somewhat contradictory system that gives job seekers the illusion of a well organized job market where all one needs to do is locate vacancy announcements, submit appropriate application forms, and wait to be called for job interviews. On the one hand, this system is characterized by a high degree of overlapping functions and redundant structures. On the other hand, it appears well organized and coherent because of new information technology adapted to the application process.

Rational Government, Naive Applicants

The federal government is confusing for many individuals who expect to encounter a well defined, rational system of governance. If it were simple and rational, the federal government would be centralized with well defined points of decision-making and entry for jobs. One would expect to respond to job announcements or submit applications to a central personnel office which, in turn, would make hiring decisions. Indeed, the federal government projects an image of rational hiring by maintaining the appearance of a unified and centralized recruitment and selection process emanating from the Office of Personnel Management.

But nothing could be further from the truth. If you stand in line with vacancy announcements in one hand and application forms in the other, you may get run over by the realities of day-to-day hiring. While the government does not have a "hidden job market" in the classic sense of the term (i.e., unannounced job vacancies), it does have lots of things happening behind the scenes that can affect your employability with federal agencies. Only naive applicants stand in line and wait and wait and wait to be called for an interview. Savvy job seekers also are proactive—they take certain actions that go beyond formal application procedures outlined by OPM to enhance their ability to land a federal job fast. Above all, they use effective job search strategies appropriate for the nature of government.

> While the government does not have a "hidden job market" in the classic sense of the term, it does have lots of things happening behind the scenes that can affect your employability.

Approach a Decentralized Structure

America's passion for decentralized political and governmental structures is offset by its commitment to achieving greater efficiency and effectiveness in government. To be efficient and effective yet decentralized and fragmented at the same time is one of the great American dilemmas of government. In trying to have their cake and eat it, government agencies are adept at presenting pictures of rational organizations responding efficiently and effectively to public needs. Today it's called "reinvented" or "re-engineered" government; tomorrow it might be called "wow" government. Each decade seems to have its own "flavor of efficiency and effectiveness" proposed to overcome the inherent defects of a democratic and decentralized government by design run by frequently frustrated politicians and bureaucrats. This image of performance may or may not have a direct relationship to the day-to-day realities of government.

Underlying the facade of organizational efficiency and effectiveness are numerous organizational jungles and management nightmares. Not only do government agencies overlap with one another and duplicate functions, internally they often are loosely structured with a great deal of autonomy given to individual departments and offices.

Decentralization and Redundancy

The structure of the federal hiring process is similar to the structure of American governments in general—exhibits an incredible amount of decentralization, fragmentation, overlap, redundancy, and chaos. The hiring system is anything but logical, efficient, and effective. For example, if you want a research intelligence position, the CIA is only one of many agencies performing these functions. The Defense Intelligence Agency in the Department of Defense, National Imagery and Mapping Agency, Intelligence and Research Bureau in the State Department, and the National Security Council in the Executive Office of the President, and the Federal Bureau of Investigation (FBI) essentially do the same type of work. Almost every department has its own police and/or investigative force—not just the FBI. Indeed, personnel at the CIA will tell you to talk to their friends at the Defense Intelligence Agency or the Intelligence and Research Bureau in the State Department—agencies they may have worked for prior to moving to the CIA. The congressional bureaucracy, through the Federal Research Division of the Library of Congress, also engages in similar functions as the CIA and DIA. These agencies duplicate each other and contribute to the overall redundancy of the federal government.

Other occupations also are represented in numerous agencies which overlap and duplicate each other. Take the case of personnel training opportunities. Most large agencies have their own training sections which conduct in-house training—not just the Office of Personnel Management. Trainers at OPM will direct you to fellow professionals in the various Departments and Independent Agencies who also conduct training. Such redundancy is uncovered when you conduct your informational interviews.

While redundancy may seem to be a waste of taxpayers' money, it may also contribute to the overall effectiveness of government by providing important internal checks and balances on policy. Whatever its costs and benefits, in a job search you need to recognize and use redundancy to your advantage. You do this by contacting several agencies for information and referrals on job opportunities in the same functional area. Remember, no single agency of government performs a unique function. Counterpart functions will be found in several agencies. Your job is to do the necessary research to uncover the counterparts.

Decentralization also should be used to your advantage. Your contacts should be developed with key personnel in the operating units or program offices—where the hiring decisions are finally made. Since units tend to be isolated from one another because of decentralization, you should conduct several informational interviews within and between agencies. In fact, it is not unusual to discover that one office does not know what another office is doing, even though it is in the same agency, housed in the same building, and even located next door!

The formal structure of hiring in the federal government overlays a great deal of decentralization, fragmentation, and chaos. It presents a deceptive picture of a centralized, organized, coordinated, and efficient government personnel system. This "public image" initially encourages people to apply but then intimidates them sufficiently enough to dissuade many from following through. Do not be intimidated nor dissuaded from achieving your objective. The key to success is in understanding the system and using this understanding to your benefit.

> Your contacts should be developed with key personnel in the operating units or program offices—where the hiring decisions are finally made.

The Office of Personnel Management, formerly known as the Civil Service Commission, is an independent executive agency. It stands at the center of the federal government's merit personnel system. Many people—including some OPM employees—believe you must apply for federal jobs through this agency. This is true in some cases, but it is not true for most federal positions. All federal agencies hire their own personnel. In so doing, they may receive direct assistance from OPM in the form of announcing vacancies, scrutinizing applications, and screening candidates. The degree of involvement with agencies depends on several factors, such as classification as exempted positions or the degree of organizational capabilities the agency has to conduct their own hiring. Nonetheless, for some federal positions, you will have to deal directly with the Office of Personnel Management.

Since the federal personnel reforms of January 1980, OPM has been decentralizing several personnel functions to individual agencies. But decentralization has not been uniform. Some agencies are capable of hiring whereas others are still more dependent upon OPM for assistance. In other cases, OPM's role increasingly is marginal to the hiring process. Overall, OPM performs general support functions for agencies, such as providing information and assisting them in the selection and training processes.

OPM does perform a few essential functions for job seekers: dispenses information on procedures and opportunities as well as automates vacancy announcements which can be accessed through the Internet and touch screen computers. It does this through its Federal Employment Information System which we outlined in Chapter 6.

Know the Formal and Informal Hiring Processes

Federal departments and agencies are highly decentralized. Each organization maintains its own personnel offices and recruitment practices. While the U. S. Office of Personnel Management develops personnel recruitment and performance standards and provides training and limited recruitment services for individual agencies and offices, most hiring takes place within particular agencies. And even within agencies, hiring tends to be decentralized to the actual operational units which have the hiring needs.

Formal organizational charts outline the basic skeleton of organizations. They indicate how organizations, under the best of circumstances, should operate according to formal authority and responsibilities. These charts are good starting points for understanding the basic structure of government. These are not, however, to be taken too seriously as indicators of how government actually functions. For within all organizations, informal structures and processes operate in spite of the formal organizational chart. Indeed, most individuals within organizations neither understand nor are interested in the formal organizational chart. Many would be hard pressed to either locate or explain the chart! Rather, they behave according to the administrative and social processes and precedents which they are most familiar with and which are identified as "the organization" within their minds.

Identifying and explaining the formal organizational chart is the easy part of conducting a job search with government. Most government offices will have a government operations manual, annual report, or telephone directory outlining their formal structure and functions. Within the federal government, the *U.S. Government Manual*, *Federal Yellow*

Book, *Congressional Yellow Book*, *Federal Directory*, *Congressional Directory*, *Washington Information Directory*, and telephone directories of departments and agencies published by the U.S. Government Printing Office adequately outline such information.

The informal structure, on the other hand, is the most important for identifying on-going realities, but also the most difficult to identify and understand. It requires research on who does what, where, when, and with what effects. It involves using investigative skills to uncover the on-going realities of organizations. The results of such investigation often uncover the negative side of organizations—the deadwood, the powerful and powerless, the perversions, the power struggles, and personnel injustices—as well as positive opportunities for you. Such investigations strip away the pictures of performance portrayed in the public relations brochures and plant one's feet firmly on the ground by reaffirming what most observers of formal and informal organizations have learned over the years: organizations are organizations are organizations; they differ considerably in terms of their structures, functions, goals, and outcomes. Some are exciting places in which to work, while others are simply dreadful. Most are difficult to change in the short-run.

> You are strongly advised to learn as much as possible about the inner workings of the organization prior to applying for and accepting a particular federal job.

Unfortunately, most job seekers develop job search strategies and expectations aimed at the formal organization and the picture of performance projected for public consumption. Few ever delve into the inner workings of government to uncover the informal structure that really determines how things get done and by whom. Such information is usually acquired while on the job—after one has made a commitment to the organization and met all the players at work. In many cases, the informal structure may be at considerable variance with what initially appeared to be the organizational reality.

We strongly urge you to try to avoid any on-the-job surprises by learning as much as possible about the inner workings of the organization prior to applying for and accepting a particular federal job. In the long-run this research may well save you many headaches.

You need to identify and use the informal structure to your advantage prior to joining an organization. Part of your research should focus on understanding this structure. While most government organizations will have a similar formal structure, their informal structures may be considerably different. You will not know this until you gather important "inside" information on an organization.

The following generalizations are valid for most government agencies. Use them as guidelines as you approach agencies for information. They will help you conduct your own investigation of agencies in an intelligent manner:

- **Most government personnel offices do not perform important hiring functions.** Their primary function is to communicate vacancies of operational units, process applications and inquiries, conduct testing, initially screen applications to pass on to the operating unit, and generally engage in routine personnel functions such as maintaining personnel files, putting employees on the payroll, and conducting limited training. They do some hiring, but normally for low level positions with which operational units would rather not be bothered.

> **Personnel offices do some hiring, but normally for low level positions.**

- **Most major hiring decisions are made at the operational levels.** Identifying vacancies, recruiting candidates, screening, and selection—are primarily made by operational units. Managers and supervisors within an office are the key decision-makers. They are the first to identify personnel needs, worry about whom to hire, and select the best individual to meet their needs. While they will share some of the hiring functions with personnel offices—normally administrative overhead and regulatory functions (issuing vacancy announcements, conducting testing and screening, ensuring equal opportunity)—they maintain a certain degree of hiring autonomy to ensure that the formal procedures will give them what they want. Appealing to higher level authorities or using political pull to force hiring decisions on these lower levels will be strongly resisted. Such actions threaten the autonomy of operating units.

- **Lengthy application procedures may or may not be necessary.** Many government jobs can be filled immediately without undergoing a lengthy recruitment and selection process. For example, it is not unusual for congressional staff aids to walk into a congressman's office and be hired on the spot! Some federal agencies participate in job fairs where they may hire an applicant on the spot. A few positions, such as nurses and border patrol agent, can be applied online by completing an electronic questionnaire. And many positions are classified as "Open Continuous Positions" and noncompetitive; they can be filled immediately upon application However, most positions will involve a waiting period precisely because the personnel office must follow a formal procedure, even though the operating unit may have already decided on a candidate prior to initiating the formal selection procedures.

- **Despite claims to the contrary, many government jobs are "wired" for particular individuals.** Vacancy announcements and equal opportunity procedures may make the hiring process look open, competitive, and legitimate, but operating units continue to engage in the notorious practice of "wiring" positions. This involves the informal pre-selection of candidates. Individuals are informally recruited for a position and then the qualifications are written around the individual's education, experience, and KSAs so that in the end he or she will probably be the best qualified candidate from the pool of so-called "qualified applicants." Some might try to sanitize this practice by calling it "benchmarking," but let's call a spade a spade—it's good ole fashioned "wiring." This practice most commonly occurs for higher level positions rather than for lower entry-level positions. As many as 70 percent of high level government vacancies may be partly wired, or at least less than fully open and competitive.

> **"Wiring" involves the informal pre-selection of candidates by writing position qualifications around a particular individual's education, experience, and KSAs. It happens a lot, especially for high level positions.**

A simple fact of life operates among those who do the wiring and hiring: they seek stability, predictability, and control over the hiring process. By all means, they wish to avoid the surprise of hiring an unknown quantity who may or may not work out for a position. For it is better to know and like your future employee ahead of time than to engage in a recruitment crap-shoot sponsored by a personnel office that doesn't really understand your needs. After all, people in personnel don't have to live with the new employee! Wiring is not an illegal practice since the formal hiring process does take place according to the rules and regulations and the final selection takes place within this system; it just "helps" the process move along a little smoother for agency personnel. But unethical? Perhaps, at least for job seekers. Unfair? Certainly. Illegal? Of course not. This is the government hiring business as usual. And it takes place in most government agencies to some degree. While OPM and agency officials will deny engaging in this long-standing practice, nonetheless, it still takes place, even in the new and improved "reinvented" government of the 1990s. All you have to do is read between the lines of many vacancy announcements, especially those that require the applicant to have "status"—only those with some kind of relationship with the federal government are eligible to apply for the position (i.e., no outsiders). Many of these announcements are so narrowly defined that one suspects they are written with a particular individual in mind—"wired" around their qualifications.

Take Effective Action

Given these guidelines and tips to the informal hiring process in the federal government, you may want to consider doing a combination of the following:

- **Do not be deceived by appearances.** Many people exaggerate their abilities, usefulness, and performance. Use your eyes and intuition as well as your ears when researching government organizations. Your goal should be to learn as much as possible about the informal organization. You want to know:

- How do things get done around here?
- Who makes the decisions?
- What kind of work environment is this?
- Do people enjoy their work?
- Who are on the "ins" and "outs"?

While difficult questions to answer as an outsider, progress toward answering them will reveal a great deal of useful information for organizing your job search with particular agencies.

- **Contact the personnel office and properly observe the formal application procedures**, but do not have high expectations or spend a great deal of time trying to get a job through this source. Personnel offices should be treated as a necessary step, but not the only one. If you let your job search stop at this office, your chances of getting a job will be minimal. To be most effective, you must go deeper into the organization.

- **Conduct research amongst those people who are most involved in making the hiring decisions**—usually the managers and supervisors in the operating units. If they have a vacancy and they like you, they may even promote you by wiring a position around your experience and qualifications, or at least make sure your application is forwarded to them from the personnel office.

- **Decide how you want to play this job search game.** Some people love to network, drop names, do investigative research, and talk about themselves. They have no qualms about being the subject of wiring, and they believe in the ethics and efficacy of "pulling their own strings." This works and is acceptable for them. On the other hand, this approach may not be for you. Many people do get good jobs without networking, wiring, or pulling strings. But don't be naive about what's going on around you. Be aware that many of your competitors are practicing these job search techniques for getting the job they want. Thus, you may be at a disadvantage. Your odds of getting a job may not be as good as they could be, but you have to live with yourself, and some things may not come naturally, are

> Many people get jobs without networking or wiring. Just don't be naive about what's going on around you.

personally objectionable, or make one feel uncomfortable. That's really your choice. Our job is to outline alternative choices and suggest different probabilities for success, regardless of your particular preferences on how you should best relate to this job market.

The Formal Application Process

While it is important to know both the formal and informal hiring processes, you must be familiar with the formal application process in order to get your foot properly positioned in the door of agencies. OPM and individual agencies outline the formal application process by advising candidates to follow these steps:

1. **Acquire position vacancy announcements and application forms:** Select from amongst OPM's alternative mediums for accessing application packages and vacancy announcements by mail, telephone, fax, touch screen computers, or the Internet as we outlined in Chapter 6 (see pages 106-109). As we noted at the beginning of this book, individuals who are Internet savvy have a distinct information advantage in this new federal hiring environment which is increasingly going high tech.

2. **Follow instructions in announcements:** Each announcement will give specific instructions on application deadlines, position description, qualifications, content of application package, tests required, and application procedures. Follow these instructions very carefully. Failure to adhere to any instruction, however minor, such as dating your application or signing it in ink, will automatically disqualify you.

3. **Complete your application:** This is the SF-171, OF-612, or federal-style resume and send it directly to the office specified in the vacancy announcement. It's usually the office that issued the vacancy announcement—the agency personnel office.

4. **Take any required tests:** If required, they will be specified in the announcement. You usually need to complete the test and receive a qualifying score before submitting your application.

5. **Wait for the agency to evaluate your qualifications and call you for an interview:** Once you complete your application and submit it to the agency, your application will be rated ("case examined") based on the information supplied in your application. The agency normally selects the top three rated candidates to interview.

6. **Wait to be selected:** If you are interviewed, you will need to wait some time before the agency makes its decision.

The one common theme running throughout this formal hiring process is that you must **wait**. Indeed, you must have a great deal of patience and perseverance from the time you review a vacancy announcement to when you are selected for a position.

> **Passive waiting is not a good job search strategy.**

While this is a very logical, and seemingly efficient, hiring process, it is not particularly effective for the individual. Passive waiting is not a good job search strategy. If you follow the formal application advice, your chances of getting a job are about as good as responding to newspaper want ads or standing in line at an employment firm—very limited.

Whatever you do in terms of seeking out vacancy announcements, don't center your job search exclusively on OPM's Federal Employment Information System. It's a great system, a wonderful way of leveling the vacancy playing field. When using this system, you are looking at a "public" stage in the hiring process. Since some vacancies may only be open for ten days, at this stage you must get the information quickly and respond in a timely fashion. Wouldn't it be nice if you learned about an impending vacancy a month or two before it was actually announced? If you would like such information, then your best job search strategy will be to target your job search on particular agencies that you have identified as being part of your job and career objective. By doing this, you will be better able to monitor impending vacancies and hopefully respond quickly and effectively to announcements.

Penetrate the Hidden Job Market

The informal federal hiring system is similar to the hidden job market found in the private sector. Since agencies continually face personnel problems because of normal turnover, they must recruit periodically. A personnel need is first identified in the operating unit and then communicated to the agency personnel office where it is formally announced in accordance with merit, affirmative action, and equal opportunity considerations. During the formal process of announcing the position, gathering applications, and selecting candidates, agency personnel often try to hedge against uncertainty by looking for qualified personnel in the informal system. This means giving information on the vacancy to friends and acquaintances in their networks in the hope of attracting qualified candidates. Fearing the unknown, officials often welcome an opportunity to meet informally with a candidate, especially in the format of an informational interview—a meeting that involves the exchange of job information and advice between a potential employer and employee.

> **Some observers estimate that over 80 percent of GS-13 and above positions are filled through agency "promotion."**

If your timing is right, you may uncover a pending vacancy in an operating unit. Again, the personnel office is often the last to learn about the vacancy in the agency. Furthermore, the position description may be written around your application or the agency may assist you in customizing your application in line with the position description. If agency personnel send you to their personnel office to rework your application, this is a good signal that you are under serious consideration for a position. Although we have no accurate figures on this phenomenon of "wiring" positions—nor is it possible to get accurate data of the practice—it probably occurs in many GS-13 and above positions. Some observers estimate that over 80 percent of these positions are filled through agency "promotion." While this may be an inaccurate estimate, the point is that such practices occur and are widespread. They most likely arise from a very basic hiring fear—the fear of hiring an unknown person who may or may not work out in the long-run. The informal screening process is a form of "correction" to the formal recruiting procedures. Many agency heads simply wish to avoid leaving critical personnel problems to chance decisions of low-level officials in personnel offices!

The informal system consists of following the same general job search steps we outlined earlier as well as adapting them to the federal personnel setting:

1. **Research federal agencies:** The more information you can gather on agency work and personnel procedures, the better your chances of getting a job with an agency.

2. **Focus on a few agencies for intensive research:** Specific jobs are found in specific agencies. The more details you gather at the level of the hiring officials, the better the probability of getting a job.

3. **Conduct informational interviews with agency personnel:** Make contacts with officials in the hiring units. Seek information, advice, and referrals. Take copies of your application with you to these interviews and leave copies for future reference.

4. **Apply for agency vacancies with a customized SF-171, OF-612, or federal-style resume:** Develop a customized application according to our advice in Chapter 7. Use this version of the application when applying for agency vacancies.

5. **Prepare to interview with the hiring supervisor:** If you pass the formal screening process with your customized application and other documents, and hiring personnel in the operating units like you, you should be called for an interview and, hopefully, offered the job.

The formal and informal systems of federal employment for GS-9 to GS-15 level positions are outlined on page 158.

We do not recommend mobilizing partisan political "pull" with agencies unless you know the President personally. Bureaucrats in general do not like to respond to blatant political pressures from elected officials. Such strategies may work wonders in some state and local governments where the "good ole boys" are still powerful—but be careful with the Feds. There are exceptions, however. Perhaps you know a Representative who is on a powerful budget or appropriations committee affecting a particular agency. The Representative and his or her

RELATIONSHIP OF FORMAL AND INFORMAL EMPLOYMENT PROCESSES

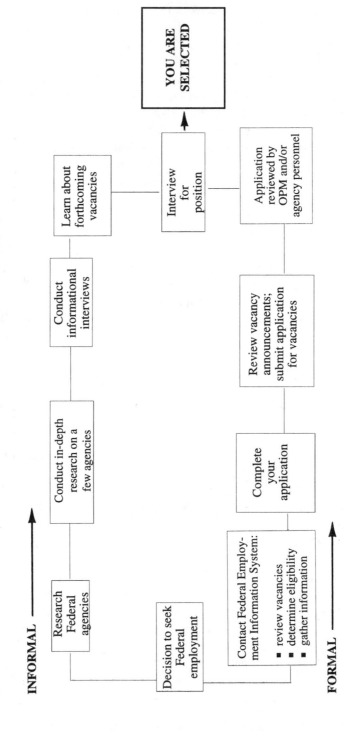

legislative assistants may know key people in the agency, and they will write you a standard letter of introduction. But do not expect miracles to happen with such a letter or by dropping names of big shots. In fact, the President of the United States only directly controls 3,000 of 3 million civilian government positions. Even the President may not be able to help you with the relatively autonomous and resistant bureaucracy!

While federal bureaucrats understand and thrive on the informal system, political patronage and political pull are considered tacky, if not illegal, these days. In this respect, government bureaucrats are no different from their counterparts in other organizations: the informal system continues to yield more reliable and trustworthy information than the formal system. Thus, the hiring goals of most government agencies are similar to those of other organizations: hire the most qualified person who is **competent, intelligent, honest, and likable**. Indeed, the 1980 personnel reforms, which are based upon the model of the private sector, already have decentralized many hiring decisions to the agency level. In this sense, conducting a job search with the federal government is remarkably similar to conducting a job search in the private sector.

> The informal system continues to yield more reliable and trustworthy information than the formal system.

Ask the Right Questions

Knowledge is always power when conducting a job search. This is especially true when seeking a federal job. While there is a great deal of general information on government, you will need to conduct research to uncover the detailed information necessary to locate the job you want as well as communicate effectively with hiring officials.

Information Needs

Your research should focus on answering five major questions for organizing your job search:

1. What are the jobs?
2. Where are the jobs?
3. Who has the power to hire?

4. How do organization X and program Y operate?
5. What do I need to do to get a job with organization X?

The first two questions can be answered by exploring OPM's Federal Employment Information System and consulting various directories and books found in most libraries as well as specialized job listing services. The last three questions can only be answered by talking with knowledgeable people associated with the organization. You need to probe as much as possible for details in order to focus your job search on particular organizations, positions, and individuals.

What Are the Jobs?

As we outlined in Chapter 6, this question can be answered by exploring OPM's Federal Employment Information System and by consulting several books and directories in the reference and government sections of your local library. The Department of Labor publishes several useful resources for surveying various job titles. At a minimum you should examine:

- *The Dictionary of Occupational Titles*
- *The Occupational Outlook Handbook*

Your library might also carry the following books on public sector jobs:

- *The Book of U.S. Government Jobs* (Dennis V. Damp)
- *Directory of Federal Jobs and Employers* (Ron and Caryl Krannich)
- *Federal Jobs: The Ultimate Guide* (Dana Morgan and Robert Goldenkoff)
- *Government Job Finder* (Daniel Lauber)
- *Guide to Federal Jobs* (Resource Directories)

Most of these and other useful guides to government are listed in the resource section at the end of the book.

In addition to conducting Internet and library research on identifying different jobs, you can write or visit various government personnel offices for detailed information on different jobs. Department and agency personnel offices, for example, will send you information on job titles, descriptions of duties and responsibilities, entrance requirements, and salaries and benefits if you telephone or write directly to them requesting the information. Each office will have its own set of literature designed to attract candidates to their operations.

You also may want to visit the touch screen computer kiosks found in federal buildings and OPM offices nationwide to access position descriptions and agency information. Also, OPM and agency personnel offices have a book which is the bible for getting information on particular positions: ***Operating Manual for Qualification Standards for General Schedule Positions*** (previously titled the ***Handbook X-118, Qualification Standards for Positions Under the General Schedule*** and still referred to as the ***Handbook X-118***). It consists of two looseleaf binders and a volume on blue-collar positions. Position descriptions written in the language of personnel offices are included for white-collar jobs (OPM's ***Handbook X-118***) and blue-collar jobs (OPM's ***Handbook X-118A***). You may have difficulty getting access to these volumes since OPM and agency personnel tend to guard them as internal documents. However, you should be able to see them by requesting to examine the books in their office.

A final source of information on identifying different types of federal jobs is the most basic and important—talk to someone in a position that interests you. Ask them about:

1. What they do.
2. How they got there.
3. Advantages and disadvantages.
4. Duties and responsibilities.
5. A typical day on the job.
6. Advancement opportunities.
7. Salaries and benefits.
8. The future.

Many people will discuss their work with you and provide you with important tips on how to enter the public service. However, many others may be too busy to see you, especially if you are making cold calls. It's always best to have a referral from a friend who is a friend of a friend or who may be a relative or a friend of a relative. A personal "connection" should yield a great deal of useful information and perhaps assistance in getting a federal job fast!

Where Are the Jobs?

This question can be answered by consulting several directories as well as many of the resources identified in the previous sections. Several directories provide addresses for locating various departments, agencies, and personnel offices. The most important ones include:

- *Congressional Directory*
- *Congressional Staff Directory*
- *Congressional Yellow Book*
- *Directory of Federal Executives*
- *Federal Executive Directory*
- *Federal Staff Directory*
- *Federal Yellow Book*
- *United States Government Manual*
- *Washington '99*
- *Washington Information Directory*

Most of these directories are found in the reference section of your local library. Some are available online.

Another source of information worth examining are **case studies** of various government departments and agencies. Many enterprising scholars, journalists, or concerned citizens have written books and articles on government operations. Several excellent books have been written on federal agencies, the most popular being TVA, FBI, CIA, Justice, Energy, and Interior. Newspaper accounts of upheavals in various departments and independent agencies provide excellent "inside" information on the internal environments of these agencies as well as their overall effectiveness in the large public and private sectors in which they operate. Such literature helps specify some of the major issues facing these agencies as well as their internal structure and current work cultures, including morale of employees.

You might also want to acquire copies of **telephone directories** for various departments and agencies. All government organizations will have an in-house telephone directory—the one document that seems to hold the organization together. This is an invaluable source of information on the internal structure of the organization as well as key contact points for making your telephone calls and visiting offices. Many of these telephone directories are organizational roadmaps. They may include a recent organizational chart, a functional breakdown of the agency by section, room number, and telephone number, and an alphabetical listing of employees with their room and telephone numbers. The federal government actually publishes and sells telephone directories for each department. You can get these publications by contacting:

Superintendent of Documents
U.S. Government Printing Office
Washington, DC 20402

Most telephone directories sell for $20-25. Many departments now have their telephone directories online. You can access them by going directly to their Web sites.

If you use the Internet, you literally have huge quantities of information at your finger tips. All departments and most agencies have their own Web sites. For example, try these URLs for the departments:

- Agriculture   *www.usda.gov*
- Commerce   *www.doc.gov*
- Defense   *www.dtic.mil*
- Education   *www.ed.gov*
- Energy   *www.doe.gov*
- Health and Human Services   *www.os.dhhs.gov*
- Housing and Urban Development   *www.hud.gov*
- Interior   *www.doi.gov*
- Justice   *www.usdoj.gov*
- Labor   *www.dol.gov*
- State   *www.state.gov*
- Transportation   *www.dot.gov*
- Treasury   *www.ustres.gov*
- Veterans Affairs   *www.va.gov*

If you're interested in working for the largest federal agency, the U.S. Postal Service, try this URL: *www.usps.gov*. The White House Web site (*www.whitehouse.gov*) functions as a gateway to executive agencies. If you're interested in working on Capitol Hill, most Senators and Congressmen have their own Web sites. For a directory to government Web site, see Bruce Maxwell's ***How to Access the Federal Government On the Internet*** (Washington, DC: Congressional Quarterly).

Federal departments and agencies produce tons of information, much of which is relevant to your job search and which is available upon request. Most publish or print organizational charts, current listings of their personnel and office locations, and statistical breakdowns of who does what and where. Some of this information is in the form of published directories, whereas other information is in the form of brochures, newsletters, or looseleaf stapled pages. For example, if you want the names and addresses of key foreign service personnel abroad, the Foreign Affairs Information Management Center of the U.S. Department of State maintains a Publishing Services Division. This unit publishes a small pocket-sized, but extremely useful, directory entitled *Key Officers of Foreign Service Posts: Guide For Business Representatives*. Regularly updated and including useful foreign mailing tips, this directory can be purchased directly from the U.S. Government Printing Office. Better still, this directory is now updated regularly on the Department of State's Web site: *www.state.gov*. A little probing on your part—either by telephone or personal visit—should uncover the information you need. However, you will need to get this type of information from offices other than personnel. Most agencies have a public information office or ombudsman whose job is to respond to such requests for information.

> **Your government is tightly wired with all departments and most agencies having their own Web sites, including members of Congress.**

Your final source of information on the "where" of government consists of the people you talk to by telephone and in person. Use your telephone extensively in gathering such information. Personal visits are the most useful for getting in-depth information, the telephone is by far the most efficient way of gathering information. If you are reluctant to make "cold calls" to strangers, consult a few books on how to become more effective on the telephone. For example, try our *Dynamite Tele-Search* which is available through Impact Publications.

Who Has the Power to Hire?

This question also will take some research effort on your part. You already know three things important for answering this question:

1. Personnel offices are in charge of conducting part of the hiring, but usually not the most important parts.

2. The program supervisors in the operating units are normally the key hiring people.

3. Several directories list the names, addresses, and telephone numbers of key officials.

Yes, what is generally the case may not be true all of the time. For example, personnel offices in some agencies play the central role in the hiring process. In other agencies they may be peripheral to the hiring process. In most agencies the personnel office will be responsible for recruiting and selecting certain types of positions.

Therefore, you need to conduct research on the particular agency that interests you. You need to ask specific questions concerning **who** normally is responsible for various parts of the hiring process:

-   Describing positions
-   Announcing vacancies
-   Receiving applications
-   Administering tests
-   Selecting eligible candidates
-   Choosing whom to interview
-   Offering the job

If you ask these questions about a specific position, you will quickly identify who has what powers to hire. Chances are the power to hire is shared between the personnel office and the operating unit. You cannot neglect the personnel office, and in some cases it will play a powerful role in all aspects of the hiring. Your research will reveal to what degree the hiring function has been centralized, decentralized, or fragmented within a particular unit of government.

How Do Agency X and Program Y Operate?

Answers to this question will help you break through the stereotypes and images of performance packaged for public consumption. You can answer this question using three approaches:

1. Read literature on the agency.
2. Attend meetings to observe, make contacts, and ask questions.
3. Interview informed individuals.

Most agencies and units of government have a great deal of printed matter about their operations. Most of this information is available to the public, although some sources may be easier to access than others. A good starting point is the annual **budget**. The budget should both raise and answer numerous questions. Most budgets tell you who is getting how much, where, and for what anticipated results. In addition, many agencies have their programs periodically evaluated. Program review or evaluation reports should be available through the planning, program evaluation, or central administration office. These reports will give you a good feel for not only the agency's goals and what it is doing at present, but also its problems and future potential. Other useful printed materials include project documents, training manuals, and operations handbooks for individual offices. You should get access to many of these documents to learn what is really going on inside the organization.

Another useful source of information is **public meetings** of officials. In addition to revealing a great deal of information on the agency, these meetings offer an opportunity for you to identify key decision-makers as well as meet them in public. Meetings of federal officials abound, from congressional committee hearings to public hearings on agency programs. In Washington, DC, for example, each day the *Washington Post* publishes the major upcoming meetings on Capitol Hill and in agencies. Thousands of meetings go on within each agency every week. You can contact the public affairs office to find out what meetings are being held when, and which ones are open to interested observers.

What Do I Need to Do to Get a Job With Agency X?

This question can only be answered by talking to people who know both the formal and informal hiring practices. As noted earlier, in government the formal system is usually well defined in terms of applications, tests, eligibility lists, and interviews. You can get this information by calling or writing the personnel office.

But in most cases you must go beyond the formal system and personnel office in order to learn how best to conduct your job search.

This means talking to people in the operational unit. Our experience is that most people in the program offices are relatively easy to talk with. They are interested in learning about potential candidates prior to initiating a time-consuming and often frustrating formal recruitment process. These busy people do not have a great deal of time to spend on the hiring process, since this is not one of their major duties and responsibilities. Therefore, information that would help them ease the hiring burden may be welcome. Contrary to what many job seekers may think, if done properly, the informational interview is not an imposition on hiring personnel. You are helping them arrive at a decision while they are helping you gain important knowledge for improving your job search. If they like you, chances are they will give you useful tips on how to get a job in their organization. There is no better information and advice than that given by the individual who will play a major role in the hiring process.

> There is no better information and advice than that given by the individual who will play a major role in the hiring process.

What Do I Do With This Information?

Your information gathering tasks involve locating important information, analyzing it, and presenting it in a **usable** form. Gathering information for "understanding" is necessary. But you must move from understanding to **application** if you are to be effective in finding a job. After analyzing and synthesizing your research findings, you must incorporate the information into an effective strategy for improving your job search. The information needs to be:

1. Incorporated into an outstanding application (Chapter 7) targeted toward specific positions.

2. Converted into effective prospecting, networking, and informational interviews.

3. Used for conducting excellent job interviews.

This means you must make incremental movements toward achieving your stated goals. More specifically, you must **discipline yourself** to explore key government Web sites on the Internet and daily monitor vacancy announcements through OPM's Federal Employment Information System. You should pick up the telephone and make three to five calls each day. You may want to take to the streets, pounding the pavement and "pressing the flesh," for useful information and job leads.

Information gathering is one important step in the job search process. More important, on a regular basis you must manage a set of discrete job search activities which are closely related to one another. Without taking action based on your research, you may "understand" a great deal, but you will go nowhere. Knowledge becomes power when it is converted to effective action.

Useful Resources

Numerous resources are available to research the federal hiring process as well as individual agencies. For a good overview of federal government opportunities and job search strategies, examine the following books:

- *Applying For Federal Jobs*, Patricia B. Wood (Moon Township, PA: Bookhaven Press, 1995)

- *The Book of U.S. Government Jobs*, Dennis V. Damp (Moon Township, PA: Bookhaven Press, 1995)

- *The Complete Guide to Public Employment*, Ron and Caryl Krannich (Manassas Park, VA: Impact Publications, 1995)

- *The Directory of Federal Jobs and Employers*, Ron and Caryl Krannich (Manassas Park, VA: Impact Publications, 1996)

- *Federal Jobs For College Graduates* (Robert Goldenkoff and Dana Morgan (New York: Prentice-Hall/Arco, 1997)

- *Federal Applications That Get Results*, Russ Smith (Manassas Park, VA: Impact Publications, 1995).

If you are particularly interested in intelligence careers with the Central Intelligence Agency (CIA), Federal Bureau of Investigation (FBI), National Security Agency (NSA), Defense Intelligence Agency (DIA), the Drug Enforcement Agency (DEA), and related agencies, consult two useful resources published by Impact Publications: *Federal Jobs in Law Enforcement* (Russ Smith, 1996) and *Alternative Careers in Secret Operations* (Mark Merritt, 1998).

Daniel Lauber's *Government Job Finder* (River Forest, IL: Planning/Communications, 1997) provides information on resources for finding jobs in federal, state, and local governments. His chapter on the federal government provides summaries and contact information on numerous such resources, including telephone numbers of agency personnel offices.

Two excellent publications provide a wealth of information on the federal personnel system, particularly on employee benefits, labor-management relations, health and retirement systems, and promotions and transfers. Each of these volumes is updated annually. Widely available in bookstores in Washington, DC, you will need to order them directly from the publishers if you live outside this area:

- *Federal Employees' Almanac*. Send $15.90 ($11.95 plus $3.95 for shipping) to: Federal Employees' News Digest, 1850 Centennial Park Drive, Suite 520, Reston, VA 20191 or call 1-800-989-3363 or fax 703/648-0265. You may prefer visiting their online bookstore at *www.fedforce.com*

- *Federal Personnel Guide*. Send $12.95 ($9.95 plus $3.00 shippping for shipping) to: Federal Personnel Guide, Key Communications Group, Inc., P.O. Box 42578, Washington, DC 20015-0578: or 5617 Warwick Place, Chevy Chase, MD 20815-5503. You can call them at 1-800-705-5353, 301/656-0450 (voice mail), or 301/656-2923 (for a real person), or fax 301/656-4554. You may prefer visiting their online bookstore at *www.fedguide.com*

The *Federal Employees' News Digest* costs $59 for a 50-issue one year subscription. It is available by writing, calling, faxing, or visiting the publisher's online bookstore:

Federal Employees' News Digest
P.O. Box 8550
Reston, VA 20195-2450
Tel. 1-800-989-3363
Fax 703/648-0265
Web site: *www.fedforce.com*

Two private firms—the Federal Research Service, Inc. and Break-through Publications—track federal job vacancies and publish bi-weekly catalogs of job vacancies available throughout the government. *Federal Career Opportunities* costs $7.95 per copy or $39 for 6 issues, $77 for 12 issues, or $175 for 26 issues. Most issues run about 64 pages and list 3400+ jobs at the GS-5 through Senior Executive Service, jobs abroad, application process and contact information, part-time and temporary positions, and "how to" articles on job hunting techniques. Contact:

Federal Research Service, Inc.
370 Maple Avenue West
P.O. Box 1059
Vienna, VA 22183-1059
Tel. 703/281-0200

The Federal Research Service also offers an electronic online service called FedJobs. This is a searchable Web version of *Federal Career Opportunities* which is updated daily. You can search the database by occupation, pay level and/or location. For a free preview, go directly to their Web site: *www.fedjobs.com*. You can subscribe to the service for $19.97 per month or $49.00 for a three-month subscription.

Another private firm publishes a similar bi-weekly listing of federal jobs—*Federal Jobs Digest*—which also comes with a "Federal Jobs Kit." Each issue of this newspaper contains about 3,000 jobs for all professions and occupations, including blue-collar jobs. Subscription rates are $34 for six issues, $59 for 12 issues, and $125 for 25 issues. For further information, contact:

Federal Jobs Digest
325 Pennsylvania Avenue, SE
Washington, DC 20003
Tel. 1-800-824-5000

Be sure to visit their Web site: *www.jobsfed.com*. The publisher (Breakthough Publications) also produces two useful federal job hunting books: *Working For Your Uncle* and *U.S. Postal Exam Text 470*.

You can also subscribe to both the *Federal Careers Opportunities* and *Federal Jobs Digest* through Impact Publications by completing the subscription information in the resource section at the end of this book.

A weekly newspaper, *The Federal Times*, also lists federal job vacancies. Contact them at: The Federal Times, ATTN: Subscription, Springfield, VA 22159-0260, Tel. 703/750-8920. Other federal jobs will be listed in the classified and/or business sections of local newspapers.

Individuals seeking legal opportunities with federal agencies can subscribe to a special job listing service. The Federal Reports, Inc. publishes a monthly listing of attorney and law-related job opportunities in both the public and private sector in the U.S. and abroad. It's called *Attorney Jobs: The National and Federal Legal Employment Report*. Subscription rates for this publication are $45 for three months, $75 for six months, and $135 for one year. Write or call them at:

Federal Reports Inc.
1010 Vermont Ave., NW, Suite 408
Washington, DC 20005
Tel. 1-800-296-9611 or 202/393-3311

You also may want to visit their Web site: *www.attorneyjobs.com*

You can also contact agency personnel offices directly to get information on vacancies. Many of these offices will send you copies of vacancy announcements. Several personnel offices also maintain a job hotline with a recorded message of vacancies.

Many federal government positions require passing a written examination for eligibility. Arco Publishing (Prentice-Hall) produces several self-study guides to help individuals prepare for various civil service examinations at all levels of government. Among the many titles relevant to federal employment are:

- *Air Traffic Controller Qualifying Test*
- *Bookkeeper-Account Clerk*
- *Civil Service Administrative Tests*
- *Civil Service Arithmetic and Vocabulary*
- *Civil Service Handbook*

- *Civil Service Psychological and Psychiatric Tests*
- *Civil Service Reading Comprehension Tests*
- *Civil Service Tests for Basic Skills Jobs*
- *Correction Officer*
- *Federal Clerk-Stenotypist*
- *General Test Practice of 101 U.S. Jobs*
- *How to Get a Clerical Job in Government*
- *Postal Exams Handbook*
- *Post Office Clerk-Carrier*
- *Rural Carrier—U.S. Postal Service*
- *Special Agent: Treasury Enforcement Agent*

Learning Express also publishes a similar series of examination and career starter books relevant to federation employment:

- *Border Patrol Exam*
- *Civil Service Career Starter*
- *Federal Clerical Exam*
- *Postal Worker Exam*

Several useful publications are available in the reference section of your local library. These are primarily directories which provide an overview of the structure of the federal government as well as provide the names and addresses of key individuals within each agency. Among the most important directories are:

- *U.S. Government Manual*
- *Federal Staff Directory*
- *Federal Yellow Book*
- *Government Phone Book 1999*
- *Taylor's Encyclopedia of Government Officials*
- *Washington Information Directory*
- *Directory of Federal Executives*
- *Washington '99: A Comprehensive Directory of the Key Institutions and Leaders of the National Capital Area*

The Office of Personnel Management and the U.S. Government Printing Office publish several informative brochures and books on federal personnel which you may wish to examine. You can purchase them directly from the Superintendent of Documents, U.S. Government Printing Office, Washington, DC 20402. If you write to them, also ask for their catalog of publications on government jobs and personnel. You may, for example, want to purchase a telephone directory for a particular agency that interests you. Remember, the U.S. Government Printing Office is the largest publisher, printer, and bookstore in the country. It produces a wealth of reports and useful guides on the various functions and agencies of government. And they are eager to sell their publications!

You should also write or call the personnel offices of the agency that interests you. Many of these offices have publications describing various jobs and careers. For example, the U.S. Immigration and Naturalization Service of the Department of Justice publishes a question and answer brochure on becoming a Border Patrol Agent. The brochure addresses the major concerns of most applicants: duties, qualifications, conditions of employment, written and medical examinations, appointments, training, uniforms, career advancement, benefits, and special retirement.

Another useful source of information on federal jobs are the numerous federal and postal employee unions and organizations. You can find the names, addresses, and telephone numbers of these groups in the following annual directories which are available in most libraries or they can be ordered directly from Impact Publications: *Encyclopedia of Associations* and *National Trade and Professional Associations*.

Job Fairs

During the past few years several federal agencies have joined together in sponsoring job fairs for recruiting personnel. Organized by private contractors, most of the fairs have been designed to quickly recruit individuals for high turnover and hard-to-fill positions, such as clerical and high-tech positions. However, given recent cutbacks and continuing uncertainty about staffing levels, few federal job fairs have been held since 1993. We would expect them to resume sometime in the future, depending on new staffing needs.

Job fairs usually consist of twenty or more agencies that come together for one or two days to provide information on career opportunities and interview potential candidates for specific positions. Each agency usually has a booth where it provides literature on the agency as well as has personnel to meet with interested candidates to discuss career opportunities within the agency.

When conducting research with agencies, be sure to check to see if they are planning to participate in an upcoming job fair that relates to your particular interests and skills. Since most job fairs with federal agencies have been for either clerical or scientific and technical positions, don't expect to find job fairs for other types of positions. If your skills match those of the job fairs, this is a good way to get an overview of several federal agencies that are recruiting for similar positions as well as to interview for specific positions. Indeed, participating in a job fair is probably the fastest way to get hired with the federal government. In some cases, one can literally be hired the same day you interview for a position at the job fair!

9

Capitol Hill and the Judiciary

W hile not normally included in most examinations of the federal employment, the legislative and judicial branches of government do provide exciting job opportunities for those who know the what, where, and how of finding employment in these two arenas. Jobs with the legislature in particular often lead to a variety of jobs and careers with other organizations that define the public sector (Chapter 4, page 58). Individuals who work on Capitol Hill, for example, frequently move to other jobs in the executive branch as well as transition to associations, law firms, contracting and consulting organizations, and nonprofit organizations.

This chapter outlines the basic principles for acquiring a job in two of the most overlooked areas of the federal government—the legislative and judicial branches. It examines legislative agencies, congressional organizations, the Supreme Court, U.S. Courts, and supporting organizations.

Opportunities

While the number of employees in the legislative and judicial branches (61,837) is relatively small compared to executive agencies (2,717,569), rewarding employment opportunities abound nonetheless. Many of the

HOUSE OF REPRESENTATIVES

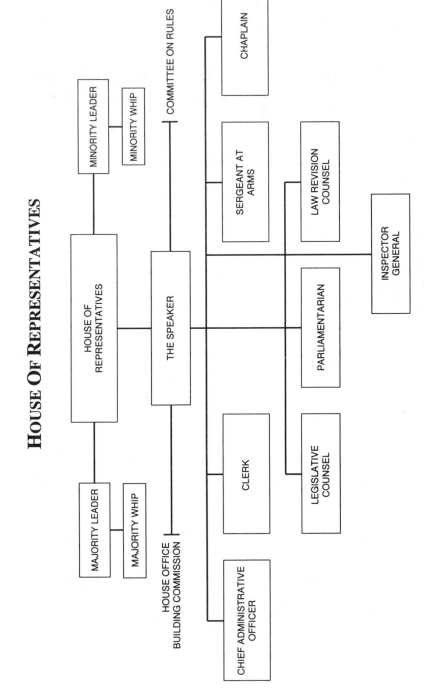

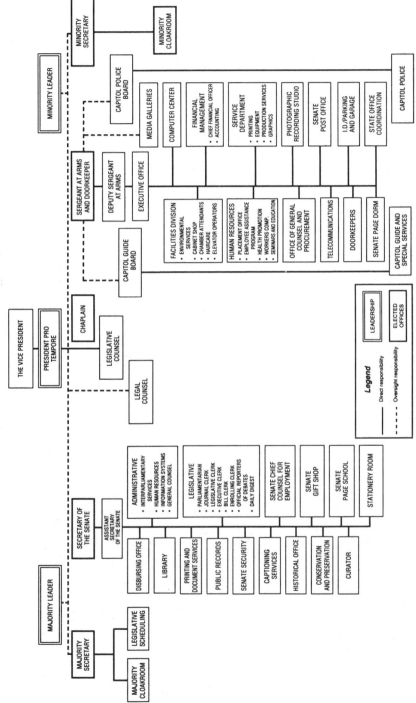

UNITED STATES SENATE

jobs lead to long-term careers within their respective branches of government. They also serve as important **stepping stones** for jobs in the executive branch as well as amongst numerous peripheral public sector institutions, especially with associations and nonprofits.

Employment Levels and Procedures

The federal legislative branch in May 1998 employed 30,745 individuals; the federal judiciary employed 31,092. While the largest number of individuals work for Congress (17,215), nearly 13,000 individuals work for four legislative agencies: Library of Congress (4,369), Government Printing Office (3,443), General Accounting Office (3,283), and the Architect of the Capitol (1,744). Other legislative agencies include the Congressional Budget Office (220), U.S. Botanic Gardens (43), and the Medicare Payment Advisory Commission (26). The Supreme Court employs 383, but the remaining federal courts employ 30,709 individuals. In fact, the federal court system is one of the fastest growing areas of government, increasing by 116 percent since 1980 (from 14,404 to 31,092 employees).

> **The federal court system is one of the fastest growing areas of government, increasing by 116 percent since 1980.**

Legislative agencies generally follow similar formal recruitment procedures as executive agencies: position announcements, application forms, testing, eligibility lists, and interviews. However, being constitutionally separate from the executive branch, the legislative branch sets its own rules and regulations for recruitment and selection. While most executive agencies classify their positions according to the General Schedule and use OPM for setting hiring standards, each legislative agency develops its own recruitment procedures separate from the GS Schedule and OPM operations. Furthermore, Congress uses its own recruitment procedures which are less structured and more personal in nature than recruitment in either executive or legislative agencies. The federal judiciary, however, is less structured; its hiring practices tend to follow a more personal approach commonly associated with jobs and careers in the legal profession.

Let's take, for example, the largest agency in Congress—the Library of Congress. This agency makes its own personnel decisions, from issuing vacancy announcements to accepting applications, screening candidates, and hiring. Unlike most executive agencies, the Library of Congress actually requires completion of the SF-171 in order to be considered for employment. Consequently, our SF-171 example in Chapter 7 is especially relevant to this congressional agency. The Library of Congress also outlines a five-step process involved in applying for a job. It's basically the same process for most executive agencies:

FIVE STEPS TO EMPLOYMENT WITH THE LIBRARY OF CONGRESS

STEP 1: Obtain a Copy of the Vacancy Announcement

Positions at the Library of Congress are advertised through "Vacancy Announcements" which are available from the Library of Congress Human Resources Office, located in Room LM-107, James Madison Memorial Building, Washington, D.C. 20540. Information concerning specific announcements, as well as copies, can be obtained by calling (202) 707-5627.

STEP 2: Read the Vacancy Announcement Carefully

Each Library of Congress Vacancy Announcement provides information on Number of Vacancies, Brief Description of Duties, and Minimum Qualifications. The Minimum Qualifications section describes those requirements including knowledge, skills, and abilities which are used to determine your basic eligibility for a position. Included in this section is a description of the necessary specialized experience, education requirements, and, for some positions, language proficiencies, which must be demonstrated on your application. Many vacancy announcements also list Quality Ranking Factors used by a Qualifications Rating Panel to determine Better Qualified candidates. READ THE VACANCY ANNOUNCEMENT CAREFULLY TO BE CERTAIN YOUR EXPERIENCE AND EDUCATION ARE QUALIFYING.

STEP 3: Prepare an Effective Application

Here are some guidelines for enhancing your application:

– Use a typewriter, if possible; otherwise, print neatly and clearly in ink; if photocopied, make sure the copy is readable.

– Provide complete information. Answer all questions and complete all blocks.

- Make the application letter-perfect in terms of correct grammar, spelling, punctuation, and neatness.

- Address in your application the minimum qualifications and Quality Ranking Factors, if present. Attach to your application a statement which highlights your Experience, Education and Training, Self-Development and Outside Activities, and Awards and Commendations in relation to the Quality Ranking Factors on the vacancy announcement.

- Include all requested attachments. Read the announcement to determine if you need to submit one or more of the following: (1) test results; (2) list of college courses; (3) writing samples, and/or (4) supplemental statements or forms.

STEP 4: Submit a Separate Application for Each Vacancy Announcement

All applicants for positions at the Library of Congress must use a Standard Form 171, Application for Federal Employment, for employment consideration. The SF-171 can be obtained from the Library of Congress Human Resources Office or from most Federal agency personnel offices. We will accept a photocopy of the application as long as it is readable with an original (not photocopied) signature and date. To receive consideration, your application must be received in the Employment Office, James Madison Memorial Building, Room LM-107, Washington, D.C. 20540, by the closing date specified on the vacancy announcement. (The closing date of a vacancy announcement MAY be extended.)

STEP 5: Be Familiar With the Selection Process

All applications received by the vacancy announcement's closing date are evaluated by the Library's Human Resources Office for basic eligibility to determine if the posted minimum requirements have been met. Should your application not meet the minimum qualifications, you are advised in a letter explaining why you do not qualify.

Many vacancies at the Library are filled through the use of a Qualifications Rating Panel which evaluates each application that has met the minimum qualifications of the vacancy announcement. Such announcements include a list of two or more Quality Ranking Factors which provide the panel with the basis for rating and ranking each application. The panel evaluates your application for information demonstrating the knowledge, skills or abilities described by the Quality Ranking Factors in terms of your Experience, Education and Training, Self-Development and Outside Activities, and Awards and Commendations. A maximum number of points determines your final standing or rank in comparison to all other candidates. Applicants determined to be the Better Qualified Candidates will be interviewed and considered further by the Recommending Officer. Some vacancies are filled without the panel process. In such cases, the vacancy announcement does not include Quality Ranking Factors and the applications of all the qualified candidates are referred to the Recommending Officer for further consideration and possible interviews.

The entire selection process takes approximately 90-120 days from the opening date of the vacancy announcement. All candidates, whether interviewed or not, are notified of the final selection.

You'll find this and a great deal of additional useful information on the Library of Congress Web site: *http://lcweb.loc.gov*

In this chapter we outline the basic principles for acquiring a job in two of the most overlooked employment arenas of the federal government—the legislative and judicial branches. It examines legislative agencies, congressional organizations, the Supreme Court, U.S. Courts, and supporting organizations.

Highly Wired and Linked Arenas

Within the past three years, both the legislative and judicial branches of government have become highly wired with numerous Web sites linked to one another—a virtual job hunter's paradise. Information on individual agencies and employment opportunities are readily available through the Internet. Indeed, all one needs to do is click on to one or more of these gateway sites and details on both branches of government quickly unfold:

> *www.whitehouse.gov*
> *www.senate.gov*
> *www.house.gov*
> *www.thomas.loc.gov*
> *www.uscourt.gov*
> *www.fjc.gov*

You'll discover a wealth of information on individual members of Congress, including congressional agencies as well as personal and congressional staffs, and the U.S. court system. We highly recommend visiting these five sites in conjunction with the material presented in this chapter. These sites yield all kinds of information for better understanding each employment arena. Best of all, these sites include linkages to personnel offices that offer online vacancy announcements, application forms, and submission procedures.

Legislative Agencies

The legislative branch maintains its own bureaucracy to perform general housekeeping functions (Architect of the Capitol), provide information for decision-making and dissemination purposes (Library of Congress and Government Printing Office), and oversee the financial operations of executive agencies (General Accounting Office). Legislative agencies are relatively small in terms of personnel and budgets, but they offer numerous opportunities for enterprising job seekers.

Functions and Linkages

The **General Accounting Office** (3,283 employees) performs important congressional oversight functions. It conducts audits of federal agencies and issues reports on how to improve the efficiency and effectiveness of government. It checks to what degree agencies have spent funds allocated by Congress. In so doing, it employs hundreds of individuals with specialties in accounting, economics, and operations research. Visit them online at *www.gao.gov*

The **Library of Congress** (4,369 employees) is Congresses' information arm as well as the nation's largest and most comprehensive library. It employs hundreds of librarians and subject matter specialists. The Congressional Research Service, for example, provides congressional committees with information as well as conducts specialized studies. The Federal Research Division is Congresses' equivalent to the CIA and DIA. Visit the Library of Congress online at *http://lcweb.loc.gov*

The **Government Printing Office** (3,443 employees) is the government's central printer and bookstore. It daily prints all major documents, such as the *Congressional Record* and the *Federal Register*, as well as pamphlets, magazines, reports, directories, and books commissioned by individual agencies. Visit the GPO online at *www.access.gpo.gov*

The **Congressional Budget Office** (220 employees) provides Congress with budgetary data, analyzes fiscal alternatives, conducts studies, and forecasts spending. This office provides an important congressional check to similar functions performed by the Office of Management and Budget in the Executive Office of the President.

The **Architect of the Capitol** (1,744 employees) is responsible for maintaining all congressional buildings and grounds, the U.S. Supreme Court building, the Thurgood Marshall Federal Judiciary Building, the Capitol Power Plant, the Capitol Police headquarters, and the Robert A. Taft Memorial. It also arranges for inaugural and other ceremonies held in the building or on the grounds. Visit them online at *www.aoc.gov*

The **United States Botanic Garden** (43 employees) collects, cultivates, and grows a large variety of plants for public exhibitions. It provides facilities for educational groups interested in the botanic garden. Information on this organization is available through the Architect of the Capitol's Web site: *www.aoc.gov*

Recruitment

Each legislative agency recruits its own personnel. Consequently, you will need to contact each agency to learn their particular procedures for announcing vacancies and selecting personnel. For example, the **General Accounting Office** issues vacancy announcements through its Office of Recruitment (Room 1165, 441 G Street, NW, Washington, DC 20548). GAO's Web site (*www.gao.gov*) includes a section called "Job Vacancies at GAO" which, in turn, provide application details.

The **Library of Congress** issues position vacancy announcements. If you want information on current employment opportunities, you can call the Employment Opportunity Hotline at 202/707-5295. The message is updated every Tuesday. If you are in Washington, you can walk into the Employment Office between the hours of 8:30am and 4:30pm, Monday through Friday, to get copies of current vacancy announcements (Room LM-107, 101 Independence Avenue, SE). This office also conducts testing for clerical and word processing positions. You also may want to visit their Web site, although it is not updated as well as one might expect: *http//:lcweb.loc.gov*. The **Congressional Research Service** also has information on employment opportunities. You can either visit their Administration Office in Room 208 of the James Madison Building to review job vacancy announcements with the CRS or call them for information at 202/707-8803.

The **Government Printing Office** has experienced a 20 percent cut in personnel since 1980 and often operates under hiring freezes. Contact the Employment Branch (202/512-1118) for general employment information. Jobs with GPO are part of the competitive service and thus the whole employment process is handled through the Office of Personnel Administration. GPO's Web site (*www.access.gpo.gov*) includes job announcements and application forms.

The **Congressional Budget Office** provides job vacancy information by telephone (202/226-2621) or by visiting their Personnel and Security Office (House Annex 2, Room 410, Second and D Streets, SW, Washington, DC). You can also visit their Web site: *www.cbo.gov*

Both the **Architect of the Capitol** and the **U.S. Botanic Garden** recruit their personnel through the Personnel Office of the Architect of the Capitol. Contact this office for vacancy announcements for both offices by calling 202/225-1231. You also can visit their Web site (*www.aoc.gov*) or office in Washington, DC to survey job vacancy announcements and ask questions about the employment process: Room 179, Second and D Streets, SW.

Start your job search by visiting the relevant Web site of each legislative agency.

Your best job search strategy with these legislative agencies will be to contact the personnel offices for job vacancy information (start with their relevant Web sites), complete any application forms required, submit your application package, and make informal contacts with key agency personnel. Follow the same procedures we outlined for the informal job search process in executive agencies.

Capitol Hill

Finding a job with Congress requires an intimate knowledge of the congressional hiring process. Both the House and Senate maintain placement offices to primarily collect resumes. But the relatively unstructured and highly personal nature of the congressional hiring process requires surfing congressional Web sites, knocking on doors, making personal contacts, and networking for jobs. This can involve anything from roaming the halls of the Dirksen and Hart Senate Office Buildings and the Cannon and Longworth House Office Buildings; contacting the Administrative Assistant and asking up front if he or she has any staff openings at present for someone with your qualifications; or networking for information, advice, and job leads by getting to know staffers who hang out at the local eating and drinking establishments, such as Hawk n' Dove, Bullfeathers, Tune Inn, Tortilla Coast, Irish Times, Dubliner, and Red River Grill as well as many bars and restaurants in Union Station and along Massachusetts Avenue.

However, before launching into such cold-calling and networking campaigns for penetrating the employment scene on Capitol Hill, you must understand the structure of Congress and the various opportunities available. For, in the end, job hunting with Congress involves 535 personal staffs and over 300 committees and subcommittees which have their own hiring practices and salary structures. In this sense, Congress consists of over 835 separate hiring systems!

Congressional work is not for everyone. Each year approximately 40 percent of all congressional employees leave for other work. While much of the work is interesting and challenging, for many people it is stressful and financially unrewarding. Few people make congressional work a career. For many, it is an important **stepping stone** to other types of public service work. Yet, this high turnover rate provides numerous opportunities for enterprising job seekers who wish to get some "Hill" experience before moving on to greener employment pastures.

> **The relatively unstructured nature of the congressional hiring requires knocking on doors, making personal contacts, and networking.**

The Rush to Downsize

Since the congressional elections of November 1994, Congress engaged in a similar crash course as the executive agencies to downsize their staffs. The House of Representatives immediately reduced its committee staffs by 37 percent, cut salaries by up to 25 percent, and increased workloads for already overworked staffs. As it reduced its staff budget, Congress also found itself operating with antiquated technology and the need to pay cash for overtime. By 1998, the cuts had been less drastic than initially envisioned—1,671 fewer congressional jobs which represented an 8.8 percent reduction in the workforce since 1994. Consequently, finding a job in Capitol Hill was increasingly difficult during the mid-1990s when Congress was under political pressure to reduce its overall personnel levels.

Personal Staffs

Most congressional job opportunities are with personal staffs or committee staffs. There are 535 personal staffs—one for each member of
Congress (100 in the Senate and 435 in the House of Representatives).
Each of these staffs are divided into Washington-based staffs and
home-district staffs. The typical Washington staff consists of 16 full-time
and four part-time employees cramped into four to six small offices in the
Russell Senate, Dirkson Senate, Rayburn House, Longworth House, or
Cannon House Buildings as well as in Senate and House Annex
buildings. The home-district offices are relatively small. They are usually
staffed by political loyalists who are primarily oriented toward maintaining a positive image and promoting the
re-election of their bosses. In the process
of doing this, they respond to a great deal
of constituent and interest group pressures.

> **Each member of Congress has a Web page that enables Internet users to quickly visit their offices.**

Each member of Congress has a Web
page that enables Internet users to visit
their offices and become acquainted with
their work and their staffs. You'll find
online linkages to their sites through the main House (*www.house.gov*)
and Senate (*www.senate.gov*) Web sites.

The Washington-based personal staffs are organized to perform
several functions for representatives. Research and subject matter
specialists work closely with the Representative in the legislative arena.
They follow legislation, conduct research, and draft bills. Other members
of the staff function as ombudsmen, responding primarily to constituent
inquiries and interest groups. And still others specialize in promoting the
present image and future reelection of their boss and performing general
housekeeping functions. An experienced Administrative Assistant, or
AA, heads this staff.

Many personal staffs operate similar to boiler-room operations. Office
space is extremely limited, work loads are unrealistic, most jobs are
understaffed, and much of the work is reactive in nature. Little time is
available for long-term planning and thoughtful analysis. Recent management studies of congressional staffs conducted by the Congressional
Management Foundation found congressional staffs in the following
situation:

- Congressional workloads have grown dramatically during the past two decades:

- The pay gap between Congressional staff salaries and federal government employees continues to grow with House salaries lagging 16 percent and Senate salaries lagging 33 percent behind their executive branch counterparts.

- High turnover rates continue for most staff positions, with average tenure being under three years for personnel in current positions.

- Women hold 56 percent of all congressional staff positions, and the pay gap between male and female staffers continues to narrow (women earn nearly 90 percent of what males earn).

- Office working conditions are less than optimal—crowded and extremely noisy, cramped with paper and files, and subject to occasional electrical failures.

Given the nature of the work, working conditions, and salaries, it's not surprising that there's nearly a 40 percent turnover rate of congressional staffers each year and that many congressional offices have difficulty recruiting qualified staff members with Hill experience.

The Washington personal staffs are comprised of different types of individuals who perform various legislative and administrative-management functions. The figure on page 188 outlines the typical hierarchical structure of these personal staffs. The exact titles of staff members will vary from office to office. For example, an "Executive Assistant" may be called a "Scheduler" or a "Legislative Assistant" may be called "Personal Staff."

Major congressional staff positions include the following:

- **Administrative Assistant/Executive Assistant (AA) or Chief of Staff:** The key staff person who is responsible for overall office functions, supervision of projects, district and Hill politics and personnel. Salary ranges: $65,000-$135,000 (average is around $95,000). Senate AA's or Chief of Staffs on average earn about $25,000 a year more than their counterparts in the House.

HIERARCHY OF PERSONAL
STAFF POSITIONS

ADMINISTRATIVE STAFF
- **Washington:**
  —Office Manager
  —Scheduler
  —Personal Assistant
  —System Administrator
  —Correspondence Assistant
- **Home District:**
  —District Office Rep.
  —Receptionist

CONSTITUENT SERVICES
- Case Worker
- Grants Specialist
- Mobile Office Operator

LEGISLATIVE STAFF
- Legislative Director
- Legislative Assistant
- Researchers

COMPUTER SERVICES
- Computer Operator
- Legislative Correspondent

OTHER STAFF
- Press Secretary
- Special Projects
- Interns

ADMINISTRATIVE ASSISTANT

MEMBER

SOURCE: Based on Kerry Dumbaugh and Gary Serota, *Capitol Jobs*
          Washington, DC: Tilden Press, 1982), p. 47

- **Legislative Director (LD):** Directs legislative program or manages the Member's committee work, including committee prep work for hearings, witnesses, testimony, and legislative proposals, as well as general issues, oversights, and initiatives, floor work, and much more. Salary range: $40,000-$110,000 (average is around $70,000). Legislative Directors in the Senate average about $30,000 more than their counterparts in the House.

- **Legislative Assistant:** Assists the LA with legislative matters. Salary range: $27,000-$90,000+ (average is around $40,000). LA's in the Senate earn about $15,000 more than their counterparts in the House.

- **Legislative Correspondent:** Primarily responsible for responding to correspondence from constituents. Salary range: $15,000-$45,000 (average is around $24,000). The average salary difference between Senate and House Legislative Corepondence is only about $1,000.

- **Press Secretary/Communications Director:** Directs publicity for Member/Senator by issuing press releases, radio and TV spots, newsletters, newspaper columns, speeches, schedule announcements, etc. Salary range: $20,000-$115,000 (average is around $50,000). Average salary difference between Senate and House is about $20,000.

- **Federal Grants Assistant/Projects Coordinator:** Responsible for obtaining federal financial assistance for the home district by helping local government entities and hometown applicants to obtain funds. Provides information on programs, deadlines, helpful agency officials, and general clarification of decisions. Salary range: $10,000-$70,000 (average is around $42,000). Average salary difference between Senate and House is about $5,000.

- **State/District Caseworker:** Handles constituent casework: initial problem identification, contacts with agencies, follow- up letters, and case resolution. Salary range: $13,000-$60,000 (average is around $30,000).Average salary difference between Senate and House is about $3,000.

As you can see from the salary range figures, salaries can vary tremendously for the same positions. Certain positions, such as a Press Secretary, that appear to be low paying may indeed be an excellent paying position in some Senator's or Representative's offices.

The Administrative Assistant (AA), or Chief of Staff, is a very prestigious position requiring a great deal of management and political expertise. This individual, as well as most other staff members, may or may not be from the Representative's district or Senator's state. Rather, staff members tend to be hired on the basis of their legislative expertise and political skills in Washington rather than on their loyalty to the district back home. The most important expertise involves the ability to conduct research, analyze, write, communicate, organize, meet deadlines, and work under extreme pressure. Writing is one of the most highly valued skills. You can quickly acquire subject matter expertise if you already possess these communication skills.

> **Getting a job on a Senator's or Representative's personal staff requires a great deal of persistence, perseverance, and luck.**

Getting a job on a Senator's or Representative's personal staff requires a great deal of persistence, perseverance, and luck. While there is a high turnover rate, there also is high competition for these staff positions. Some offices will receive 1,000 resumes for a single vacancy. They regularly receive unsolicited resumes from job seekers who "shotgun" Capitol Hill with their paper qualifications. Many individuals wish to work for a particular Representative and thus they continually monitor staff vacancies in one office. Others are eager to work anywhere on the "Hill" so they can get experience to strengthen their resume and make important contacts.

While there are several congressional placement services available to help job seekers circulate their resumes, your best job search strategy will be to make personal contacts with key people on the Hill. You must plug into the word-of-mouth networks. The key person you need to know—the one who normally has the power to hire—is the Administrative Assistant. Above all, research individual staff offices to identify impending vacancies and to determine who has the power to hire. The high turnover rate on Capitol Hill virtually assures that hiring will be done on ad hoc, emergency bases. The more you can get into the networks to let people know about your interests, skills, abilities, and availability, the better your chances of getting a job.

If you don't know someone to start networking on Capitol Hill, at least contact your Representative. His or her staff should, as a courtesy to a constituent, get you started by providing you with useful advice on how to initiate a "Capitol Hill" search. They may give you names of people to talk to and review your resume for future reference. At the same time, you can use the "cold turkey" approach: call a Representative's office and pointblank ask *"Who makes the hiring decisions in this office?"* Once you get this information, try to get an appointment to see this person. If you can't get an appointment, try someone else on the staff who will at least give you information and job leads. The easiest way to make staff contacts is to initially visit the Web sites of each member of Congress. Many of these sites include the names of key staff members

> **The high turnover rate on Capitol Hill virtually assures that hiring will be done on ad hoc, emergency bases.**

and their relevant responsibilities. As noted earlier, you can quickly find the Web addresses of all House and Senate members on these two URLs: *www.house.gov* and *www.senate.gov*

Since you do not have to be from a Representative's district to get a personal staff job, 535 personal staffs offer similar job opportunities for you. Given the lack of a central personnel office for these staff positions, your most effective job search strategy will involve networking. You must contact individual offices to identify job vacancies and advertise your qualifications. The Washington-based positions are biased toward individuals who are physically present in Washington and who can make the necessary networking telephone calls and personal visits. However, you also can conduct a long-distance job search via the Web.

Your job search will go much easier if you know someone who knows a member Congress. This person, in turn, can give you an introduction and recommendation. Using this contact, you can call a Representative's office and ask to speak to the AA or his or her assistant. You want to conduct several informational and referral interviews. Mention that Mr. or Ms. Smith *"recommended that I contact you concerning possible staff vacancies on Capitol Hill."* Ask for an appointment to discuss your interests. Be sure to make this a general request for information rather than ask for a job on the AA's staff. Chances are there are no vacancies at present, but the AA and other staff members often know about vacancies on others' staffs. When a vacancy does arise, it is frequently filled through word-of-mouth referrals. If you happen to be in the right place at the right time, you may be considered for the position.

Since the job search on Capitol Hill primarily involves networking, it will take time, and you can expect numerous deadends and rejections. However, you must continue networking until your timing is right in relation to unexpected vacancies. Remember, competition for Capitol Hill positions is very keen. When you land a job, most likely it will occur unexpectedly because the hiring process is somewhat unpredictable.

Committee Staff

The bulk of Congresses' work is done through various committees: standing, select, joint, and ad hoc. Standing committees are permanent committees with full time professional staffs. These staff members conduct research, write reports, and draft legislation for committee members. The committees also are subdivided into subcommittees which have their own staffs. Altogether, there are more than 300 committees and subcommittees in both the House and Senate. The major committees include:

- Agriculture
- Appropriations
- Armed Services
- Banking, Finance, and Urban Affairs
- Budget
- District of Columbia
- Education and Labor
- Energy and Commerce
- Foreign Affairs
- Government Operations
- House Administration
- Judiciary
- Merchant Marine and Fisheries
- Natural Resources
- Post Office and Civil Service
- Public Works and Transportation

- Rules
- Science, Space, and Technology
- Small Business
- Standards of Official Conduct
- Veterans' Affairs
- Ways and Means

The Senate has similar committees, subcommittees, and task forces as well as several Select and Joint Committees with the House, and a variety of Boards, Commissions, and Advisory Organizations; many have their own staffs as well as functioning subcommittees. The House and Senate Web sites include information on these committees and subcommittees.

As we go to press, several of these committees, subcommittees, boards, commissions, and advisory organizations are undergoing restructuring or are being eliminated. For information on the structure of the current Congress, visit the House and Senate Web sites or consult the latest editions of the *Congressional Directory, Congressional Yellow Book,* and the *Congressional Staff Directory.*

> **Professionalism, along with politics, play key roles in getting committee and subcommittee positions.**

Committee and subcommittee work is both interesting and hectic. Many staff members receive a great deal of job satisfaction because they help formulate important legislation. At the same time, these jobs involve long hours attendant with unrealistic work loads and deadlines.

Since each committee and subcommittee focuses on a particular policy area, many of these professional positions require highly qualified subject matter specialists. While many members of personal staffs are young and inexperienced generalists, in contrast, committee and subcommittee staff members tend to be older and experienced specialists. Committee and subcommittee staff positions also tend to pay better than personal staff positions.

Similar to finding a job on a personal staff, getting a job on a committee or subcommittee staff requires a great deal of networking, persistence, and perseverance. There are no formal hiring procedures, and hiring practices will differ from one committee to another. Therefore, you need to do a great deal of research on each committee and subcommittee in determining the best job search strategies.

Professionalism, along with politics, play key roles in getting committee and subcommittee positions. The most important hiring individual is the Chair of the committee or subcommittee. If the Chair is a Republican, the committee and subcommittee staff members will most likely be Republicans. If the chair shifts from a Republican to a Democrat, the staff too will change. Therefore, entry into these positions begins with the Chair of the committee or subcommittee.

When conducting a job search with these committees and subcommittees, it is best to start with the committee or subcommittee chairperson's AA. This individual usually will be responsible for staffing his or her bosses' committee or subcommittee. Use a similar networking approach as you would use in landing a personal staff position. Research the committee or subcommittee, try to get a contact to the Chair, contact the AA for an informational interview, and request information, advice, and referrals to this Senator's or Representative's committees or subcommittees. If you have sufficient subject matter expertise, are persistent, and indicate a political preference, you will be in a strong position for landing one of these jobs.

Changing the Guard

One of the best times to conduct a "Capitol Hill" job search is immediately following a congressional election. Indeed, given the relatively high turnover rates of House and Senate members these days, job opportunities on Capitol Hill are numerous. Newly elected members need to quickly form a staff in Washington. Should House and Senate majority control shift from one political party to another—as happened in the historic congressional elections of November 1994—numerous job vacancies will arise amongst the various committees and subcommittees. Indeed, nearly 3,000 Democratic staffers lost their jobs in the November 1994 elections—the highest turnover in such positions in over 40 years. The 1994 elections created a job hunter's paradise for Republicans interested in personal and committee staff positions. Hundreds of long-time Democratic staffers quickly joined the unemployment lines. Those who found jobs in the new 104th Congress faced a congressional political feeding frenzy to cutback committee staffs and reduce staff salaries. This was not the best of times to find a job on Capitol Hill!

If you closely monitor congressional elections and identify newly elected members, you should be able to locate individuals who have immediate staffing needs. Although they will bring a few of their district-level campaign workers and loyalists to Washington for key staff positions, members of Congress must recruit many of their staffers from among the pool of applicants based in Washington.

Your best strategy is to call the newly elected Senator's or Representative's office as soon as you learn of their election. Your goal should be to arrange an interview rather than send a resume. After all, the Senator or Representative may receive hundreds of unsolicited resumes from past and present Capitol Hill staffers who are either losing their jobs because of election defeat or are looking for greener, and less stressful, pastures.

Useful Resources

In addition to the Web sites noted earlier, several useful print resources are available to guide you through the congressional maze. You should begin by reading a wonderful insider's guide to finding a job on Capitol Hill:

Capitol Hill: An Insider's Guide to Finding a Job in Congress, Kerry Dumbaugh and Gary Serota (1984)

Although now out of print and very dated, you may be able to find a copy of this book in a few libraries. This book is both a primer on the internal structure of Congress and a how-to guide to pulling the right strings. It includes a wealth of useful information, including tips on "Hill speak," networking strategies, and names and addresses of bars and restaurants most frequented by congressional staffers.

After orienting yourself with *Capitol Jobs*, you should begin targeting your job search on various personal, committee, or subcommittee staffs. Our companion volume—*The Directory of Federal Jobs and Employers* (Impact Publications)—includes the names, addresses, and phone numbers of key contacts in Congress. In addition to this book, you may want to consult the latest editions of the following directories for the names, addresses, and telephone numbers of key representatives, staff people, and committees and subcommittees:

- *The American Almanac of Politics*
- *Congressional Yellow Book*
- *Congressional Staff Directory*
- *Congressional Directory*

The House and Senate also publish telephone directories which you should consult: *United States Senate Telephone Directory* and *Telephone Directory: United States House of Representatives*. Costing between $15 and $20, both directories can be purchased directly from the U.S. Government Printing Office, Washington, DC 20402.

You may wish to leave a copy of your resume with the non-partisan **congressional placement offices**. These offices provide job application, interview, and referral services for both personal staff and committee positions. The House Office of Human Resources is located at 263 Cannon Office Building, Washington, DC 20515-6610. For information on House job vacancies and its Resume Referral Service, call 202/226-6731 for a recorded message. You'll be instructed to mail or fax (202/226-0098) your resume and cover letter, along with salary requirements, to the House Office of Human Resources. If you choose to enter your resume in the Resume Referral Service, it will remain in the database for three months. After three months, you'll need to send an updated resume to get re-entered into the database. The Resume Referral Service assists personal and committee staffs in identifying quality personnel. For example, if a House member or Committee Staff needs a particular type of employee, it may contact this office for information on applicants. The office, in turn, will refer candidates to the appropriate staff.

The Senate Placement Office is located in the Hart Senate Office Building, Room 142, Washington, DC 20510. Similar to the House Placement Office, this office operates on a walk-in basis. Interviewing hours are 10am to 12noon and 1pm to 3pm, Monday through Thursday. On Friday this office is open 10am to 12noon and from 1pm to 2pm. This office primarily interviews individuals to identify interests and then refers them to the proper hiring officials with the Senators' and Staff's offices. For more information, call 202/224-9167. This office also operates a Job Hotline at 202/228-JOBS.

Please keep in mind that these offices are not designed to find you a job. Providing assistance only in the form of testing and referrals, these placement offices primarily collect resumes and forward them upon request to various offices which already have numerous unsolicited resumes. They can give you useful tips on the recruitment process on Capitol Hill. Therefore, it does not hurt to cover all bases by contacting these offices and getting your resume in their files.

The Congressional Management Foundation (CMF) monitors personnel developments on Capitol Hill. Every two years it publishes a survey of job descriptions and salaries with congressional offices as well as conducts numerous seminars for Hill staffs. Its two major publications include:

- *House Staff Employment: Salaries, Tenure, Demographics and Benefits* (new edition for 1998)

- *Senate Staff Employment: Salaries, Tenure, Demographics and Benefits* (new edition for 1999)

They also publish a useful manual for Capitol Hill interns: *A Congressional Intern Handbook.* You can contact them at:

> Congressional Management Foundation
> 513 Capitol Court, NE, Suite 300
> Washington, DC 20002
> Tel. 202/546-0100

You also may want to visit their Web site: *www.cmfweb.org.* This site includes an online bookstore with CMF publications. If you click onto the House and Senate employment reports, you can access summaries of salary information and staffing trends for most congressional staff positions.

Two other resources provide useful financial information on various staff positions. *The Report of the Clerk of the House*, published quarterly, provides details on the financial structure of each Representative's office. This document will give you all the information you need for researching House salaries. You can get a copy from the House Document Room which is located in Room H226 of the Capitol Building. A similar document, *The Report of the Secretary of the Senate*, is available on Senate staff salaries. It is free for the asking through the Senate Documents Room (Room B04) in the Hart Senate Office Building.

A variety of other publications are available on various aspects of Congress. Before venturing into this arena, you should have a thorough understanding of the structure and functions of the House and Senate. Your local library should have such basic reference works as the *Congressional Directory*, *Congressional Staff Directory*, and the *Congres-*

sional Yellow Book. They also should have the ***Congressional Quarter-ly***, ***The Almanac of American Politics***, and several books on how Congress works and how to lobby Congress. The lobbying books are especially useful, because they are written in a how-to format. They reveal the internal structure of congressional organizations and outline useful strategies for influencing each organization—strategies which can be directly adapted to your job search. You, in effect, want to "lobby" congressional organizations with your resume, experience, and skills.

The Judiciary

The judicial branch, the fastest growing branch of government, consists of the Supreme Court, a variety of U.S. Courts, and supporting organizations. Altogether, these organizations employed 31,092 individuals in May, 1998, which represents a 116 percent increase in personnel since September 1980. While employment with the Supreme Court only increased by 14 percent during this same period—from 336 to 383—most of the increase took place outside Washington, DC in the U.S. Courts. These courts went from 14,847 employees in September 1980 to 30,709 in May 1998.

Finding employment within the judiciary is similar to finding employment in the legislative branch—networking and direct application. And similar to other branches of government, the judiciary is highly wired via the Internet. You can access a great deal of information on the court system as well as job vacancies by examining their two gateway sites to the judiciary:

www.uscourts.gov
www.fjc.gov

To go directly to employment opportunities, with vacancy announcements and application procedures, visit:

www.uscourts.gov/employment/opportunity.html

The Supreme Court is a relatively small organization with only 383 employees. Court employees consist of the Clerk of the Court, Marshall, Reporter of Decisions, Press Officer, Librarian and their staffs as well as messengers and security officers. These individuals are appointed by the

Court. Law clerks, on the other hand, are appointed by the Justices.

The Clerk of the Court has the largest staff, consisting of more than 30 individuals. The Marshall of the Court is responsible for seating arrangements, paying the Justices' salaries, and dispersing court funds. The Reporter of Decisions has general editing, printing, and publication responsibilities relevant to court opinions. The Press Officer provides public information. The Librarian is responsible for maintaining a 250,000 volume library. Messengers are selected by the Marshall of the Court; they replaced the former page system and work directly with the Justices. Four law clerks provide staff assistance to each Justice.

Several other individuals and groups work directly with the court, but they are not court employees. These consist of:

- **Office of Solicitor General:** The third highest ranking Department of Justice official who is responsible for representing the federal government before the Court.

- **Supreme Court Bar:** Admits 6,000 individuals to the Supreme Court Bar each year.

- **U.S. Judicial Conference:** The "Board of Trustees" for the federal judicial system. Receives staff assistance from the Administrative Office of the U. S. Courts.

- **Administrative Office of the U.S. Courts:** Supervises the administration, salaries, and benefits of federal court support personnel—except the Supreme Court. Prepares and submits budgets of all U.S. district courts as well as the 11 circuit courts of appeal. The Washington, DC staff consists of over 650 employees. Contact the Human Resources Division at 202/273-1270 for information concerning jobs in the court system. For information on jobs with the Administrative Office of the U.S. Courts, call 202/273-2777.

- **Federal Judicial Center:** The research, training, and development arm of the federal judiciary. It has a staff of 128. While they normally advertise vacancies in the *Washington Post* and list vacancies online rather than take phone calls, you can contact them as follows for personnel information: Office of

ADMINISTRATIVE OFFICE OF THE U.S. COURTS

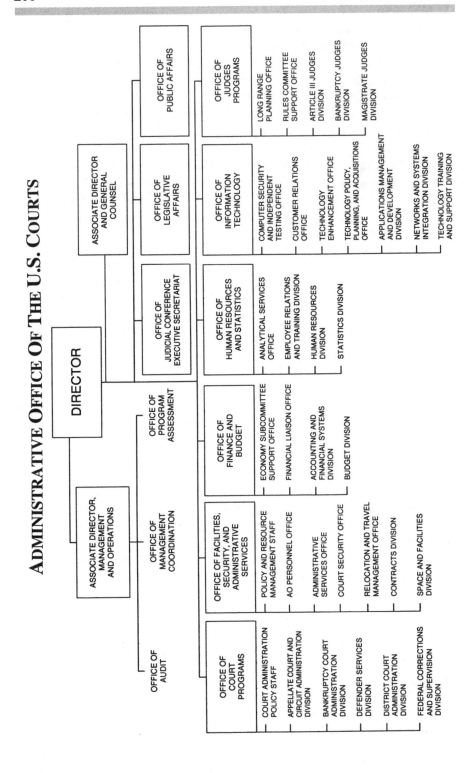

Personnel, Federal Judicial Center, Thurgood Marshall Federal Judiciary Building, One Columbus Circle, NE, Washington, DC 20002, Tel. 202/273-4165 or fax 202/273-4019. The Federal Judicial Center also operates an excellent gateway Web site to the federal judiciary which includes employment information: *www.fjc.gov*

- **Supreme Court Historical Society:** Nonprofit group organized to educate the public about the federal judiciary. It has a staff of 15. Located at 111 Second Street, NE, Washington, DC 20002, you can contact them at 202/543-0400.

- **U.S. Sentencing Commission:** Develops sentencing policies and practices for the federal criminal justice system, including guidelines prescribing the appropriate form and severity of punishment for offenders convicted of federal crimes. You can contact them at the United States Sentencing Commission, Suite 2-500 South Lobby, One Columbus Circle, NE, Washington, DC 20002-8002, Tel. 202/273-4500.

The bulk of job opportunities with the federal judiciary are found among the various lower and special courts located throughout the U.S. Altogether, they employ 30,709 individuals or 98.8 percent of all judicial branch employees. These consist of:

Lower Courts

- U. S. Courts of Appeals (13 judicial circuits) and the U.S. Court of Appeals for the Armed Forces
- U.S. Court of Appeals for the Federal Circuit (before 1982 known as the U.S. Court of Customs and Patent Appeals and the U.S. Court of Claims)
- U.S. District Courts (includes trial courts of general federal jurisdictions and bankruptcy units in each district court—94 U.S. District Courts, including DC and Puerto Rico)

Special Courts

- U.S. Court of Federal Claims
- U.S. Tax Court

- U.S. Court of Veterans Appeals
- United States Court of International Trade
- District of Columbia: Court of Appeals and Superior Court

Each of these courts and organizations employs two types of individuals: legal specialists and administrative support staff.

Finding employment opportunities with the various courts and supporting organizations of the federal judiciary requires a great deal of investigation and networking on your part. Remember, this is the legal field where many positions require formal legal training, law degrees, and bar certification; access to employment tends to follow the "ole boy" system of classmate, alumni, and law firm connections. Job vacancies tend to be announced through the informal word-of-mouth system. Without a law degree, numerous connections, and a link into the word-of-mouth system, you may have difficulty gaining access to many jobs in this arena. On the other hand, these courts and judicial organizations do hire a large number of support personnel through normal hiring channels, including vacancy announcements placed in newspapers and professional publications as well as through law school career planning and placement offices.

> Without a law degree, numerous connections, and a link into the word-of-mouth system, you may have difficulty gaining access to many jobs in this arena.

Nonetheless, enterprising job seekers can gain access by developing a job search particularly geared toward the unique characteristics of the federal judicial system. The first thing you need to do is to understand how the federal judiciary is structured and functions. Good starting points are the gateway Web sites mentioned earlier and *Your Nation's Court Series* which consists of two volumes published by Want Publishing Co. (420 Lexington Ave., Suite 300, New York, NY 10170, Tel. 212/687-3774 or Fax 212/687-3779). The first volume is *Want's Federal-State Court Directory* ($35.00 plus $4.50 shipping). This directory provides an overview of the structure of the court system. If you are interested in state and county court systems, you should get the second volume: *Directory of State Court Clerks and County Courthouses* ($65.00 plus $4.50 shipping). Information on these books is available on the publisher's Web site: *www.wantpublishing.com*

You also may want to call the Supreme Court Public Information Office, United States Supreme Court Building, 1 First Street, NE, Washington, DC 20543, Tel. 202/479-3211, for information on the various judicial organizations. They can refer you to the necessary sources. From there, you should directly contact each judicial organization—both court and support groups—for information and advice. In the case of federal courts outside Washington, DC, contact the court directly as well as the local bar association or law school for information and advice. The Administrative Office of the United States Courts (Washington, DC 20544, Tel. 202/273-1530) will also provide information on the lower courts. Many law schools maintain placement offices which can provide advice on how to best approach the federal circuit and district courts within their geographic area. And don't forget to check with one of the major job search resources focusing on attorneys who are interested in federal employment which we mentioned in Chapter 8 (page 171)—Federal Reports, Inc. (*www.attorneyjobs.com*).

10

Take Effective Action

F inding a federal job fast requires immediate action on your part. In the previous chapters we attempted to provide you with an understanding of how the federal hiring system operates as well as outline useful strategies and contact information that will help you get a job with each branch of the federal government. Now it's time to focus on action and results. You're not finished with this process until you get the job you want.

Organized For Success

While you may be one of the few who lands a federal job within a few days, chances are you will take more time as you methodically develop your SF-171, OF-612, or federal-style resume, research and target agencies, and network for information, advice, and referrals. Our point throughout this book has been to organize yourself for success rather than quit prematurely because of some mistaken belief that the federal hiring process is very complicated, time consuming, and slow. It can be for those who don't know what they are doing and thus waste a great deal of time using ineffective approaches to getting a federal job. No longer do you need to be a part of this tradition of frustration and ineffectiveness.

Understanding without action is a waste of time. And buying a how-to book without implementing it is a waste of money. Many people read how-to books, attend how-to seminars, and do nothing other than read more books, attend more seminars, and engage in more wishful thinking. While these activities become forms of therapy for some individuals, they should lead to positive actions for you. If you want a federal job, you must take action to land a job that is right for you.

> **Understanding without action is a waste of time. And buying a how-to book without implementing it is a waste of money.**

From the very beginning of this book we stressed the importance of understanding how the federal job market operates in both theory and practice as well as developing appropriate job search strategies linked to specific agencies for getting the job you want. We make no assumptions nor claim any magic is contained in this book. Rather, we have attempted to assemble useful information to help individuals realistically approach the federal job market. We have done our part in getting you to the implementation stage. What happens next is your responsibility.

Motivated For Success

Assuming you have a firm understanding of how to get a federal job, what do you do next? The next steps involve **hard work**. Just how motivated are you to seek a federal job? Our experience is that individuals need to be sufficiently **motivated** to make the first move and do it properly. If you go about your job search half-heartedly—you just want to "test the federal waters"—to see what's out there—don't expect to be successful. You must be committed to achieving specific goals. Make the decision to properly develop and implement your job search and be prepared to work hard in achieving your goals.

Once you've convinced yourself to take the necessary steps to find a federal job, you need to find the **time** to properly implement your job search. The sooner you do this, the faster you will find a federal job. This requires setting aside specific blocks of time for identifying your skills, developing your application, writing letters, making telephone calls, and conducting the necessary research and networking required for success. If you are a busy person, like most of us, you simply must make the time.

Practice your own versions of time management or cutback management. Get better organized, give some things up, or cut back on all your activities. If, for example, you can set aside one hour each day to devote to your job search, you will spend seven hours a week or 28 hours a month on your search. However, you should and can find more time than this for these activities.

Time and again we find successful job hunters are ones who routinize a job search schedule and keep at it. They make contact after contact, conduct numerous informational interviews, submit many applications, and keep repeating these activities in spite of rejections. Success is just a few more "nos" and informational interviews away!

You may find it useful to commit yourself in writing to achieving job search success. This is a very useful way to get both motivated and directed for action. Start by completing the job search contract on page 207 and keep it near you—in your briefcase or on your desk.

In addition, you should complete weekly performance reports. These reports identify what you actually accomplished rather than what your good intentions were. Make copies of the performance and planning report form on page 208 and use one each week to track your actual progress and to plan your activities for the next week.

If you fail to meet these written commitments, issue yourself a revised and updated contract. But if you do this three or more times, we strongly suggest you stop kidding yourself about your motivation and commitment to find a federal job fast. Start over again, but this time find a friend or consult a professional career counselor who can provide you with the necessary structure to make progress in finding a job.

We wish you well as you navigate through the sea of agencies, programs, and people that make up the sprawling federal government complex. If you approach this decentralized hiring process with an excellent application (SF-171, OF-612, or federal-style resume) and a well organized job search that targets particular agencies, you should indeed find a federal job fast!

JOB SEARCH CONTRACT

1. I will begin my job search on _____.

2. I will involve _____ with my job search.
   (individual/group)

3. I will complete my skills identification step by _____.

4. I will complete my objective statement by _____.

5. I will complete my application by _____.

6. Each week I will:

   ■ make ___ new job contacts.

   ■ conduct ___ informational interviews.

   ■ follow-up on ___ referrals.

7. My first job interview will take place during the week of
   _____.

8. I will begin my new federal job on _____.

9. I will manage my time so that I can successfully complete my
   job search and find a high quality job.

   Signature: _____

   Date: _____

Weekly Job Search Performance And Planning Report

1. The week of: _____.

2. This week I:

   - wrote __ job search letters.
   - sent __ applications to agencies.
   - made __ job search telephone calls.
   - completed __ hours of job research.
   - set up __ appointments for informational interviews.
   - conducted __ informational interviews.
   - received __ invitations to a job interview.
   - followed up on __ contacts and __ referrals.

3. Next week I will:

   - write __ job search letters.
   - submit __ applications to potential employers.
   - make __ job search telephone calls.
   - complete __ hours of job research.
   - set up __ appointments for informational interviews.
   - conduct __ informational interviews.
   - follow up on __ contacts and __ referrals.

4. Summary of progress this week in reference to my Job Search Contract commitments:

   _____

   _____

   _____

   _____

Appendix A

Federal Employment Information Sources

As we noted in Chapter 6 (pages 106-108), the Federal Employment Information System is available in both on-line and off-line versions. If you use the Internet, you can access a wealth of information on the employment process, vacancy announcements, and agencies by visiting a variety of sites which we outline in Chapters 8 and 9 and in Appendix B. If you do not use the Internet, you can call or fax several numbers or visit the special kiosks which have Touch Screen Computers. The following locations have kiosks with Touch Screen Computers that enable users to survey current federal job opportunities and request application packages.

ALABAMA: Huntsville
520 Wynn Dr., NW.

ALASKA: Anchorage
Federal Bldg., 222 W. 7th Ave.
Rm. 156

ARIZONA: Phoenix
VA Medical Center
650 E. Indian School Rd.
Bldg. 21, Rm. 141

ARKANSAS: Little Rock
Federal Bldg., 700 W. Capitol
1st Floor Lobby

CALIFORNIA: Sacramento
801 I ("I") St.

COLORADO: Denver
Dept. of Social Services
Employment Center
2200 West Alameda Avenue, #5B

CONNECTICUT: Hartford
Federal Bldg., 450 Main St., Lobby

DISTRICT OF COLUMBIA:
Washington, DC, Theodore Roosevelt
Federal Bldg., 1900 E St., NW.
Rm. 1416

FLORIDA: Miami
Downtown Jobs and Benefits Center
Florida Job Service Center
401 NW. 2nd Ave., Suite N-214

Orlando
Florida Job Service Center, 1001
Executive Center Dr., First Floor

GEORGIA: Atlanta
Richard B. Russell Federal Bldg.
Main Lobby, Plaza Level
75 Spring St., SW.

HAWAII: Honolulu
Federal Bldg., Rm. 5316
300 Ala Moana Blvd.

Fort Shafter
Department of Army, Army
Civilian Personnel Office
Army Garrison, Bldg. T-1500

ILLINOIS: Chicago
77 West Jackson Blvd.
1st Floor Lobby

INDIANA: Indianapolis
Minton-Capehart Federal Bldg.
575 N. Pennsylvania St., Rm. 339

LOUISIANA: New Orleans
Federal Bldg., 423 Canal Street
1st Floor Lobby

MAINE: Augusta
Federal Office Bldg.
40 Western Ave.

MARYLAND: Baltimore
George H. Fallon Bldg., Lombard St.
and Hopkins Plaza, Lobby

MASSACHUSETTS: Boston
Thomas P. O'Neill, Jr., Federal
Bldg., 10 Causeway St., 1st Floor

MICHIGAN: Detroit
477 Michigan Ave., Rm. 565

MINNESOTA: Twin Cities
Bishop Henry Whipple Federal
Bldg., 1 Federal Dr., Rm. 501
Ft. Snelling

MISSOURI: Kansas City
Federal Bldg., 601 E. 12th St.
Rm. 134

NEW HAMPSHIRE: Portsmouth
Thomas McIntyre Federal Bldg.
80 Daniel St., 1st Floor Lobby

NEW JERSEY: Newark
Peter J. Rodino Federal Bldg., 970
Broad St., 2nd Floor near Cafeteria

NEW MEXICO: Albuquerque
New Mexico State Job Service
501 Mountain Rd. NE., Lobby

NEW YORK: Albany
Leo W. O'Brian Federal Bldg.
Clinton Ave. & North Pearl
Basement Level

Buffalo
Thaddeus T. Dulski Federal Bldg.
111 West Huron St., 9th Floor

New York City
Jacob K. Javits Federal Bldg.
26 Federal Plaza, Lobby

New York City
World Trade Center, Cafeteria

Syracuse
James M. Hanley Federal Bldg.
100 S. Clinton St.

OHIO: Dayton
Federal Bldg., 200 W. 2nd St.
Rm. 509

OKLAHOMA: Oklahoma City
Career Connection Center
7401 NE. 23rd St.

OREGON: Portland
Federal Bldg., Rm. 376
1220 SW. Third Ave.

    Bonneville Power Admin.
    905 NE 11th Ave.

    Dept. of Army & Corps of
    Engineers, Duncan Plaza

PENNSYLVANIA: Harrisburg
Harrisburg Federal Bldg.
228 Walnut St., Rm. 168

    Philadelphia
    William J. Green, Jr.
    Federal Bldg.
    600 Arch St., 2nd Floor

    Pittsburgh Federal Bldg.
    1000 Liberty Ave.
    1st Floor Lobby

    Reading
    Reading Postal Service
    2100 N. 13th St.

PUERTO RICO: San Juan
U.S. Federal Bldg.
150 Carlos Chardon Ave., Rm. 328

RHODE ISLAND: Providence
380 Westminster, Mall Lobby

TENNESSEE: Memphis
Naval Air Station Memphis
Transition Assistance Center
7800 3rd Ave., Bldg.
South 239, Millington

TEXAS: Dallas
Federal Bldg., 1st Floor Lobby
1100 Commerce St.

    El Paso
    Federal Bldg., 700 East San
    Antonio St., Lobby

    Houston
    Mickey Leland Federal Bldg.
    1919 Smith St., 1st Floor Lobby

    San Antonio
    Federal Bldg., 1st Floor Lobby
    727 East Durango

UTAH: Salt Lake City
Utah State Job Service
720 South 2nd East, Reception Area

VERMONT: Burlington
Federal Bldg., 11 Elmwood Ave.
1st Floor Lobby

VIRGINIA: Norfolk
Federal Bldg., 200 Granby St.

WASHINGTON: Seattle
Federal Bldg., 915 Second Ave.
Rm. 110

WASHINGTON, DC: Theodore
Roosevelt Federal Bldg.
1900 E St., NW., Rm. 1416

    The federal government also maintains a nationwide automated phone system (*Career America Connection*) which operates 24-hours a day, 7 days a week. If you call these numbers, you'll be able to access information on current employment opportunities (nationwide and worldwide); special programs for students, veterans, and people with disabilities; the

Presidential Management Intern Program; and salaries and benefits. You also can request application materials. Call the number nearest you:

ALABAMA, Huntsville
205-837-0894

CALIFORNIA, San Francisco
415-744-5627

COLORADO, Denver
303-969-7050

DISTRICT OF COLUMBIA,
Washington
202-606-2700

GEORGIA, Atlanta
404-331-4315

HAWAII, Honolulu
808-541-2791

ILLINOIS, Chicago
312-353-6192

MICHIGAN, Detroit
313-226-6950

MINNESOTA, Twin Cities
612-725-3430

MISSOURI, Kansas City
816-426-5702

NORTH CAROLINA, Raleigh
919-790-2822

OHIO, Dayton
937-225-2720

PENNSYLVANIA, Philadelphia
215-597-7440

TEXAS, San Antonio
210-805-2402

VIRGINIA, Norfolk
757-441-3355

WASHINGTON, Seattle
206-553-0888

**or, FROM ANYWHERE IN THE
NATION OR THE WORLD**
912-757-3000

NATIONWIDE TDD SERVICE
912-744-2299

To use the **FedFax System**, which provides employment information and forms by fax 24-hours a day, 7 days a week, use these numbers:

Atlanta	404/331-5267
Denver	303/969-7764
Detroit	313/226-2593
San Francisco	415/744-7002
Washington, DC	202/606-2600

Appendix B

Key Web Sites

As we've noted throughout this book, the federal government is highly wired via the Internet. Information on agency operations, vacancy announcements, and application procedures can be easily accessed through several gateway Web sites as well as individual agency sites. Also, be sure to check out several extra-governmental sites that focus on federal government operations, such as professional associations and publishers specializing in federal employment resources.

Federal Government Gateway Sites

- Federal government:

  www.whitehouse.gov
  www.fedworld.gov
  www.usajobs.opm.gov
  http://eden.cs.umass.edu/govbot
  www.law.vill.edu/fed-agency/fedwebloc.html

- Legislature:

  www.thomas.loc.gov

  – Senate:
  – House:

  www.senate.gov
  www.house.gov

- Judiciary:

  www.uscourt.gov
  www.fjc.gov

213

Executive Branch

Cabinet Departments

- Agriculture   *www.usda.gov*
- Commerce   *www.doc.gov*
- Defense   *www.dtic.mil*
  – Army   *www.army.mil*
  – Navy   *www.ncts.navy.mil*
  – Air Force   *www.af.mil*
- Education   *www.ed.gov*
- Energy   *www.doe.gov*
- Health and Human Services   *www.os.dhhs.gov*
- Housing and Urban Development   *www.hud.gov*
- Interior   *www.doi.gov*
- Justice   *www.usdoj.gov*
- Labor   *www.dol.gov*
- State   *www.state.gov*
- Transportation   *www.dot.gov*
- Treasury   *www.ustres.gov*
- Veterans Affairs   *www.va.gov*

Agencies, Commissions, Boards, Corporations

- Agency For International Development   *www.info.usaid.gov*
- Arms Control and Disarmament Agency   *www.acda.gov*
- Central Intelligence Agency (CIA)   *www.odci.gov*
- Commodity Futures Trading Commission   *www.cftc.gov*
- Consumer Product Safety Commission   *www.state.gov*
- Corporation For National Service   *www.cns.gov*
- Defense Intelligence Agency (DIA)   *www.dia.mil*
- Environmental Protection Agency (EPA)   *www.epa.gov*
- Export-Import Bank   *www.exim.gov*
- Federal Bureau of Investigation (FBI)   *www.fbi.gov*
- Federal Communications Commission   *www.fcc.gov*
- Federal Deposit Insurance Corporation   *www.fdic.gov*
- Federal Election Commission   *www.fec.gov*
- Federal Emergency Management Agency   *www.fema.gov*
- Federal Housing Finance Board   *www.fhfb.gov*
- Federal Reserve System   *www.bog.frb.fed.us*
- Federal Trade Commission   *www.ftc.gov*
- General Services Administration   *www.gsa.gov*
- Merit Protection Board   *www.access.gpo.gov/mspb*
- National Aeronautics & Space Administration   *www.nasa.gov*
- National Archives & Records Administration   *www.nara.gov*

- National Credit Union Administration   *www.ncua.gov*
- National Endowment For the Arts   *http://artsendow.gov*
- National Endowment For the Humanities   *www.nehfed.us*
- National Labor Relations Board   *www.nlrb.gov*
- National Performance Review   *www.npr.gov*
- National Science Foundation   *www.nsf.gov*
- National Security Agency   *www.nsa.gov:8080/*
- National Technology Transfer Center   *www.nttc.edu*
- Nuclear Regulatory Commission   *www.nrc.gov*
- Office of Personnel Management   *www.opm.gov*
- Peace Corps   *www.peacecorps.gov*
- Pension Benefit Guaranty Corporation   *www.pbgc.gov*
- Railroad Retirement Board   *www.rrb.gov*
- Securities & Exchange Commission   *www.sec.gov*
- Selective Service System   *www.sss.gov*
- Small Business Administration   *www.sba.gov*
- Smithsonian Institution   *www.si.edu*
- Social Security Administration   *www.ssa.gov*
- Tennessee Valley Authority   *www.tva.gov*
- U.S. Information Agency   *www.usia.gov*
- U.S. International Trade Commission   *www.usitc.gov*
- U.S. Office of Special Counsel   *www.access.gpo.gov/osc*
- U.S. Postal Service   *www.usps.gov*

Legislature and Legislative Agencies

- U.S. House of Representatives   *www.house.gov*
- U.S. Senate   *www.senate.gov*
- Architect of the Capitol   *www.aoc.gov*
- Congressional Budget Office   *www.cbo.gov*
- General Accounting Office   *www.gao.gov*
- Government Printing Office   *www.access.gpo.gov*
- Library of Congress   *http://lcweb.loc.gov*
- U.S. Botanic Garden   *www.aoc.gov*

Judiciary

- Administrative Office of the U.S. Courts   *www.uscourts.gov*
- Federal Judicial Center   *www.fjc.gov*
- U.S. Sentencing Commission   *www.ussc.gov*

Useful Associations

- American Federation of Govt. Employees   *www.afge.org*
- American Foreign Service Association   *www.afsa.org*
- American Postal Workers Union   *www.apu.org*

- Association of U.S. Army — *www.bignet.org*
- Council For Excellence in Government — *www.excelgov.org*
- Federal Managers Association — *www.fpm.com*
- Federally Employed Women, Inc. — *www.few.org*
- National Air Traffic Controllers Association — *www.natca.org*
- National Association of Govt. Communicators — *www.nagc.com*
- National Association of Letter Carriers — *www.nalc.org*
- National Treasury Employees Union — *www.nteu.org*
- National Weather Service Employees Organization — *www.nwseo.org*
- Retired Officers Association — *www.troa.org*

Publishers

- Bookhaven — *http://members.aol.com/govjobs*
- Breakthrough Publications — *www.jobsfed.com*
- DataTech Software — *www.federaljobs.com*
- Federal Employees' News Digest — *www.fedforce.com*
- Federal Reports, Inc. — *www.attorneyjobs.com*
- Federal Research Service — *www.fedjobs.com*
- Federal Times — *www.federaltimes.com*
- FEDweek — *www.fedweek.com*
- Government Executive Magazine — *www.govexec.com*
- Impact Publications — *www.impactpublications.com*
- Key Communications Group — *www.fedguide.com*
- Planning/Communications — *http://jobfindersonline.com*
- Resume Place, Inc. — *www.resume-place.com*

Appendix C

Sample Application Forms

A s we noted in Chapter 7, the federal government no longer requires the Standard Form 171 (SF-171) when applying for a federal job. While agencies still accept the SF-171, application options now include the OF-612 and federal-style resumes. While other options also are permitted, over 90 percent of agencies accept SF-171s, OF-612s, and federal-style resumes.

The SF-171 is 8½ x 11 inches in size. We've reduced the size for ease of reference on pages 219-224. While OPM no longer prints and distributes the SF-171, you can get a copy online from the FedWorld Information Network (*www.fedworld.gov*). It's also found on DataTech's popular federal application software program, *Quick & Easy Federal Jobs Kit*. Chapter 7 provides information on how to customize this form.

Please refer to this form during our discussion in Chapter 7 on how to complete each item on the SF-171. For a more in-depth discussion of each item, including examples of work statements which include the critical KSAs, refer to *The Right SF-171 Writer* and *The KSA Sampler*. Both workbooks are available through Impact Publications.

The OF-612 form appearing on pages 225-226 includes much of the same information requested on the SF-171. However, most of the background information requested on the SF-171 is not required on the OF-612 form. Most of this information in now requested on the OF-306 (Declaration for Federal Employment) which appears on pages 227-228. While all applicants will need to complete the OF-306 sometime during the application process, they need not do so immediately upon application.

If you elect to use the OF-612, you may want to use continuation sheets that enable you to expand the critical "Work Experience" and "Other Qualifications" sections. These sheets can be purchased separately by acquiring Federal Research Service's *Reinvented Federal Job Application Forms Kit* ($6.95). This kit also includes the SF-171, a sample federal-style resume, the SF-171, continuation sheets for the SF-171, supplemental statement, performance appraisal form, college courses and certification of scholastic achievement form, and a vacancy tracking log form.

For assistance in completing all of these forms, see Russ Smith's book *Federal Applications That Get Results: From SF-171s to Federal-Style Resumes,* and the computer software program (Windows only) produced by DataTech, *Quick and Easy Federal Jobs Kit.* Both products are available through Impact Publications.

If you choose to produce a federal-style resume, we recommend Kathryn K. Troutman's *The Federal Resume Guidebook* which also is available through Impact Publications.

Standard Form 171 Application for Federal Employment

Read The Following Instructions Carefully Before You Complete This Application

- DO NOT SUBMIT A RESUME INSTEAD OF THIS APPLICATION.
- TYPE OR PRINT CLEARLY IN DARK INK.
- IF YOU NEED MORE SPACE for an answer, use a sheet of paper the same size as this page. On each sheet write your name, Social Security Number, the announcement number or job title, and the item number. Attach all additional forms and sheets to this application at the top of page 3.
- If you do not answer all questions fully and correctly, you may delay the review of your application and lose job opportunities.
- Unless you are asked for additional material in the announcement or qualification information, do not attach any materials, such as: official position descriptions, performance evaluations, letters of recommendation, certificates of training, publications, etc. Any materials you attach which were not asked for may be removed from your application and will not be returned to you.
- We suggest that you keep a copy of this application for your use. If you plan to make copies of your application, we suggest you leave items 1, 48 and 49 blank. Complete these blank items each time you apply. YOU MUST SIGN AND DATE, IN INK, EACH COPY YOU SUBMIT.
- To apply for a specific Federal civil service examination (whether or not a written test is required) or a specific vacancy in an Federal agency:
  — Read the announcement and other materials provided.
  — Make sure that your work experience and/or education meet the qualification requirements described.
  — Make sure the announcement is open for the job and location you are interested in. Announcements may be closed to receipt of applications for some types of jobs, grades, or geographic locations.
  — Make sure that you are allowed to apply. Some jobs are limited to veterans, or to people who work for the Federal Government or have worked for the Federal Government in the past.
  — Follow any directions on "How to Apply". If a written test is required, bring any material you are instructed to bring to the test session. For example, you may be instructed to "Bring a completed SF 171 to the test." If a written test is not required, mail this application and all other forms required by the announcement to the address specified in the announcement.

Work Experience *(Item 24)*

- Carefully complete each experience block you need to describe your work experience. Unless you qualify based on education alone, your rating will depend on your description of previous jobs. Do not leave out any jobs you held during the last ten years.
- Under Description of Work, write a clear and brief, but complete description of your major duties and responsibilities for each job. Include any supervisory duties, special assignments, and your accomplishments in the job. We may verify your description with your former employers.
- If you had a major change of duties or responsibilities while you worked for the same employer, describe each major change as a separate job.

Veteran Preference in Hiring *(Item 22)*

- DO NOT LEAVE Item 22 BLANK. If you do not claim veteran preference, place an "X" in the box next to "NO PREFERENCE".
- You cannot receive veteran preference if you are retired or plan to retire at or above the rank of major or lieutenant commander, unless you are disabled or retired from the active military Reserve.
- To receive veteran preference your separation from active duty must have been under honorable conditions. This includes honorable and general discharges. A clemency discharge does not meet the requirements of the Veteran Preference Act.
- Active duty for training in the military Reserve and National Guard programs is not considered active duty for purposes of veteran preference.
- To qualify for preference you must meet ONE of the following conditions:
  1. Served on active duty anytime between December 7, 1941, and July 1, 1955; (If you were a Reservist called to active duty between February 1, 1955 and July 1, 1955, you must meet condition 2, below.)
     or
  2. Served on active duty any part of which was between July 2, 1955 and October 14, 1976 or a Reservist called to active duty between February 1, 1955 and October 14, 1976 and who served for more than 180 days;
     or
  3. Entered on active duty between October 15, 1976 and September 7, 1980 or a Reservist who entered on active duty between October 15, 1976 and October 13, 1982 and received a Campaign Badge or Expeditionary Medal or are a disabled veteran;
     or
  4. Enlisted in the Armed Forces after September 7, 1980 or entered active duty other than by enlistment on or after October 14, 1982 and:
     a. completed 24 months of continuous active duty or the full period called or ordered to active duty, or were discharged under 10 U.S.C. 1171 or for hardship under 10 U.S.C. 1173 and received or were entitled to receive a Campaign Badge or Expeditionary Medal; or
     b. are a disabled veteran.
- If you meet one of the four conditions above, you qualify for 5-point preference. If you want to claim 5-point preference and do not meet the requirements for 10-point preference, discussed below, place an "X" in the box next to "5-POINT PREFERENCE".
- If you think you qualify for 10-Point Preference, review the requirements described in the Standard Form (SF) 15, Application for 10-Point Veteran Preference. The SF 15 is available from any Federal Job Information Center. The 10-point preference groups are:
  — Non-Compensably Disabled or Purple Heart Recipient.
  — Compensably Disabled (less than 30%).
  — Compensably Disabled (30% or more).
  — Spouse, Widow(er) or Mother of a deceased or disabled veteran.
- If you claim 10-point preference, place an "X" in the box next to the group that applies to you. To receive 10-point preference you must attach a completed SF 15 to this application together with the proof requested in the SF 15.

DETACH THIS PAGE—NOTE SF 171-A ON BACK

Application for Federal Employment -- SF 171

Read the instructions before you complete this application. *Type or print clearly in dark ink.*

Form Approved
OMB No. 3206-0012

GENERAL INFORMATION

1 What kind of job are you applying for? *Give Title and announcement no. (if any)*

2 Social Security Number

3 Sex
☐ Male ☐ Female

4 Birth date *(Month, Day, Year)*

5 Birthplace *(City and State or Country)*

6 Name *(Last, First, Middle)*

Mailing address *(include apartment number, if any)*

City   State   ZIP Code

7 Other names ever used *(e.g., maiden name, nickname, etc.)*

8 Home Phone
Area Code | Number

9 Work Phone
Area | Extension

10 Were you ever employed as a civilian by the Federal Government? If **"NO"**, go to **Item 11**. If **"YES"**, mark each type of job you held with an **"X"**.

☐ Temporary ☐ Career-Conditional ☐ Career ☐ Excepted
What is your **highest** grade, classification series and job title?

Dates at **highest** grade: FROM   TO

AVAILABILITY

11 When can you start work? *(Month and Year)*

12 What is the **lowest** pay you will accept? *(You will not be considered for jobs which pay less than you indicate)*

Pay $_____ per _____ OR Grade _____

13 In what geographic area(s) are you willing to work?

14 Are you willing to work:

	YES	NO
A. 40 hours per week *(full-time)*?		
B. 25-32 hours per week *(part-time)*?		
C. 17-24 hours per week *(part-time)*?		
D. 16 or fewer hours per week *(part-time)*?		
E. An intermittent job *(on-call/seasonal)*?		
F. Weekends, shifts, or rotating shifts?		

15 Are you willing to take a temporary job lasting:

A. 5 to 12 months *(sometimes longer)*? ....
B. 1 to 4 months? ....
C. Less than 1 month? ....

16 Are you willing to travel away from home for:

A. 1 to 5 nights each month? ....
B. 6 to 10 nights each month? ....
C. 11 or more nights each month? ....

MILITARY SERVICE AND VETERAN PREFERENCE

17 Have you served in the United States Military Service? *If your only active duty was training in the Reserves or National Guard, answer "NO". If "NO", go to item 22* ....

YES NO

18 Did you or will you retire at or above the rank of major or lieutenant commander? ....

DO NOT WRITE IN THIS AREA

FOR USE OF EXAMINING OFFICE ONLY

Date entered register

Form reviewed:
Form approved:

Option	Grade	Earned Rating	Veteran Preference	Augmented Rating
			☐ No Preference Claimed	
			☐ 5 Points (Tentative)	
			☐ 10 Pts. (30% Or More Comp. Dis.)	
			☐ 10 Pts. (Less Than 30% Comp. Dis)	
			☐ Other 10 Points	

Initials and Date

☐ Disallowed ☐ Being Investigated

FOR USE OF APPOINTING OFFICE

Preference has been verified through proof that the separation was under honorable conditions, and other proof as required.

☐ 5-Point ☐ 10-Point—30% or More Compensable Disability ☐ 10-Point—Less Than 30% Compensable Disability ☐ 10-Point—Other

Signature and Title

Agency   Date

MILITARY SERVICE AND VETERAN PREFERENCE *(Cont.)*

19 Were you discharged from the military service under honorable conditions? *(If your discharge was changed to "honorable" or "general" by a Discharge Review Board, answer "YES". If you received a clemency discharge, answer "NO".)* If **"NO"**, provide below the date and type of discharge you received.

YES NO

Discharge Date *(Month, Day, Year)*	Type of Discharge

20 List the dates *(Month, Day, Year)*, and branch for all **active duty** military service.

From	To	Branch of Service

21 If all your active military duty was after October 14, 1976, list the full names and dates of all campaign badges or expeditionary medals you received or were entitled to receive.

22 **Read the instructions that came with this form before completing this item.** When you have determined your eligibility for veteran preference from the instructions, place an **"X"** in the box next to your veteran preference claim.

☐ NO PREFERENCE

☐ 5-POINT PREFERENCE -- You must show proof when you are hired.

10-POINT PREFERENCE -- If you claim 10-point preference, place an **"X"** in the box below next to the basis for your claim. **To receive 10-point preference you must also complete a Standard Form 15, Application for 10-Point Veteran Preference, which is available from any Federal Job Information Center. ATTACH THE COMPLETED SF 15 AND REQUESTED PROOF TO THIS APPLICATION.**

☐ Non-compensable disabled or Purple Heart recipient.
☐ Compensably disabled, less than 30 percent.
☐ Spouse, widow(er), or mother of a deceased or disabled veteran.
☐ Compensably disabled, 30 percent or more.

THE FEDERAL GOVERNMENT IS AN EQUAL OPPORTUNITY EMPLOYER
PREVIOUS EDITION USABLE UNTIL 12-31-90
Page1

NSN 7540-00-935-7150   171-110

Standard Form 171 (Rev. 6-88)
U.S. Office of Personnel Management
FPM Chapter 295

WORK EXPERIENCE *If you have no work experience, write "NONE" in A below and go to 25 on page 3.*

23 May we ask your present employer about your character, qualifications, and work record? *A "NO" will not affect our review of your qualifications. If you answer "NO" and we need to contact your present employer before we can offer you a job, we will contact you first.* . . . . | YES | NO |

24 READ **WORK EXPERIENCE** IN THE INSTRUCTIONS BEFORE YOU BEGIN.

- Describe your current or most recent job in Block **A** and work backwards, describing each job you held **during the past 10 years**. If you were **unemployed** for longer than **3 months** within the past 10 years, list the dates and your address(es) in an experience block.

- You may sum up in one block work that you did **more than 10 years ago**. But if that work **is related** to the type of job you are applying for, describe each related job in a separate block.

- INCLUDE VOLUNTEER WORK *(non-paid work)*--**If the work** *(or a part of the work)* **is like the job you are applying for,** complete all parts of the experience block just as you would for a paying job. You may receive credit for work experience with religious, community, welfare, service, and other organizations.

- INCLUDE MILITARY SERVICE--You should complete **all** parts of the experience block just as you would for a non-military job, including all supervisory experience. Describe each major change of duties or responsibilities in a separate experience block.

- IF YOU NEED MORE SPACE TO DESCRIBE A JOB--Use sheets of paper the same size as this page (be sure to include **all** information we ask for in **A** and **B** below). On **each** sheet show your name, Social Security Number, and the announcement number or job title.

- IF YOU NEED MORE EXPERIENCE BLOCKS use the SF 171-A or a sheet of paper.

- IF YOU NEED TO UPDATE (ADD MORE RECENT JOBS), use the SF 172 or a sheet of paper as described above.

A | Name and address of employer's organization *(include ZIP Code, if known)* | Dates employed *(give month, day and year)* From: To: | Average number of hours per week | Number of employees you supervise |

| Salary or earnings | Your reason for wanting to leave |
| Starting $ per |
| Ending $ per |

Your immediate supervisor Name | Area Code | Telephone No. | Exact title of your job | If Federal employment *(civilian or military)* list series, grade or rank, and, if promoted in this job, the date of your last promotion

Description of work: Describe your specific duties, responsibilities and accomplishments in this job, **including** the job title(s) of any employees you supervise. *If you describe more than one type of work (for example, carpentry and painting, or personnel and budget), write the approximate percentage of time you spent doing each.*

For Agency Use (skill codes, etc.)

B | Name and address of employer's organization *(include ZIP Code, if known)* | Dates employed *(give month, day and year)* From: To: | Average Number of hours per week | Number of employees you supervised |

| Salary or earnings | Your reason for leaving |
| Starting $ per |
| Ending $ per |

Your immediate supervisor Name | Area Code | Telephone No. | Exact title of your job | If Federal employment *(civilian or military)* list series, grade or rank, and, if promoted in this job, the date of your last promotion

Description of work: Describe your specific duties, responsibilities and accomplishments in this job, **including** the job title(s) of any employees you supervised. *If you describe more than one type of work (for example, carpentry and painting, or personnel and budget), write the approximate percentage of time you spent doing each.*

For Agency Use (skill codes, etc.)

◄──── **ATTACH ANY ADDITIONAL FORMS AND SHEETS HERE**

EDUCATION

25 Did you graduate from high school? *If you have a GED high school equivalency or will graduate within the next nine months, answer "YES".*

26 Write the name and location *(city and state)* of the last high school you attended or where you obtained your GED high school equivalency.

YES	If **"YES"**, give month and year graduated or received GED equivalency: . . . .
NO	If **"NO"** give the highest grade you completed:

27 Have you ever attended college or graduate school?

YES ➤ If **"YES"**, continue with **28**.
NO ➤ If **"NO"**, go to **31**.

28 NAME AND LOCATION *(city, state and ZIP Code)* OF COLLEGE OR UNIVERSITY. *If you expect to graduate within nine months, give the **month** and **year** you expect to receive your degree:*

	Name	City	State	ZIP Code	MONTH AND YEAR ATTENDED From	To	NUMBER OF CREDIT HOURS COMPLETED Semester	Quarter	TYPE OF DEGREE (e.g. B.A., M.A.)	MONTH AND YEAR OF DEGREE
1)										
2)										
3)										

29

CHIEF UNDERGRADUATE SUBJECTS *Show major on the first line*	NUMBER OF CREDIT HOURS COMPLETED Semester	Quarter
1)		
2)		
3)		

30

CHIEF GRADUATE SUBJECTS *Show major on the first line*	NUMBER OF CREDIT HOURS COMPLETED Semester	Quarter
1)		
2)		
3)		

31 If you have completed any **other courses or training related to the kind of jobs you are applying for** *(trade, vocational, Armed Forces, business)* give information below.

NAME AND LOCATION *(city, state and ZIP Code)* OF SCHOOL	MONTH AND ATTENDED From	To	CLASS-ROOM HOURS	SUBJECT(S)	TRAINING COMPLETED YES	NO
School Name 1) City State ZIP Code						
School Name 2) City State ZIP Code						

SPECIAL SKILLS, ACCOMPLISHMENTS AND AWARDS

32 Give the title and year of any honors, awards or fellowships you have received. List your special qualifications, skills or accomplishments that may help you get a job. *Some examples are: skills with computers or other machines; most important publications (do not submit copies); public speaking and writing experience; membership in professional or scientific societies; patents or inventions; etc.*

33 How many words per minute can you: TYPE? TAKE DICTATION?

Agencies may test your skills before hiring you.

34 List **job-related** licenses or certificates that you have, such as: *registered nurse; lawyer; radio operator; driver's; pilot's; etc.*

LICENSE OR CERTIFICATE	DATE OF LATEST LICENSE OR CERTIFICATE	STATE OR OTHER LICENSING AGENCY
1)		
2)		

35 Do you speak or read a language other than English *(include sign language)*? *Applicants for jobs that require a language other than English may be given an interview conducted solely in that language.*

YES ➤ If **"YES"**, list each language and place an **"X"** in each column that applies to you.
NO ➤ If **"NO"**, go to **36**.

LANGUAGE(S)	CAN PREPARE AND GIVE LECTURES Fluently	With Difficulty	CAN SPEAK AND UNDERSTAND Fluently	Passably	CAN TRANSLATE ARTICLES Into English	From English	CAN READ ARTICLES Easily	With Difficulty
1)								
2)								

REFERENCES

36 List three people who are not related to you and are not supervisors you listed under **24** who know your qualifications and fitness for the kind of job for which you are applying. At least **one** should know you well on a personal basis.

FULL NAME OF REFERENCE	TELEPHONE NUMBER(S) *(Include Area Code)*	PRESENT BUSINESS OR HOME ADDRESS *(Number, street and city)*	STATE	ZIP CODE
1)				
2)				
3)				

BACKGROUND INFORMATION--*You must answer each question in this section before we can process your*

			YES	NO
37	Are you a citizen of the United States? (In most cases you must be a U.S. citizen to be hired. You will be required to submit proof identity and citizenship at the time you are hired.) If "NO", give the country or countries you are a citizen of:			

NOTE: **It is important that you give complete and truthful answers to questions 38 through 44.** If you answer **"YES"** to any of them, provide your explanation(s) in Item 45. Include convictions resulting from a plea of nolo contendere (*no contest*). Omit: 1) traffic fines of $100.00 or less; 2) any violation of law committed before your 16th birthday; 3) any violation of law committed before your 18th birthday, if finally decided in juvenile court or under a Youth Offender law; 4) any conviction set aside under the Federal Youth Corrections Act or similar State law; 5) any conviction whose record was expunged under Federal or State law. We will consider the date, facts, and circumstances of each event you list. In most cases you can still be considered for Federal jobs. However, **if you fail to tell the truth or fail to list all relevant events** or circumstances, this may be grounds for not hiring you, for firing you after you begin work, or for criminal prosecution (18 USC 1001).

		YES	NO
38	During the last **10 years**, were you **fired from any job** for any reason, did you **quit after being told that you would be fired**, or did you leave by mutual agreement because of specific problems?		
39	Have you **ever** been convicted of, or forfeited collateral for **any felony violation**? *(Generally, a felony is defined as any violation of law punishable by imprisonment of longer than 1 year, except for violations called misdemeanors under State law which are punishable by imprisonment of two years or less.)*		
40	Have you **ever** been convicted of, or forfeited collateral for **any firearms or explosives violation**?		
41	Are you **now** under charges for **any** violation of law?		
42	During the last **10 years** have you forfeited collateral, been convicted, been imprisoned, been on probation, or been on parole? Do **not** include violations reported in 39, 40, or 41, above.		
43	Have you **ever** been convicted by a military **court-martial**? If no military service, answer "NO"		
44	Are you **delinquent** on any Federal debt? (Include delinquencies arising from Federal taxes, loans, overpayment of benefits, and other debts to the U.S. Government **plus** defaults on Federally guaranteed or insured loans such as student and home mortgatge loans) . .		

45 If "YES" in: 38 - Explain for each job the problem(s) and your reason(s) for leaving. Give the employer's name and address.
               39 through 43 - Explain each violation. Give place of occurrence and name/address of police or court involved.
               44 - Explain the type, length and amount of the delinquency or default, and steps you are taking to correct errors or repay the debt. Give
                     any identification number associated with the debt and the address of the Federal agency involved.

NOTE: If you need more space, use a sheet of paper, and include the item number.

Item No.	Date (Mo./Yr.)	Explanation	Mailing Address
			Name of Employer, Police, Court, or Federal Agency
			City State ZIP Code
			Name of Employer, Police, Court, or Federal Agency
			City State ZIP

		YES	NO
46	Do you receive, or have you ever applied for retirement pay, pension, or other pay based on military, Federal civilian, or District of Columbia Government service?		
47	Do any of your relatives work for the United States Government or the United States Armed Forces? Include: *father; mother; husband; wife; son; daughter; brother; sister; uncle; aunt; first cousin; nephew; niece; father-in-law; mother-in-law; son-in-law; daughter-in-law; brother-in-law; sister-in-law; stepfather; stepmother; stepson; stepdaughter; stepbrother; stepsister; half brother; and half sister.*		

If **"YES"**, provide details below. If you need more space, use a sheet of paper.

Name	Relationship	Department, Agency or Branch of Armed Forces

SIGNATURE, CERTIFICATION, AND RELEASE OF INFORMATION

YOU MUST SIGN THIS APPLICATION. Read the following carefully before you sign.

- A false statement on any part of your application may be grounds for not hiring you, or for firing you after you begin work. Also, you may be punished by fine or imprisonment (U.S. code, title 18, section 1001).
- If you are a male born after December 31, 1959 you must be registered with the Selective Service System or have a valid exemption in order to be eligible for Federal employment. You will be required to certify as to your status at the time of appointment.
- **I understand** that any information I give may be investigated as allowed by law or Presidential order.
- **I consent** to the release of information about my ability and fitness for Federal employment by *employers, schools, law enforcement agencies and other individuals and organizations,***to** *investigators, personnel staffing specialists, and other authorized employees of the Federal Government.*
- **I certify** that, to the best of my knowledge and belief, **all** of my statements are true, correct, complete, and made in good faith.

48 SIGNATURE *(Sign each application in dark ink)*	**49** DATE SIGNED *(Month, day, year)*

Standard Form 171-A-- *Continuation Sheet for SF 171*

Form Approved
OMB No. 3206-0012

● Attach all SF 171-A's to your application at the top of page 3.

1. Name *(Last, First, Middle Initial)*	2. Social Security Number

3. Job Title or Announcement Number You Are Applying For	4. Date Completed

ADDITIONAL WORK EXPERIENCE BLOCKS

C | Name and address of employer's organization *(include ZIP Code, if known)* | Dates employed *(give month, day and year)* From: To: | Average number of hours per week | Number of employees you supervised |

Salary or earnings
Starting $ per
Ending $ per

Your reason for leaving

| Your immediate supervisor Name | Area Code | Telephone No. | Exact title of your job | If Federal employment *(civilian or military)* list series, grade or rank, and, if promoted in this job, the date of your last promotion |

Description of work: Describe your specific duties, responsibilities and accomplishments in this job, **including** the job title(s) of any employees you supervised. *If you describe more than one type of work (for example, carpentry and painting, or personnel and budget), write the approximate percentage of time you spent doing each.*

For Agency Use (skill codes, etc.)

D | Name and address of employer's organization *(include ZIP Code, if known)* | Dates employed *(give month, day and year)* From: To: | Average Number of hours per week | Number of employees you supervised |

Salary or earnings
Starting $ per
Ending $ per

Your reason for leaving

| Your immediate supervisor Name | Area Code | Telephone No. | Exact title of your job | If Federal employment *(civilian or military)* list series, grade or rank, and, if promoted in this job, the date of your last promotion |

Description of work: Describe your specific duties, responsibilities and accomplishments in this job, **including** the job title(s) of any employees you supervised. *If you describe more than one type of work (for example, carpentry and painting, or personnel and budget), write the approximate percentage of time you spent doing each.*

For Agency Use (skill codes, etc.)

Form Approved
OMB No. 3206-0219

OPTIONAL APPLICATION FOR FEDERAL EMPLOYMENT - OF 612

You may apply for most jobs with a resume, this form, or other written format. If your resume or application does not provide all the information requested on this form and in the job vacancy announcement, you may lose consideration for a job.

1 Job title in announcement	**2** Grade(s) applying for	**3** Announcement number

4 Last name	First and middle names	**5** Social Security Number

6 Mailing Address	**7** Phone Numbers (incl area code) Day ( )
City State Zip Code	Eve ( )

WORK EXPERIENCE

8 Describe your paid and nonpaid work experience related to the job for which you are applying. Do not attach job descriptions.

1) Job Title (if Federal, include series and grade)

From (MM/YY)	To (MM/YY)	Salary $	per	Hours per week

Employer's name and address | Supervisor's name and phone number ( )

Describe your duties and accomplishments

2) Job Title (if Federal, include series and grade)

From (MM/YY)	To (MM/YY)	Salary $	per	Hours per week

Employer's name and address | Supervisor's name and phone number ( )

Describe your duties and accomplishments

9 May we contact your current supervisor?

    YES [ ] NO [ ] if we need to contact your current supervisor before making an offer, we will contact you first.

EDUCATION

10 Mark highest level completed. **Some HS [ ] HS/GED [ ] Associate [ ] Bachelor [ ] Master [ ] Doctoral [ ]**

11 Last high school (HS) or GED school. Give the school's name, city, State, ZIP Code (if known), and year diploma or GED received.

12 Colleges and universities attended. Do **not** attach a copy of your transcript unless requested.

1) Name			Total Credits Earned		Major(s)	Degree - Year
			Semester	Quarter		(if any) Received
City	State	Zip Code				
2)						
3)						

OTHER QUALIFICATIONS

13 Job-related training courses (give title and year). **Job-related** skills (other languages, computer software/hardware, tools, machinery, typing speed, etc.). **Job-related** certificates and licenses (current only). **Job-related** honors, awards, and special accomplishments (publications, memberships in professional/honor societies, leadership activities, public speaking, an d performance awards). Give dates, but do **not** send documents unless requested.

GENERAL

14 Are you a U.S. citizen?   **YES [ ] NO [ ]◆** Give the country of your citizenship. _____

15 Do you claim veterans' preference? **NO [ ] YES [ ]◆** Mark your claim of 5 or 10 points below.
    5 points [ ]◆ Attach your DD 214 or other proof. 10 points [ ]◆ Attach an *Application for 10-Point Veterans' Preference* (SF 15) and proof required.

16 Were you ever a federal civilian employee?

    NO [ ] YES [ ]◆ For highest civilian grade give: Series   Grade   From   To

17 Are you eligible for reinstatement based on career or career-conditional Federal status?

    NO [ ] YES [❭ if requested, attach SF 50 proof.

APPLICANT CERTIFICATION

18 I certify that, to the best of my knowledge and belief, all of the information on and attached to this application is true, correct, complete and made in good faith. **I understand** that false or fraudulent information on or attached to this application may be grounds for not hiring me or for firing me after I begin work, and may be punishable by fine or imprisonment. **I understand** that any information I give may be investigated.

SIGNATURE   **DATE SIGNED**

PRIVACY ACT AND PUBLIC BURDEN STATEMENT

The Office of Personnel Management is authorized to request this information under sections 1302, 3301, 3304, and 8716 of title 5 of the U.S. Code. Section 1104 of title 5 allows the Office of Personnel Management to delegate personnel management functions to other Federal agencies. If neces- sary, and usually in conjunction with another form or forms, this form may be used in conducting an investigation to determine your suitability or your ability to hold a security clearance, and it may be disclosed to authorized officials making similar, subsequent determinations.

Public burden reporting for this collection of information is estimated to vary from 5 to 30 minutes with an average of 15 minutes per response, including time for reviewing instructions, searching existing data sources, gathering the data needed, and completing and reviewing the collection of information. Send comments regarding the burden estimate or any other aspect of the collection of information, including suggestions for reducing this burden, to Report and Forms Management Officer, U.S. Office of Personnel Management, 1900 E Street, N.W., Washington, D.C. 20415.

ROUTINE USES: Any disclosure of this record or information in this record is in accordance with routine uses found in System Notice OPM/GOVT-1, General Personnel Records. This system allows disclosure of information to training facilities; organizations deciding claims for retirement, insurance, unemployment, or health benefits; officials in litigation or administrative proceeding where the Government is a party; law enforcement agencies concerning a violation of law or regulation; Federal agencies for statistical reports and studies; officials of labor organizations recognized by law in connection with representing employees; Federal agencies or other sources requesting information for Federal agencies in connection with hiring or retaining, security clearance, security or suitability investigations, classifying jobs, contracting, or issuing licenses, grants, or other benefits; public and private organizations, including news media, which grant or publicize employee recognition and awards; the Merit Systems Protection Board, the Office of Special Counsel, the Equal Employment Opportunity Commission, the Federal

Labor Relations Authority, the National Archives, the Federal Acquisitions Institute, and Congressional offices in connection with their official functions; prospective non-Federal employers concerning tenure of employ- ment, civil service status, length of service, and the date and nature of action for separation as shown on the SF 50 (or authorized exception) of a specifically identified individual; requesting organizations or individuals concerning the home address and other relevant information on those who might have contracted an illness or been exposed to a health hazard; authorized Federal and non-Federal agencies for use in computer matching; spouses or dependent children asking whether the employee has changed from a self-and-family to a self-only health benefits enrollment; individuals working on a contract, service, grant, cooperative agreement, or job for the Federal government; non-agency members of an agency's performance or other panel; and agency- appointed representatives of employees con- cerning information issued to the employee about fitness-for-duty or agency-filed disability retirement procedures.

Optional Form 306 (EG) September 1994 U.S. Office of Personnel Management	Form Approved: O.M.B. No. 3206-0182

Declaration for Federal Employment

GENERAL INFORMATION

1 FULL NAME

▶

2 SOCIAL SECURITY NUMBER

▶

3 PLACE OF BIRTH *(Include City and State or Country)*

▶

4 DATE OF BIRTH *(MM/DD/YY)*

▶

5 OTHER NAMES EVER USED *(For example, maiden name, nickname, etc.)*

▶

▶

6 PHONE NUMBERS *(Include Area Codes)*

DAY ▶

NIGHT ▶

MILITARY SERVICE

7 Have you served in the United States Military Service? *If your only active duty was training in the Reserves or National Guard, answer "NO".* . . . .

	Yes	No

If you answered "YES", list the branch, dates (MM/DD/YY), and type of discharge for all active duty military service.	BRANCH	FROM	TO	TYPE OF DISCHARGE

BACKGROUND INFORMATION

For all questions, provide all additional requested information under item 15 or on attached sheets. The circumstances of each event you list will be considered. However, in most cases you can still be considered for Federal jobs.

For questions 8, 9, and 10, your answers should include convictions resulting from a plea of nolo contendere *(no contest)*, but omit (1) traffic fines of $300 or less, (2) any violation of law committed before your 16th birthday, (3) any violation of law committed before your 18th birthday if finally decided in juvenile court or under a Youth Offender law, (4) any conviction set aside under the Federal Youth Corrections Act or similar State law, and (5) any conviction whose record was expunged under Federal or State law.

		Yes	No
8	During the last 10 years, have you been convicted, been imprisoned, been on probation, or been on parole? (Includes felonies, firearms or explosives violations, misdemeanors, and all other offenses.) *If "Yes", use item 15 to provide the date, explanation of the violation, place of occurrence, and the name and address of the police department or court involved.*		
9	Have you been convicted by a military court-martial in the past 10 years? (If no military service, answer "NO".) *If "Yes", use item 15 to provide the date, explanation of the violation, place of occurrence, and the name and address of the military authority or court involved.*		
10	Are you now under charges for any violation of law? *If "Yes", use item 15 to provide the date, explanation of the violation, place of occurrence, and the name and address of the police department or court involved.* . .		
11	During the last 5 years, were you fired from any job for any reason, did you quit after being told that you would be fired, did you leave any job by mutual agreement because of specific problems, or were you debarred from Federal employment by the Office of Personnel Management? *If "Yes", use item 15 to provide the date, an explanation of the problem and reason for leaving, and the employer's name and address.*		
12	Are you delinquent on any Federal debt? (Includes delinquencies arising from Federal taxes, loans, overpayment of benefits, and other debts to the U.S. Government, plus defaults of Federally guaranteed or insured loans such as student and home mortgage loans.) *If "Yes", use item 15 to provide the type, length, and amount of the delinquency or default, and steps that you are taking to correct the error or repay the debt.* . .		

ADDITIONAL QUESTIONS

		Yes	No
13	Do any of your relatives work for the agency or organization to which you are submitting this form? (Includes father, mother, husband, wife, son, daughter, brother, sister, uncle, aunt, first cousin, nephew, niece, father-in-law, mother-in-law, son-in-law, daughter-in-law, brother-in-law, sister-in-law, stepfather, stepmother, step-son, stepdaughter, stepbrother, stepsister, half brother, and half sister.) *If "Yes", use item 15 to provide the name, relationship, and the Department, Agency, or Branch of the Armed Forces for which your relative works.*		
14	Do you receive, or have you ever applied for, retirement pay, pension, or other pay based on military, Federal civilian, or District of Columbia Government service?		

Designed using Perform Pro, WHS/DIOR, Jan 95

CONTINUATION SPACE/AGENCY OPTIONAL QUESTIONS

15 Provide details requested in items 8 through 13 and 17c in the continuation space below or on attached sheets. Be sure to identify attached sheets with your name, Social Security Number, and item number, and to include ZIP Codes in all addresses. If any questions are printed below, please answer as instructed (these questions are specific to your position, and your agency is authorized to ask them).

CERTIFICATIONS/ADDITIONAL QUESTION

APPLICANT: If you are applying for a position and have not yet been selected. Carefully review your answers on this form and any attached sheets. When this form and all attached materials are accurate, complete item 16/16a.

APPOINTEE: If you are being appointed. Carefully review your answers on this form and any attached sheets, including any other application materials that your agency has attached to this form. If any information requires correction to be accurate as of the date you are signing, make changes on this form or the attachments and/or provide updated information on additional sheets, initialing and dating all changes and additions. When this form and all attached materials are accurate, complete item 16/16b and answer item 17.

16 I certify that, to the best of my knowledge and belief, all of the information on and attached to this Declaration for Federal Employment, including any attached application materials, is true, correct, complete, and made in good faith. **I understand** that a false or fraudulent answer to any question on any part of this declaration or its attachments may be grounds for not hiring me, or for firing me after I begin work, and may be punishable by fine or imprisonment. **I understand** that any information I give may be investigated for purposes of determining eligibility for Federal employment as allowed by law or Presidential order. **I consent** to the release of information about my ability and fitness for Federal employment by *employers, schools, law enforcement agencies,* and *other individuals and organizations* to *investigators, personnel specialists, and other authorized employees of the Federal Government.* **I understand** that for financial or lending institutions, medical institutions, hospitals, health care professionals, and some other sources of information, a separate specific release may be needed, and I may be contacted for such a release at a later date.

16a Applicant's Signature ▶   Date ▶
    (Sign in ink)

16b Appointee's Signature ▶   Date ▶   APPOINTING OFFICER: Enter Date of Appointment or Conversion
    (Sign in ink)   ▶

17 Appointee Only *(Respond only if you have been employed by the Federal Government before):* Your elections of life insurance during previous Federal employment may affect your eligibility for life insurance during your new appointment. These questions are asked to help your personnel office make a correct determination.

	Date *(MM/DD/YY)*

17a When did you leave your last Federal job? . . . .

	Yes	No	Don't Know
17b When you worked for the Federal Government last time, did you waive Basic Life Insurance or any type of optional life insurance?			
17c If you answered "Yes" to item 17b, did you later cancel the waiver(s)? *If your answer to item 17c is "No," use item 15 to identify the type(s) of insurance for which waivers were not cancelled.*			

Optional Form 306 (Back)   September 1994

Optional Form 306   Form Approved:
U.S. Office of Personnel   **Declaration for Federal Employment**   O.M.B. No. 3206-0182
Management

INSTRUCTIONS

The information collected on this form is used to determine your acceptability for Federal employment and your enrollment status in the Government's Life Insurance program. You may be asked to complete this form at any time during the hiring process. Follow instructions that the agency provides. If you are selected, you will be asked to update your responses on this form and on other materials submitted during the application process and then to recertify that your answers are true before you are appointed.

Your Social Security Number is needed to keep our records accurate, because people may have the same name and birthdate. Executive Order 9397 also asks Federal agencies to use this number to help identify individuals in agency records. Giving us your SSN or other information is voluntary. However, if you do not give us your SSN or

any other information requested, we cannot process your application. Incomplete addresses and ZIP Codes may also slow processing.

You must answer all questions truthfully and completely. A false statement on any part of this declaration or attached forms or sheets may be grounds for not hiring you, or for firing you after you begin work. Also, you may be punished by fine or imprisonment (U.S. Code, title 18, section 1001.)

Either type your responses to this form or print clearly in dark ink. If you need additional space, attach letter-size sheets (8.5" X 11"), including your name, Social Security Number, and item number on each sheet. It is recommended that you keep a photocopy of your completed form for your records.

Index

229

The Authors

Ronald L. Krannich, Ph.D. and Caryl Rae Krannich, Ph.D., are two of America's leading career and travel writers who have authored more than 40 books. They currently operate Development Concepts Inc., a training, consulting, and publishing firm. A former Peace Corps Volunteer and Fulbright Scholar, Ron received his Ph.D. in Political Science from Northern Illinois University. Caryl received her Ph.D. in Speech Communication from Penn State University.

Ron and Caryl are former university professors, high school teachers, management trainers, and government consultants. As trainers and consultants, they have completed numerous projects on management, career development, local government, population planning, and rural development in the United States and abroad.

The Krannichs' career and business work encompasses nearly 30 books they have authored on a variety of subjects: key job search skills, public speaking, government jobs, international careers, nonprofit organizations, and career transitions. Their work represents one of today's most extensive and highly praised collections of career and business writing: *101 Dynamite Answers to Interview Questions, 101 Secrets of Highly Effective Speakers, 201 Dynamite Job Search Letters, The Best Jobs For the 21st Century, Change Your Job Change Your Life, The Complete Guide to International Jobs and Careers, Discover the Best Jobs For You, Dynamite Cover Letters, Dynamite*

Resumes, Dynamite Salary Negotiations, Get a Raise in 7 Days, Dynamite Tele-Search, The Educator's Guide to Alternative Jobs and Careers, From Air Force Blue to Corporate Gray, From Army Green to Corporate Gray, From Navy Blue to Corporate Gray, Resumes and Job Search Letters For Transitioning Military Personnel, High Impact Resumes and Letters, International Jobs Directory, Interview For Success, Jobs and Careers With Nonprofit Organizations, Jobs For People Who Love Travel, and *Dynamite Networking For Dynamite Jobs.* Their books are found in most major bookstores, libraries, and career centers as well as can be ordered directly from Impact's Web site: *www.impactpublications.com.* Many of their works are available interactively on CD-ROM (*The Ultimate Job Source*).

Ron and Caryl live a double career life. Authors of 13 travel books, the Krannichs continue to pursue their international interests through their innovative and highly acclaimed Impact Guides travel series (*"The Treasures and Pleasures....Best of the Best"*) which currently encompasses separate titles on Italy, France, China, Hong Kong, Thailand, Indonesia, Singapore, Malaysia, India, and Australia. When not found at their home and business in Virginia, they are probably somewhere in Europe, Asia, Africa, the Middle East, the South Pacific, or the Caribbean pursuing one of their major passions—researching and writing about quality arts and antiques.

The Krannichs reside in Northern Virginia. Frequent speakers and seminar leaders, they can be contacted through the publisher or by email: *krannich@impactpublications.com*

Career Resources

C ontact Impact Publications for a free annotated listing of career resources or visit their World Wide Web site for a complete listing of career resources: *www.impactpublications.com*.
The following career resources, many of which were mentioned in previous chapters, are available directly from Impact Publications. Complete the following form or list the titles, include postage (see formula at the end), enclose payment, and send your order to:

IMPACT PUBLICATIONS
9104-N Manassas Drive
Manassas Park, VA 20111-5211
1-800-361-1055 (orders only)
Tel. 703/361-7300 or Fax 703/335-9486
E-mail address: *fed@impactpublications.com*

Orders from individuals must be prepaid by check, moneyorder, Visa, MasterCard, or American Express. We accept telephone and fax orders.

Qty.	TITLES	Price	TOTAL
Government and Law Enforcement Jobs			
___	Alternative Careers in Secret Operations	19.95	___
___	Applying For Federal Jobs	17.95	___
___	Barron's Guide to Law Enforcement Careers	13.95	___
___	Book of U.S. Government Jobs	18.95	___
___	Book of U.S. Postal Jobs	18.95	___
___	Careers in Government	17.95	___
___	Complete Guide to Public Employment	19.95	___

___	Directory of Federal Jobs and Employers	21.95	___
___	Federal Applications That Get Results	23.95	___
___	Federal Jobs: The Ultimate Guide	15.95	___
___	Federal Jobs in Law Enforcement	14.95	___
___	Federal Personnel Guide (1999)	9.95	___
___	Federal Resume Guidebook (with disk)	34.95	___
___	Find a Federal Job Fast	15.95	___
___	Government Job Finder	16.95	___
___	Government Phone Book, 1999	225.00	___
___	How to Get a Federal Job	15.00	___
___	Jobs For Lawyers	14.95	___
___	KSA Sampler	12.95	___
___	KSA Workbook	12.95	___
___	Opportunities in the Federal Government	14.95	___
___	Paralegal Career Guide	24.95	___
___	Post Office Jobs	17.95	___
___	Right SF-171 Writer	19.95	___
___	Using Today's Reinvented Vacancy Announcement	12.95	___

Examination Books

___	Border Patrol Exam	17.95	___
___	Federal Clerical Exam	14.95	___
___	Postal Worker Exam	12.95	___
___	Treasury Enforcement Agent Exam	17.95	___

Federal Application Software

___	Quick & Easy Federal Application Kit (single user)	49.95	___
___	Quick & Easy Federal Application Kit (2 users)	59.95	___
___	Quick & Easy Federal Application Kit (3-8 users)	129.95	___
___	Quick & Easy Federal Application Kit (unlimited users)	399.95	___

Federal Job Listings—Bi-Weekly Subscriptions

___	Federal Career Opportunities (6 issues)	39.00	___
___	Federal Career Opportunities (26 issues)	175.00	___
___	Federal Jobs Digest (6 issues)	35.00	___
___	Federal Jobs Digest (25 issues)	125.00	___

Job Search Strategies and Tactics

___	Change Your Job, Change Your Life	17.95	___
___	Complete Idiot's Guide to Getting the Job You Want	24.95	___
___	Complete Job Finder's Guide to the 90's	13.95	___
___	Five Secrets to Finding a Job	12.95	___
___	How to Succeed Without a Career Path	13.95	___
___	Me, Myself, and I, Inc	17.95	___
___	New Rites of Passage at $100,000+	29.95	___
___	The Pathfinder	14.00	___

___	What Color Is Your Parachute?	16.95 ___
___	Who's Running Your Career	14.95 ___

Best Jobs and Employers For the 21st Century

___	50 Coolest Jobs in Sports	15.95 ___
___	Adams Jobs Almanac 1998	15.95 ___
___	American Almanac of Jobs and Salaries	20.00 ___
___	Best Jobs For the 21st Century	19.95 ___
___	Breaking and Entering: Jobs in Film Production	17.95 ___
___	Great Jobs Ahead	11.95 ___
___	Jobs 1998	15.00 ___
___	The Top 100	19.95 ___

Key Directories

___	American Salaries and Wages Survey	110.00 ___
___	Business Phone Book USA 1999	160.00 ___
___	Careers Encyclopedia	39.95 ___
___	Complete Guide to Occupational Exploration	39.95 ___
___	Consultants & Consulting Organizations Directory	605.00 ___
___	Dictionary of Occupational Titles	47.95 ___
___	Encyclopedia of American Industries 1998	520.00 ___
___	Encyclopedia of Associations 1999 (all 3 volumes)	1260.00 ___
___	Encyclopedia of Associations 1998 (National only)	490.00 ___
___	Encyclopedia of Careers & Vocational Guidance	149.95 ___
___	Enhanced Guide For Occupational Exploration	34.95 ___
___	Enhanced Occupational Outlook Handbook	34.95 ___
___	Job Hunter's Sourcebook	70.00 ___
___	National Job Bank 1999	350.00 ___
___	National Trade & Professional Associations 1998	129.00 ___
___	Occupational Outlook Handbook, 1998-99	22.95 ___
___	O*NET Dictionary of Occupational Titles	49.95 ___
___	Professional Careers Sourcebook	99.00 ___
___	Specialty Occupational Outlook: Professions	49.95 ___
___	Specialty Occupational Outlook: Trade & Technical	49.95 ___
___	Vocational Careers Sourcebook	82.00 ___

Education Directories

___	Free and Inexpensive Career Materials	19.95 ___
___	Internships 1999	24.95 ___
___	Peterson's Guide to Graduate & Professional Programs	239.95 ___
___	Peterson's Two- and Four-Year Colleges 1999	45.95 ___
___	Scholarships, Fellowships, & Loans 1999	165.00 ___

Electronic Job Search

___	CareerXroads 1998	22.95 ___
___	Guide to Internet Job Search	14.95 ___

___   How to Get Your Dream Job Using the Web   29.99 _____

Best Companies

___   Hidden Job Market 1999   18.95 _____
___   Hoover's Top 2,500 Employers   22.95 _____
___   Job Vault   20.00 _____
___   JobBank Guide to Computer & High-Tech Companies 16.95 _____
___   JobBank Guide to Health Care Companies   16.95 _____

$100,000+ Jobs

___   The $100,000 Club   25.00 _____
___   100 Winning Resumes For $100,000+ Jobs   24.95 _____
___   201 Winning Cover Letters For $100,000+ Jobs   24.95 _____
___   1500+ KeyWords For $100,000+ Jobs   14.95 _____
___   New Rites of Passage at $100,000+   29.95 _____
___   Six-Figure Consulting   17.95 _____

Finding Great Jobs

___   100 Best Careers in Casinos and Casino Hotels   15.95 _____
___   101 Ways to Power Up Your Job Search   12.95 _____
___   110 Biggest Mistakes Job Hunters Make   19.95 _____
___   Alternative Careers in Secret Operations   19.95 _____
___   Back Door Guide to Short-Term Job Adventures   19.95 _____
___   Careers For College Majors   32.95 _____
___   College Grad Job Hunter   14.95 _____
___   Directory of Executive Recruiters 1998   44.95 _____
___   Get Ahead! Stay Ahead!   12.95 _____
___   Get a Job You Love!   19.95 _____
___   Get What You Deserve!   23.00 _____
___   Great Jobs For Liberal Arts Majors   11.95 _____
___   In Transition   12.50 _____
___   Job Hunting Made Easy   12.95 _____
___   Job Search: The Total System   14.95 _____
___   Job Search 101   12.95 _____
___   Jobs & Careers With Nonprofit Organizations   15.95 _____
___   Knock 'Em Dead   12.95 _____
___   New Relocating Spouse's Guide to Employment   14.95 _____
___   No One Is Unemployable   29.95 _____
___   Non-Profits and Education Job Finder   16.95 _____
___   Perfect Pitch   13.99 _____
___   Professional's Job Finder   18.95 _____
___   Strategic Job Jumping   20.00 _____
___   Top Career Strategies For the Year 2000 & Beyond 12.00 _____
___   What Do I Say Next?   20.00 _____
___   What Employers Really Want.   14.95 _____
___   Work Happy Live Healthy   14.95 _____
___   You Can't Play the Game If You Don't Know the Rules 14.95 _____

Assessment

___	Discover the Best Jobs For You	14.95	___
___	Discover What You're Best At	12.00	___
___	Do What You Are	16.95	___
___	Finding Your Perfect Work	16.95	___
___	I Could Do Anything If Only I Knew What It Was	19.95	___

Inspiration & Empowerment

___	100 Ways to Motivate Yourself	15.99	___
___	Chicken Soup For the Soul Series	75.95	___
___	Doing Work You Love	14.95	___
___	Emotional Intelligence	13.95	___
___	Personal Job Power	12.95	___
___	Power of Purpose	20.00	___
___	Seven Habits of Highly Effective People	14.00	___
___	Survival Personality	12.00	___
___	Your Signature Path	24.95	___

Resumes

___	100 Winning Resumes For $100,000+ Jobs	24.95	___
___	101 Best Resumes	10.95	___
___	101 Quick Tips For a Dynamite Resume	13.95	___
___	1500+ KeyWords For $100,000+ Jobs	14.95	___
___	Adams Resumes Almanac & Disk	19.95	___
___	America's Top Resumes For America's Top Jobs	19.95	___
___	Asher's Bible of Executive Resumes	29.95	___
___	Better Resumes in Three Easy Steps	12.95	___
___	Complete Idiot's Guide to Writing the Perfect Resume	16.95	___
___	Designing the Perfect Resume	12.95	___
___	Dynamite Resumes	14.95	___
___	Encyclopedia of Job-Winning Resumes	16.95	___
___	Gallery of Best Resumes	16.95	___
___	Heart and Soul Resumes	15.95	___
___	High Impact Resumes & Letters	19.95	___
___	Internet Resumes	14.95	___
___	New 90-Minute Resumes	15.95	___
___	New Perfect Resume	12.00	___
___	Portfolio Power	14.95	___
___	Ready-to-Go Resumes	29.95	___
___	Resume Catalog	15.95	___
___	Resume Shortcuts	14.95	___
___	Resumes & Job Search Letters For Transitioning Military Personnel	17.95	___
___	Resumes For Dummies	12.99	___
___	Resumes For Re-Entry	10.95	___
___	Resumes in Cyberspace	14.95	___
___	Resumes That Knock 'Em Dead	14.95	___

___	Sure-Hire Resumes	14.95 ___

Cover Letters

___	175 High-Impact Cover Letters	10.95 ___
___	201 Dynamite Job Search Letters	19.95 ___
___	201 Killer Cover Letters	16.95 ___
___	201 Winning Cover Letters For $100,000+ Jobs	24.95 ___
___	Complete Idiot's Guide to the Perfect Cover Letter	14.95 ___
___	Cover Letters For Dummies	12.99 ___
___	Cover Letters That Knock 'Em Dead	10.95 ___
___	Dynamite Cover Letters	14.95 ___

Networking

___	Dynamite Networking For Dynamite Jobs	15.95 ___
___	Dynamite Telesearch	12.95 ___
___	Great Connections	19.95 ___
___	How to Work a Room	11.99 ___
___	People Power	14.95 ___
___	Power Networking	14.95 ___
___	Power Schmoozing	12.95 ___
___	Power to Get In	24.95 ___

Interview & Communication Skills

___	90-Minute Interview Prep Book	15.95 ___
___	101 Dynamite Answers to Interview Questions	12.95 ___
___	101 Dynamite Questions to Ask At Your Job Interview	14.95 ___
___	101 Secrets of Highly Effective Speakers	14.95 ___
___	111 Dynamite Ways to Ace Your Job Interview	13.95 ___
___	Complete Idiot's Guide to the Perfect Job Interview	14.95 ___
___	Complete Q & A Job Interview Book	14.95 ___
___	Interview For Success	15.95 ___
___	Job Interview For Dummies	12.99 ___

Salary Negotiations

___	Dynamite Salary Negotiations	15.95 ___
___	Get a Raise in 7 Days	14.95 ___
___	Get More Money On Your Next Job	14.95 ___
___	Negotiate Your Job Offer	14.95 ___

International & Travel

___	Complete Guide to International Jobs & Careers	24.95 ___
___	Great Jobs Abroad	14.95 ___
___	International Jobs Directory	19.95 ___
___	Jobs For People Who Love Travel	15.95 ___
___	Jobs in Paradise	14.95 ___

___	Jobs In Russia & the Newly Independent States	15.95 ___
___	Jobs Worldwide	17.95 ___

Job and Career Series

___	*"AMERICA'S TOP JOBS"* **SERIES**	**134.95** ___
___	▪ 50 Fastest Growing Jobs	14.95 ___
___	▪ Federal Jobs	14.95 ___
___	▪ Top 300 Jobs	18.95 ___
___	▪ Top Jobs For College Graduates	14.95 ___
___	▪ Top Jobs For People Without College	12.95 ___
___	▪ Top Industries	14.95 ___
___	▪ Top Medical and Human Service Jobs	12.95 ___
___	▪ Top Military Jobs	19.95 ___
___	▪ Top Office, Management and Sales Jobs	12.95 ___
___	*"CAREERS IN..."* **CAREER GUIDANCE SERIES**	**379.95** ___
___	▪ Accounting ('97)	17.95 ___
___	▪ Advertising ('96)	17.95 ___
___	▪ Business ('91)	17.95 ___
___	▪ Child Care ('94)	17.95 ___
___	▪ Communications ('94)	17.95 ___
___	▪ Computers ('96)	17.95 ___
___	▪ Education ('97)	17.95 ___
___	▪ Engineering ('93)	17.95 ___
___	▪ Environment ('95)	17.95 ___
___	▪ Finance ('93)	17.95 ___
___	▪ Government ('94)	17.95 ___
___	▪ Health Care ('95)	17.95 ___
___	▪ High Tech ('92)	17.95 ___
___	▪ Horticulture & Botany ('97)	17.95 ___
___	▪ International Business ('96)	17.95 ___
___	▪ Journalism ('95)	17.95 ___
___	▪ Law ('97)	17.95 ___
___	▪ Marketing ('95)	17.95 ___
___	▪ Medicine ('97)	17.95 ___
___	▪ Science ('96)	17.95 ___
___	▪ Social & Rehabilitation Services ('94)	17.95 ___
___	▪ Travel, Tourism, & Hospitality ('97)	17.95 ___
___	*"CAREERS FOR YOU"* **SERIES**	**449.95** ___
___	▪ Animal Lovers ('91)	14.95 ___
___	▪ Bookworms ('95)	14.95 ___
___	▪ Car Buffs ('97)	14.95 ___
___	▪ Caring People ('95)	14.95 ___
___	▪ Computer Buffs ('93)	14.95 ___
___	▪ Courageous People ('97)	14.95 ___
___	▪ Crafty People ('93)	14.95 ___
___	▪ Culture Lovers ('91)	14.95 ___
___	▪ Cybersurfers ('97)	14.95 ___

___	▪ Environmental Types ('93)	14.95	___
___	▪ Fashion Plates ('96)	14.95	___
___	▪ Film Buffs ('93)	14.95	___
___	▪ Foreign Language Aficionados ('92)	14.95	___
___	▪ Good Samaritans ('91)	14.95	___
___	▪ Gourmets ('93)	14.95	___
___	▪ Health Nuts ('96)	14.95	___
___	▪ High Energy People ('97)	14.95	___
___	▪ History Buffs ('94)	14.95	___
___	▪ Kids at Heart ('94)	14.95	___
___	▪ Music Lovers ('97)	14.95	___
___	▪ Mystery Buffs ('97)	14.95	___
___	▪ Nature Lovers ('92)	14.95	___
___	▪ Night Owl ('95)	14.95	___
___	▪ Numbers Crunchers ('93)	14.95	___
___	▪ Plant Lovers ('95)	14.95	___
___	▪ Self Starters ('97)	14.95	___
___	▪ Shutterbugs ('94)	14.95	___
___	▪ Sports Nuts ('91)	14.95	___
___	▪ Stagestruck ('97)	14.95	___
___	▪ Travel Buffs ('92)	14.95	___
___	▪ Writers ('95)	14.95	___

SUBTOTAL ___

Virginia residents add 4½% sales tax ___

POSTAGE/HANDLING ($5 for first
product and 8% of SUBTOTAL over $30) $5.00

8% of SUBTOTAL over $30 -------------------------- ___

TOTAL ENCLOSED ------------------------ ___

NAME _____

ADDRESS _____

_____

❑ I enclose check/moneyorder for $ _____ made payable to
IMPACT PUBLICATIONS.

❑ Please charge $ _____ to my credit card:
❑ Visa   ❑ MasterCard   ❑ American Express   ❑ Discover
Card # _____

Expiration date: _____/_____ Phone _____/_____
Signature _____

Your One-Stop Online Superstore
Hundreds of Terrific Resources Conveniently Available On the World Wide Web 24-Hours a Day, 365 Days a Year!

Ever wanted to know what are the newest and best books, directories, newsletters, wall charts, training programs, videos, CD-ROMs, computer software, and kits available to help you land a job, negotiate a higher salary, or start your own business? What about finding a job in Asia or relocating to San Francisco? Are you curious about how to find a job 24-hours a day by using the Internet or what you'll be doing five years from now? Trying to keep up-to-date on the latest career resources but not able to find the latest catalogs, brochures, or newsletters on today's "best of the best" resources?

Welcome to the first virtual career bookstore on the Internet. Now you're only a "click" away with Impact Publication's electronic solution to the resource challenge. Impact Publications, one of the nation's leading publishers and distributors of career resources, offers the most comprehensive "Career Superstore and Warehouse" on the Internet. The bookstore is jam-packed with the latest job and career resources on:

- Alternative jobs and careers
- Self-assessment
- Career planning and job search
- Employers
- Relocation and cities
- Resumes
- Cover Letters
- Dress, image, and etiquette
- Education
- Recruitment
- Military
- Salaries
- Interviewing
- Nonprofits
- Empowerment
- Self-esteem
- Goal setting
- Executive recruiters
- Entrepreneurship
- Government
- Networking
- Electronic job search
- International jobs
- Travel
- Law
- Training and presentations
- Minorities
- Physically challenged

The bookstore also includes sections for ex-offenders and middle schools.

"This is more than just a bookstore offering lots of product," say Drs. Ron and Caryl Krannich, two of the nation's leading career experts and authors and developers of this on-line bookstore. *"We're an important resource center for libraries, corporations, government, educators, trainers, and career counselors who are constantly defining and redefining this dynamic field. Of the thousands of career resources we review each year, we only select the 'best of the best.'"*

Visit this rich site and you'll quickly discover just about everything you ever wanted to know about finding jobs, changing careers, and starting your own business—including many useful resources that are difficult to find in local bookstores and libraries. The site also includes tips for job search success and monthly specials. Its shopping cart and special search feature make this one of the most convenient Web sites to use. Impact's Internet address is:

www.impactpublications.com